THE COMPLETE BOOK OF
GRAMMAR AND PUNCTUATION
Grades 3-4

Send all inquiries to:
School Specialty Publishing
8720 Orion Place
Columbus, OH 43240-2111

ISBN 0-7696-4332-9

3 4 5 6 7 8 9 10 POH 11 10 09 08 07 06

AMERICAN
EDUCATION
PUBLISHING™

Columbus, Ohio

Table of Contents

Sentences (continued)

Name _____

Nouns

A **noun** names a person, place, or thing.

Examples:

person — sister, uncle, boy, woman

place — building, city, park, street

thing — workbook, cat, candle, bed

Directions: Circle the nouns in each sentence.

Example: The (dog) ran into the (street).

1. Please take this book to the librarian.

2. The red apples are in the kitchen.

3. That scarf belongs to the bus driver.

4. Get some blue paper from the office to make a card.

5. Look at the parachute!

6. Autumn leaves are beautiful.

7. The lion roared loudly at the visitors.

Directions: Write each noun you circled in the correct group.

People	Places	Things	
librarian	street	dog	

Name _____

Nouns

Directions: Write nouns that name people.

1. Could you please give this report to my _____?

2. The _____ works many long hours to plant crops.

3. I had to help my little _____ when he wrecked his bike yesterday.

Directions: Write nouns that name places.

1. I always keep my library books on top of the _____ so I can find them.

2. We enjoyed watching the kites flying high in the _____.

3. Dad built a nice fire in the _____ to keep us warm.

Directions: Write nouns that name things.

1. The little _____ purred softly as I held it.

2. Wouldn't you think a _____ would get tired of carrying its house around all day?

3. The _____ scurried into its hole with the piece of cheese.

4. I can tell by the writing that this _____ is mine.

5. Look at the _____ I made in art class.

6. His _____ blew away because of the strong wind.

Name _____

Nouns

A **noun** is a word that names a person, place, or thing.

Examples: **person**

- chef
- postman
- florist

place

- meadow
- beach
- island

thing

- bowl
- doorknob
- jacket

Directions: Read the story below and circle all the nouns.

There is a magical chef who lives on a small, windy island off the coast of Ireland. His name is Happy O'Reilly. People travel from all over the world to see Happy. He has jolly red cheeks, twinkling blue eyes, and a smile for everybody.

He lives by himself in a small, stone cottage that has a giant stone fireplace right in the middle. In that magical fireplace, he makes his potato bread and vegetable beef stew that will cure any sickness. In the summertime, he makes his apple cobbler dessert that will keep a smile on your face for an entire year! Go visit Happy O'Reilly— if you can find him!

Name _____

Idea Nouns

Nouns can also name ideas. **Ideas** are things we cannot see or touch, such as bravery, beauty, or honesty.

Directions: Underline the "idea" nouns in each sentence.

1. Respect is something that you must earn.

2. Truth and justice are two things that people value.

3. The beauty of the flower garden was breathtaking.

4. You must learn new skills in order to master new things.

5. His courage impressed everyone.

6. She finds peace out in the woods.

7. Their friendship was amazing.

8. The man's honesty in the face of such hardship was refreshing.

9. The dog showed its loyalty toward its owner.

10. Trouble is brewing.

11. The policeman's kindness calmed the the scared child.

12. The boy had a fear of the dark.

Name _____

Common Nouns

Common nouns are nouns that name any member of a group of people, any place, or any thing instead of a specific person, place, or thing.

Directions: Read the sentences below. Write the common noun found in each sentence.

Example: _____socks_____ My socks do not match.

1. _____ The bird could not fly.

2. _____ Ben likes to eat jelly beans.

3. _____ Jill is going to the store.

4. _____ We will go swimming in the lake tomorrow.

5. _____ I hope the flowers will grow quickly.

6. _____ We colored eggs together.

7. _____ It is easy to ride a bicycle.

8. _____ Cousin Ed is taller than a tree!

9. _____ Ted and Jane went fishing in their boat.

10. _____ They won a prize yesterday.

11. _____ She fell down and twisted her ankle.

12. _____ My brother was born in a hospital.

13. _____ She went down the slide.

14. _____ Ray went to the doctor today.

Name _____

Proper Nouns

Proper nouns are names of specific people, places, or things. A proper noun begins with a capital letter.

Directions: Read the sentences below. Circle the proper nouns in each sentence.

Example: (Aunt Frances) gave me a puppy for my birthday.

1. We lived on Jackson Street before we moved to our new house.

2. Angela's birthday party is tomorrow night.

3. We drove through Cheyenne, Wyoming on our way home.

4. Dr. Charles always gives me a treat for not crying.

5. George Washington was our first president.

6. Our class took a field trip to the Johnson Flower Farm.

7. Uncle Jack lives in New York City.

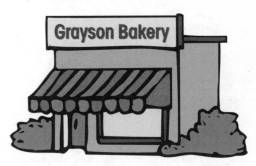

8. Amy and Elizabeth are best friends.

9. We buy doughnuts at the Grayson Bakery.

10. My favorite movie is *E.T.*

11. We flew to Miami, Florida in a plane.

12. We go to the Great American Ballpark to watch the baseball games.

13. Mr. Fields is a wonderful music teacher.

14. My best friend is Tom Dunlap.

Name _____

Proper Nouns

Directions: Write about you! Write a proper noun for each category below. Capitalize the first letter of each proper noun.

1. Your first name: _____

2. Your last name: _____

3. Your street: _____

4. Your city: _____

5. Your state: _____

6. Your school: _____

7. Your best friend's name: _____

8. Your teacher: _____

9. Your favorite book character: _____

10. Your favorite vacation place: _____

Common and Proper Nouns

A **common noun** does not begin with a capital letter unless it is the first word in a sentence. A **common noun** names any person, place, or thing.

Examples: skater, ice

A **proper noun** begins with a capital letter. A **proper noun** names a specific person, place, or thing.

Examples: Peggy Fleming, Michelle Kwan

Directions: Read the story. Circle each common noun and underline each proper noun.

Peggy Fleming

Peggy Fleming is a famous iceskater. She was born in California and began skating when she was nine years old. She won many iceskating competitions as a child. In 1964, Peggy competed in the Winter Olympics in Austria. She came in sixth place.

Peggy took ballet classes to become a better iceskater. This helped her win a gold medal in the 1968 Winter Olympics in France.

After the Olympics, Peggy became a professional skater and toured the country doing ice shows. After her skating career, Peggy became a commentator for television.

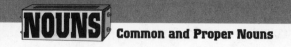

Name _____

Common and Proper Nouns

Common nouns are nouns that name any person, place, or thing. **Proper nouns** are nouns that name specific people, places, or things. A proper noun always starts with a capital letter.

Examples: **common:** boy
            proper: Robert

Directions: Underline the common nouns and circle the proper nouns in the story below.

Crafty Critters Give Police the Slip

When the Gambezi Brothers' Circus passed the town library, Jeremiah Clank blew his trumpet loudly. The noise scared Ellie the Elephant, Harriet the Hyena, and Grumbles the Tiger. A stampede followed.

An emergency police call from Captain Courageous went out over the radio and television: "Emergency! Alert! Everyone should be on the lookout for the circus animals that have escaped from the Gambezi Brothers' Circus."

Thankfully, the police were able to capture all the circus animals and no one was injured. Jeremy Clank will spend the week cleaning the cages of the animals that he scared.

Name _____

Singular and Plural Nouns

A **noun** names a person, place, or thing.

A **singular noun** names one person, place, or thing.

A **plural noun** names more than one person, place, or thing.

Add **s** to change most singular nouns to plural nouns.

  Example: dog = dogs

Add **es** to singular nouns that end in **sh**, **ch**, **s**, **x**, or **z** to make them plural.

  Example: wish = wishes

Directions: Circle the correct spelling of the plural noun.

1.	elephant	elephants	elephantes
2.	box	boxes	boxs
3.	drum	drumes	drums
4.	clown	clownes	clowns
5.	swing	swings	swinges
6.	horse	horses	horsees
7.	tent	tentes	tents
8.	ticket	tickets	ticketes
9.	costume	costumees	costumes
10.	bicycle	bicycles	bicyclees
11.	flash	flashs	flashes
12.	announcer	announceres	announcers
13.	trampoline	trampolines	trampolinees
14.	punch	punches	punchs
15.	cannon	cannones	cannons

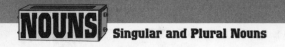

Name _____

Singular and Plural Nouns

A **singular noun** names one person, place, or thing.

> Example: **The class** went on a **field trip** to the **forest**.

A **plural noun** names more than one person, place, or thing.

> Example: **The classes** went on **field trips** to the **forests**.

Directions: Draw one line under each singular noun. Draw two lines under each plural noun.

1. One girl saw three foxes run across the field.

2. Squirrels were running up and down the sides of the trees.

3. A bunny scurried under a bush.

4. As the child watched, some bluebirds flew overhead.

5. Pictures in books helped the students identify many animals.

Directions: Write a sentence for each of these singular or plural nouns.

(apples)_____

(town) _____

(trees) _____

(boys) _____

(girls) _____

(cake) _____

Name _____

Plural Nouns

A **plural** form of most nouns is formed by adding the letter **s**. Some plural nouns are formed by:

- adding **s** to nouns ending in a **vowel** and a **y**.

- adding **es** to nouns ending in **s**, **x**, **z**, **ch**, and **sh**.

- changing **y** to an **i** and adding **es** if the noun ends with a consonant and a **y**.

Examples: boy = boys
fox = foxes
family = families

Directions: Write the plural form above each underlined noun.

1. Aunt Betty took the <u>box</u> of gold <u>fruit</u> and carefully put them in the box for the <u>boy</u> and <u>girl</u>.

2. Aunt Betty wrapped the box of <u>toy</u> with <u>bow</u> and <u>ribbon</u>.

3. On one of the <u>box</u>, Aunt Betty drew some red <u>fox</u>.

4. On the box for the <u>baby</u>, Aunt Betty put pink and blue <u>ribbon</u>.

5. In the box with the <u>dish</u>, she put lots and lots of <u>tissue</u>.

6. In one of the boxes she put watercolor <u>paint</u> and <u>paintbrush</u>.

7. Then, in each of the picnic <u>basket</u>, she packed four peanut butter and jelly <u>sandwich</u>.

8. She also packed several <u>book</u> and two small <u>peach</u>.

Name _____

Plural Nouns

Directions: Write the plural of each noun to complete the sentences below. Remember to change the **y** to **ie** before you add **s**!

1. I am going to two birthday _____ this week.
   (party)

2. Sandy picked some _____ for Mom's pie.
   (cherry)

3. At the store, we saw lots of _____ .
   (bunny)

4. My change at the candy store was three _____ .
   (penny)

5. All the _____ baked cookies for the bake sale.
   (lady)

6. Thanksgiving is a special time for _____ to gather together.
   (family)

7. Boston and New York are very large _____ .
   (city)

Name _____

Plural Nouns

To make **plural nouns**:

Add **s** to a singular noun ending in a vowel and an **o**.

　　Example:　　rodeo = rodeos

Add **es** to a singular noun ending in a consonant and an **o**.

　　Example:　　tomato = tomatoes

Change the **f** to **v** and add **es** to a singular noun ending in **f**.

　　Example:　　leaf = leaves

Directions: Circle the correct plural form of each noun.

1. potato	potatoes	potatos	potatose
2. half	halfs	halves	halvs
3. mosquito	mosquitoes	mosquitoz	mosquitos
4. hero	heros	heroes	herose
5. loaf	loaves	loafs	loafes
6. zero	zeroes	zeros	zeroz
7. calf	calfs	calves	calfz
8. leaf	leaves	leafs	leafes
9. shelf	shelfs	shelvs	shelves
10. hoof	hooves	hoofs	hoofes

Name _____

Plural Nouns

Some words have special plural forms.

Example: leaf = leaves

Directions: Some of the words in the Word Bank are special plurals. Finish each sentence with a plural noun from the Word Box. Then, write the letters from the boxes in the blanks at the bottom to solve the puzzle.

Word Bank

tooth	teeth	mouse	mice
child	children	woman	women
foot	feet	man	men

1. I lost my two front ___ ___ ___ ▢ ___ !

2. My sister has two pet ___ ___ ___ ▢ .

3. Her favorite book is *Little* ___ ___ ___ ▢ ___ .

4. The circus clown had big ___ ___ ___ ▢ .

5. The teacher played a game with the

   ___ ▢ ___ ___ ___ ___ ___ ___ .

Take good care of this pearly plural!

___ ___ ___ ___ ___
 1   2   3   4   5

Name _____

Collective Nouns

Collective nouns are used to represent a group. They are used with a singular verb.

Example: **The mob of children was** excited for the parade to start.

Directions: First, underline the collective noun in each sentence. Then, circle the singular verb that goes with each collective noun.

1. The crowd of people (was, were) scared by Aunt Betty's monster truck.

2. The army (wear, wears) blue uniforms in the parade.

3. The scout troop (throw, throws) candy to the children.

4. The football team (marches, march) behind the scout troop.

5. The largest group in the parade (is, are) the high school marching band.

6. The parade committee (ride, rides) on a float covered with yellow daisies.

7. The public (follows, follow) the last float to the community park.

8. The school (has, have) a picnic for everyone in the parade.

9. The school choir (sing, sings) several songs for the people.

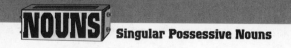

Name _____

Singular Possessive Nouns

A **singular possessive noun** shows ownership. To form a singular possessive noun, add an **apostrophe** and the letter **s** (**'s**) to the end of a singular noun.

Example: Susan **Moore's** lunchbox
Tony's baseball

Directions: Read Mrs. Goldfinger's will. Write the correct possessive noun above each sentence that uses a phrase like **belongs to**.

Example: Mrs. Goldfinger's Last Will and Testament

~~Last Will and Testament of Mrs. Goldfinger~~

Being of sound mind,

I leave the antique chair in my living room, which belonged to my Aunt

Minnie, to the Toon Town Oldies-but-Goodies Museum. I give to Digger J.

Goldfinger my collection of herbs that belonged to my mother. The flag

that belonged to my father will go to the school that is run by my aunt

Theodora Tutor. The book collection that once belonged to my aunt will

be donated to the college. I give my gold-plated yo-yo, which

belonged to my friend, Millie Molly, to my mailman, Lawrence

Letter. Finally, to my nephew, Harry Hoo, I give the owl that

belonged to my Uncle Hugh.

Singular Possessive Nouns

To make a singular noun show **possession** or ownership, add an **apostrophe** and the letter **s ('s)**.

| **Examples:** | **Deandre** | **Deandre's** hiking shoes are muddy. |
| | **tree** | The **tree's** limbs are heavy with snow. |

Directions: Change each noun to its possessive form.

1. snake _____

2. rock _____

3. bird _____

4. lizard _____

5. plant _____

6. shrub _____

7. turtle _____

Directions: Write a sentence using the possessive form of each word.

1. Kelly _____

2. truck _____

3. insect _____

4. rope _____

5. spider _____

Name _____

Plural Possessive Nouns

A **plural possessive noun** shows that something belongs to more than one person, place, or thing. To make a plural noun possessive, add only an **apostrophe** after the **s** or **es** ending. If the plural does not end in **s**, add an **apostrophe** and **s** (**'s**).

Examples: the toys of the brothers = the brothers' toys
the shoes of the women = the women's shoes

Directions: Change the words below to show the plural possessive nouns.

the truck belonging to the twins

_____

the bows the girls are wearing

_____

the toys of the children

_____

the trays of the waiters

_____

the ties belonging to the men

_____

the lawns of our neighbors

_____

the books belonging to the teachers

_____

the book projects of all the classes

_____

the flowers belonging to the gardeners

_____

the bones for the dogs

_____

Plural Possessive Nouns

To make a plural noun that ends with **s** show **possession** or ownership, add an **apostrophe** after the **s**.

> **Examples:** **boys**   The **boys'** mother took them to the skate park.

If the plural noun does not end in **s**, add an **apostrophe** and the letter **s**.

> **Examples:** **men**   The **men's** fitting room is on the left.

Directions: Change each plural noun to its possessive form.

1. cups _____
2. hamburgers _____
3. french fries _____
4. workers _____
5. straws _____

6. children _____
7. parents _____
8. milkshakes _____
9. sundaes _____
10. fish _____

Directions: Write a sentence using the possessive form of each plural noun.

1. girls _____
2. women _____
3. hats _____
4. snacks _____
5. yo-yos _____

Name _____

Articles

An **article** is a word that comes before a noun. **A**, **an**, and **the** are articles. We use **a** before a word that begins with a consonant. We use **an** before a word that begins with a vowel.

Example: **a peach**   **an apple**

Directions: Write **a** or **an** in the sentences below.

Example: My bike had _____a_____ flat tire.

1. They brought _____ goat to the farm.

2. My mom wears _____ old pair of shoes to mow the lawn.

3. We had _____ party for my grandfather.

4. Everybody had _____ ice-cream cone after the game.

5. We bought _____ picnic table for our backyard.

6. We saw _____ lion sleeping in the shade.

7. It was _____ evening to be remembered.

8. He brought _____ blanket to the game.

9. _____ exit sign was above the door.

10. They went to _____ orchard to pick apples.

11. He ate _____ orange for lunch.

Name _____

Articles

A, **an**, and **the** are special words called **articles**. **A** and **an** are used to introduce singular nouns. Use **a** when the next word begins with a consonant sound. Use **an** when the next word begins with a vowel sound.

Examples: **a** chair   **an** antelope

The is used to introduce both singular and plural nouns.

Examples: **the** beaver   **the** flowers

Directions: Underline the correct article for each word.

1. (the, an)   field
2. (a, an)   award
3. (an, the)   ball
4. (a, the)   wheels
5. (a, an)   inning
6. (an, the)   sticks
7. (the, a)   goalposts
8. (a, an)   obstacle
9. (a, an)   umpire
10. (an, the)   quarterback
11. (a, the)   outfield
12. (the, an)   surfboard
13. (an, the)   team
14. (an, the)   shin guards
15. (a, an)   helmet

16. (a, an)   glove
17. (the, an)   net
18. (a, the)   skates
19. (a, the)   tennis shoes
20. (a, an)   touchdown
21. (a, the)   ice
22. (a, an)   wave
23. (the, an)   skateboard
24. (a, the)   water
25. (the, a)   goggles
26. (an, the)   scoreboard
27. (a, the)   spectators
28. (the, an)   uneven bars
29. (a, the)   hurdles
30. (a, an)   time-out

Name _____

Articles

A, an, and **the** are words called **articles**. **A** and **an** refer to any one thing. Use **a** before a word that starts with a consonant sound. Use **an** before a word that starts with a vowel sound or a silent h. **The** refers to a specific thing.

Examples: Every duck in **the** pond wanted **a** bath.
It was **an** easy thing to do in **an** hour.

Directions: Complete the story below by filling in the articles **a, an,** or **the.**

_____ park on Saturday was full of animals. _____ ant was nibbling on my sandwich before I could get it in my mouth! _____ deer was behind _____ fence watching all _____ animals and people. _____ children were running and leaping through_____ grass, chasing _____ chipmunk. _____ park ranger made sure _____ picnic area was kept clean. When I looked down by my feet, I spotted _____ apple slice there. It wasn't there for long, though. Before I could pick it up, _____ squirrel snatched it and ran away! _____ sun was peeking through _____ thick-leaved trees and casting just enough warmth for_____ turtle who was wading in _____ pond. Even though I was only at_____ park for _____ hour, it was my most exciting visit ever.

Directions: Write the article **a** or **an** before each animal listed below.

_____ hippopotamus   _____ flamingo   _____ emperor penguin
_____ cockatoo   _____ California condor   _____ sloth
_____ chameleon   _____ robin   _____ sailfish
_____ falcon   _____ beetle   _____ blue macaw
_____ giraffe   _____ flying squirrel   _____ anteater
_____ starfish   _____ owl   _____ eel
_____ elephant   _____ albatross   _____ shark

Name _____

Articles

A, **an**, and **the** are called **articles**. **A** and **an** are articles that come before any person, place, or thing. **A** comes before a word that begins with a consonant. **An** comes before a word that begins with a vowel. **The** is the article that comes before a specific person, place, or thing.

Example: I saw **a** Tyrannosaurus Rex and **an** Allosaurus in **a** museum, and I saw **the** most complete dinosaur in Haddonfield, New Jersey.

Directions: Finish each sentence by filling in the correct article.

1. _____ bone was found about ten feet under the ground.

2. _____ crew member who found it dusted it carefully to remove dirt.

3. Once in the lab, Dr. Dexterous examined _____ find.

4. Three of _____ dino-diggers took _____ airplane to Phoenix where they had special equipment to date the bone.

5. At _____ university, the scientists used _____ special process to figure out how old _____ bone was.

6. They also found out that _____ bone was not from _____ dinosaur but from _____ human.

Name _____

Action Words – Verbs

A **verb** is a word that tells what is happening in a sentence.

Word Bank			
answers	play	studies	race
read	eats	yell	hugs
dances	swims	chats	

Directions: Write each verb from the Word Bank in the correct blank.

Sara has a busy day at school.

First, she _____ the teacher's

question, and then she _____

for her spelling test. At 11:30 a.m., she

_____ her lunch and

_____ with her friends.

On the playground at recess, the kids

_____ each other and _____ at the top of their lungs!

Sara likes to _____ quietly or _____ checkers instead!

Directions: Choose three of your favorite action words from the Word Bank. Then, write one or two sentences using all three words.

_____

_____

_____

_____

Name _____

Action Verbs

Action verbs show some kind of action. We use them to show what someone or something does, did, or will do.

Example: We **hike** down the trail.

Directions: Underline the action verbs in each rule.

Hiking Rules

1. You should walk, not run, on the trails.

2. Throw away your trash.

3. Do not drop or throw rocks into the canyon.

4. When you hike down to the bottom, you may camp only in the campground.

5. You may build fires only in marked areas.

6. Store your food in a nearby tree.

7. Be polite to other hikers. Stop to let them pass you.

8. On hot days, take plenty of water and wear a hat.

Action Verbs

Verbs are action words. They tell what is happening in a sentence. Some verbs are boring and used too often. You can make your writing clearer and more exciting by changing some verbs.

Examples: Barbara **put** peanut butter on her bread.
Barbara **slathered** peanut butter on her bread.

Directions: Change the underlined word in each sentence to a verb from the Word Bank to make the sentence more exciting.

Word Bank				
thundered	streaked	explained	scurried	splashed
danced	grumbled	pitched	cried	hopped
steered	gathered	rescued	sailed	shrieked

1. _____ Dad <u>drove</u> the car toward the beach.

2. _____ The seagulls <u>played</u> at the edge of the water.

3. _____ Waves <u>broke</u> on the sand.

4. _____ Tomas <u>found</u> seashells at the seashore.

5. _____ "What's that?" Petra <u>said</u>.

6. _____ "It's a sand crab," Bobby <u>said</u>.

7. _____ The sand crabs <u>went</u> away when he lifted the rock.

8. _____ Sam <u>ran</u> across the hot sand.

9. _____ Jessica <u>swam</u> in the surf.

10. _____ The beach ball <u>went</u> through the air.

Action Verbs

Action verbs tell what the subject of the sentence is doing.

Examples: run, jump, talk, throw, load, fight, read

Directions: Read the story below. Underline each action verb.

The Unexpected Fall

One Saturday, Mac and his father hiked in the desert near Superstition Mountain. Mac ran ahead, anxious to see if he could find the Lost Dutchman's gold mine. Mac and his father looked up at the rocky mountain. Saguaro cactuses stood guard. White clouds scurried across the noon sky. The puffy white balls looked so close that Mac reached up to touch them.

As he jumped up, his father shouted, "Watch out!"

Mac saw the *Beware! Danger!* sign too late. Suddenly, his feet went out from under him, and he slid down a hole. When he stopped sliding, he was underground in the dark. He was in a cave. He heard his father yell, "Are you okay?"

 **Action Verbs**

Action Verbs

Directions: Answer each question using a verb from the Word Bank. Write a sentence using that verb.

Word Bank					
stir	clap	drag	hug	plan	grab

Which verb means to put your arms around someone?

_____

_____

Which verb means to mix something with a spoon?

_____

_____

Which verb means to pull something along the ground?

_____

_____

Which verb means to take something suddenly?

_____

_____

Name _____

Action Verbs

A word that tells what is happening in a sentence is called a **verb**. Verbs are **action words**.

Directions: Finish each sentence with the correct action word from the Word Bank.

Word Bank				
discovers	eats	shoots	dances	drives

Duffy _____ his new, red car.

The lady _____ on the stage.

Coby _____ the arrow at the target.

Judy _____ pumpkin pie.

The archaeologist _____ the hidden doorway.

Directions: Choose two action words from the Word Bank that you like. Then, write a sentence using both of the words.

Word Bank				
creates	builds	scrubs	hammers	mows

_____

_____

_____

_____

Name _____

Action Verbs

A **verb** is the action word in a sentence that tells what something or someone does.

   Examples: run, jump, skip

Directions: Draw a box around the verb in each sentence below.

1. Spiders spin webs of silk.

2. A spider waits in the center of the web for its meals.

3. A spider sinks its sharp fangs into insects.

4. Spiders eat many insects.

5. Spiders make their nests with silk.

6. Female spiders wrap silk around their eggs to protect them.

Directions: Finish each sentence with the correct word from the Word Bank.

Word Bank				
hides	swims	eats	grabs	hurt

1. A crab spider _____ deep inside a flower where it cannot be seen.

2. The crab spider _____ insects when they land on the flower.

3. The wolf spider is good because it _____ wasps.

4. The water spider _____ under water.

5. Most spiders will not _____ people.

Name _____

The Verb "Be"

Most verbs name an action. The verb **be** is different. It tells about someone or something. **Am**, **is**, and **are** are forms of the the verb **be**.

Use **is** with one person, place, or thing.

Example: Mr. Wu **is** my teacher.

Use **are** with more than one person, place, or thing or with the word **you**.

Examples: We **are** studying mummies.
              You **are** happy.

Use **am** with the word **I**.

Example: I **am** happy today.

Directions: Fill in each blank with the correct form of the verb **be** (**is**, **am**, or **are**).

1. My house _____ brown.

2. My favorite color _____ blue.

3. We _____ baking cookies today.

4. I _____ going to the movies on Saturday.

5. My friends _____ going with me.

6. What _____ your phone number?

7. You _____ standing on my foot.

8. I _____ four feet tall.

9. The firefighter _____ driving the engine.

10. Charles and I _____ playing football.

11. The band _____ playing "The Star-Spangled Banner."

12. Denver _____ east of Los Angeles.

13. You _____ a nice person.

14. _____ I your best friend?

Name _____

Linking Verbs

A **linking verb** does not show action. It links the subject of the sentence with a noun or adjective. Forms of **to be** are linking verbs.

   Example: Thomas Jefferson **was** a president of the United States.

Directions: Write a linking verb in each blank.

1. The class's writing assignment _____ a report on U.S. Presidents.

2. The due date for our report _____ tomorrow.

3. I _____ glad I chose to write about Thomas Jefferson.

4. He _____ the youngest delegate to the First Continental Congress.

5. The colonies _____ angry at England.

6. Thomas Jefferson _____ a great writer, so he was asked to help write the Declaration of Independence.

7. The signing of that document _____ an important historical event.

8. As President, Jefferson _____ responsible for organizing the Louisiana Purchase.

9. He _____ the second president to live in the White House.

10. Americans _____ fortunate for the part Thomas Jefferson played in our country's history.

Name _____

Linking Verbs

A **linking verb** connects the subject in a sentence to the words in the **predicate**. The predicate is the part of the sentence that contains the verb. Forms of the verb **to be** (**is**, **are**, and **am**) are the most commonly used linking verbs.

Example: I **am** sick.
Mrs. Potter **is** our neighbor.

Directions: Finish each sentence with the correct linking verb from the Word Bank. You can use the same word twice.

Word Bank
is   am   was   are   were

1. The oldest saguaro cactus _____ over 250 years old.

2. The cactus wrens _____ in the hole.

3. The coyotes _____ wild.

4. I _____ cold as I paddle down the river.

5. The saguaro cactus _____ a flowering plant.

6. The flower of the saguaro cactus _____ the state flower of Arizona.

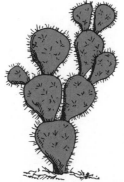
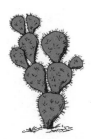

Name _____

Linking Verbs

Linking verbs connect the noun to a descriptive word. Linking verbs are often forms of the verb **be**.

Directions: The linking verb is underlined in each sentence. Circle the two words that are being connected.

Example: The (cat) is (fat).

1. My favorite food <u>is</u> pizza.

2. The car <u>was</u> red.

3. I <u>am</u> tired.

4. Books <u>are</u> fun!

5. The garden <u>is</u> beautiful.

6. Pears <u>taste</u> juicy.

7. The airplane <u>looks</u> large.

8. Rabbits <u>are</u> furry.

Helping Verbs

A **helping verb** is a word used with an action verb.

Examples: might, shall, are

Directions: Finish each sentence with an appropriate helping verb from the Word Bank.

		Word Bank	
can	could	must	might
may	would	should	will
shall	did	does	do
had	have	has	am
are	were	is	
be	being	been	

Example: Tomorrow, I ____might____ play soccer.

1. Mom _____ buy my new soccer shoes tonight.

2. Yesterday, my old soccer shoes _____ ripped by the cat.

3. I _____ going to ask my brother to go to the game.

4. He usually _____ not like soccer.

5. But he _____ go with me because I am his sister.

6. He _____ promised to watch the entire soccer game.

7. He has _____ helping me with my homework.

8. I _____ spell a lot better because of his help.

9. Maybe I _____ finish the semester at the top of my class.

Name _____

Helping Verbs

Sometimes an **action verb** needs help from another verb called a **helping verb**.

Common Helping Verbs					
am	can	does	is	shall	will
are	could	had	may	should	would
be	did	has	might	was	
been	do	have	must	were	

Directions: Underline the action verb in each sentence. Then, finish each sentence with the best helping verb.

1. Jasmine's family _____ planning a recycling project.
   (is, had, are)

2. They _____ talking to their neighbors.
   (is, may, are)

3. Mr. Chavez _____ look for old newspapers and magazines.
   (will, do, were)

4. The Ong children _____ gathering bags to collect plastic bottles.
   (should, are, did)

5. Jasmine _____ open a lemonade stand to keep us cool.
   (have, was, might)

6. Mrs. Zanuto said she _____ drive us to the recycling center. (would, be, are)

7. We _____ respect our planet.
   (have, must, are)

Name _____

Helping Verb

A **helping verb** "helps" another verb to show action.

Examples: I **was** turning.
He **should have** turned.
They **must have been** turning.

Directions: Finish each sentence below. Fill in the verb phrase by using the verb shown and adding a helping verb from the Word Bank. Try to use a different helping verb in each sentence.

Example: The flowers _____ are growing _____ tall.
(to grow)

1. Freddie _____ in class.
(to listen)

2. Lori _____ her vegetables.
(to eat)

3. I _____ my homework later.
(to do)

4. They _____ to the movie.
(to go)

Word Bank				
could	would	does	been	are
can	should	do	being	am
must	will	had	be	is
might	shall	have	were	was
may	did	has		

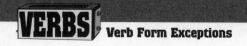

Name _____

Verbs "Went" and "Gone"

The word **went** is used without a helping verb.

Examples:
Correct: Susan **went** to the store.
Incorrect: Susan **has went** to the store.

The word **gone** is used with a helping verb.

Examples:
Correct: Susan **has gone** to the store.
Incorrect: Susan **gone** to the store.

Directions: Write **C** in the blank if the verb is used correctly. Draw an **X** in the blank if the verb is not used correctly.

Example: ___C___ She has gone to my school since last year.

1. _____ Has not he been gone a long time?

2. _____ He has went to the same class all year.

3. _____ I have went to that doctor since I was born.

4. _____ She is long gone!

5. _____ Who among us has not gone to get a drink yet?

6. _____ The class has gone on three field trips this year.

7. _____ The class went on three field trips this year.

8. _____ Who has not went to the board with the right answer?

9. _____ We have not went on our vacation yet.

10. _____ Who is went for the pizza?

11. _____ The train has been gone for two hours.

12. _____ The family had gone to the movies.

13. _____ Have you went to visit the new bookstore?

14. _____ He has gone on and on about how smart you are!

Name _____

The Verb "Be"

Some forms of the verb **to be** can be used as **main verbs** or **helping verbs**.

Examples: **main:** They **are** quiet.
helping: They **are being** quiet.

Directions: Circle the form of **to be** in each sentence below. Then, write **main** or **helping** in the blank to show how the verb is being used.

1. _____ Ruth has been playing soccer every day this week.

2. _____ He was teaching us to read.

3. _____ The lunches were good.

4. _____ Janie was planning on leaving school.

5. _____ My baby sister is unhappy.

Directions: Circle the correct form of **to be** in each sentence. Then, rewrite the sentence.

1. Julie (been, has been) the best student in our class.

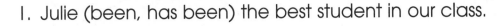
_____

2. Emily (be, will be) a very good scientist.

_____

3. Soon, he (been, will be) a student hall monitor.

_____

4. Our school year (been, has been) good so far.

_____

5. Brendan and Janie (be, are) both shy.

_____

Name _____

Verbs

Verbs are the action words in a sentence. There are three kinds of verbs: **action verbs**, **linking verbs**, and **helping verbs**.

An **action verb** tells the action of a sentence.

Examples: run, hop, skip, sleep, jump, talk, snore
Michael **ran** to the store.

A **linking verb** joins the subject and predicate of a sentence.

Examples: am, is, are, was, were
Michael **was** at the store.

A **helping verb** is used with an action verb to "help" the action of the sentence.

Examples: am, is, are, was, were
Matthew **was** helping Michael.

Directions: Underline the verbs in each sentence. Above the verb, write **A** if it is an action verb, **L** if it is a linking verb, or **H** if it is a helping verb.

Example: Amy <u>jumps</u> rope.
                       A

1. Paul was jumping rope, too.

2. They were working on their homework.

3. The math problem requires a lot of thinking.

4. Addition problems are fun to do.

5. The baby sleeps in the afternoon.

6. Grandma is also napping.

7. Sam is going to bed.

8. John paints a lovely picture of the sea.

9. The colors in the picture are soft and pale.

Name _____

Present-Tense Verbs

When something is happening right now, it is in the **present tense**. There are two ways to write verbs in the present tense: in the **simple present tense** and in **present tense with a helping verb**.

Examples: simple present tense: The dog **walks**.
present tense with a helping verb: The dog **is walking**.

Directions: Rewrite each sentence using a different form of the verb.

Example: He lists the numbers.
He is listing the numbers.

1. She is pounding the nail.

_____

2. My brother toasts the bread.

_____

3. They search for the robber.

_____

4. The teacher lists the pages.

_____

5. They are spilling the water.

_____

6. Ken and Amy load the packages.

_____

Name _____

Present-Tense Verbs

When a **present-tense verb** tells what one person or thing is doing now, it often ends in **s**.

 Example: She **sings**.

When a verb is used with **you**, **I**, or **we**, we do not add an **s**.

 Example: I **sing**.

Directions: Write the correct verb in each sentence.

 Example: I ____write____ a newspaper about   **writes, write**
             our street.

1. My sister _____ me sometimes.   **helps, help**

2. She _____ the pictures.   **draw, draws**

3. We _____ them together.   **delivers, deliver**

4. I _____ the news to all the people.   **tell, tells**

5. Mr. Macon _____ the most beautiful flowers.   **grow, grows**

6. Mrs. Jones _____ to her plants.   **talks, talk**

7. Kevin Turner _____ his dog loose every day.   **lets, let**

8. Little Mikey Smith _____ lost once a week.   **get, gets**

9. You may _____ I live on an interesting street.   **thinks, think**

10. We _____ it's the best street in town.   **say, says**

Present-Tense Verbs

Directions: Use each verb below in two sentences that tell about something that is happening now. Write the verb as both simple present tense and present tense with a helping verb.

Example: run

Mia runs to the store.
(simple present tense)

Mia is running to the store.
(present tense + helping verb)

1. hatch _____

_____

2. check _____

_____

3. spell _____

_____

4. blend _____

_____

5. lick _____

_____

6. cry _____

_____

7. write _____

_____

8. dream _____

_____

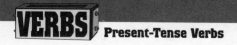

Name _____

Present-Tense Verbs

The **present tense** of a verb tells about something that is happening now, happens often, or is about to happen. These verbs can be written in **simple present tense** (The bird sing**s**.) or in **present tense with a helping verb** (The bird is sing**ing**.).

Directions: Write each sentence again, using the verb **is** and writing the **ing** form of the verb.

> **Example:** He cooks the cheeseburgers.
>
> He is cooking the cheeseburgers.

1. Sharon dances to that song.

   _____

2. Frank washed the car.

   _____

3. Mr. Benson smiles at me.

   _____

Directions: Finish each sentence below. Tell something that is happening now. Be sure to use the helping verb **is** and the **ing** form of the action verb.

> **Example:** The big, brown dog is barking _____.

1. The little baby _____.

2. Most nine-year-olds _____.

3. The monster on television _____.

Name _____

Past-Tense Verbs

The **past tense** of a verb tells about something that has already happened. We add a **d** or an **ed** to most verbs to show that something has already happened.

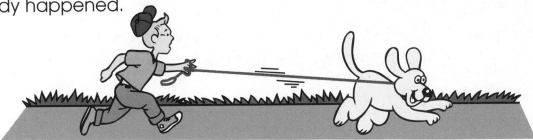

Directions: Use the verb from the first sentence to complete the second sentence.

Example: Please **walk** the dog.   I already _____walked_____ her.

1. The flowers look good.   They _____ better yesterday.

2. Please accept my gift.   I _____ it for my sister.

3. I wonder who will win.   I _____ about it all night.

4. He will saw the wood.   He _____ some last week.

5. Fold the paper neatly.   She _____ her paper.

6. Let's cook outside tonight.   We _____ outside last night.

7. Do not block the way.   They _____ the entire street.

8. Form the clay this way.   He _____ it into a ball.

9. Follow my car.   We_____ them down the street.

10. Glue the pages like this.   She _____ on the flowers.

Name _____

Past-Tense Verbs

When you write about something that has already happened, you add **ed** to most verbs. There is another way to write about something in the past tense.

Examples: The dog walked. = The dog was walking.
                  The cats played. = The cats were playing.

Directions: Write each sentence again, using the verb in a different way.

Example: The baby pounded the pans.

<u>The baby was pounding the pans.</u>

1. Gary loaded the car by himself.

   _____

2. They searched for a long time.

   _____

3. The water spilled over the edge.

   _____

4. Dad toasted the rolls.

   _____

Name _____

Past-Tense Verbs

To write about something that already happened, you can add **ed** to the verb.

Example: Yesterday, we **talked**.

You can also use the helping verbs **was** and **were** and add **ing** to the action verb.

Example: Yesterday, we **were talking**.

When a verb ends with **e**, you usually drop the **e** before adding **ing**.

Examples: grade = was grading   weave = were weaving
tape = was taping   sneeze = were sneezing

Directions: Write two sentences for each verb below. Tell about something that has already happened. Write the verb both ways.

Example: stream
The rain **streamed** down the window.
The rain **was streaming** down the window.

1. grade

_____

_____

2. tape

_____

_____

3. weave

_____

_____

4. sneeze

_____

_____

53

Name _____

Past-Tense Verbs

To make many verbs past tense, add **ed**.

    Examples: cook = cooked   wish = wished   play = played

When a verb ends in a **silent e**, drop the **e** and add **ed**.

    Examples: hope = hoped   hate = hated

When a verb ends in **y** after a consonant, change the **y** to **i** and add **ed**.

    Examples: hurry = hurried   marry = married

When a verb ends in a single consonant after a single short vowel, double the final consonant before adding **ed**.

    Examples: stop = stopped   hop = hopped

Directions: Make the present-tense verb past-tense.

    Example: call <u>called</u>

1. copy _____
2. frown _____
3. smile _____
4. live _____
5. talk _____
6. name _____
7. list _____
8. spy _____
9. phone _____

10. reply _____
11. top _____
12. clean _____
13. scream _____
14. clap _____
15. mop _____
16. soap _____
17. choke _____
18. scurry _____

Name _____

Past-Tense Verbs

Present-tense verbs tell what is happening now. **Past-tense verbs** tell what happened in the past.

To change most action verbs to past tense, add **ed**.
 Example: jump = jumped

To change verbs that end in **e** to past tense, add **d**.
 Example: race = raced

To change verbs that end in a consonant followed by a **y** to past tense, change the **y** to **i** and add **ed**.
 Example: try = tried

To change verbs that end with a vowel followed by a consonant to past tense, double the consonant and add **ed**.
 Example: stop = stopped

Directions: Fill in each blank with the past tense of the verb.

I was _____ to a birthday party. So, my mom, my sister, and I
     (invite)

_____ to the mall to buy a gift. We_____ off the elevator.
(hurry)   (hop)

"Don't touch anything!" Mom said. So, I _____ everything. I
                                    (touch)

_____ the sweaters off the tables. I_____ on all the hats. I
(pull)   (try)

_____ hide-and-seek with my sister. She_____ when I
(play)   (cry)

_____ her. I _____ her to make her feel better.
(trip)   (hug)

We _____ at a candy shop. I _____ my lips when I saw the
     (stop)   (lick)

chewy bears. I_____ my mom to buy some. She_____ .
            (beg)   (refuse)

I _____ to get my friend chewy bears. I _____
   (decide)   (smile)

as the salesperson_____ the gift. I_____ the
                    (wrap)   (carry)

candy out to the car. What do you think _____
                                        (happen)

to the gift?

Name _____

Irregular Verbs

Irregular verbs are verbs that you do not change from the present tense to the past tense by adding **d** or **ed**.

Example: sing = sang

Directions: Read the sentence and underline the verbs. Choose the past-tense form of the verb from the Word Bank and write it next to the sentence.

Word Bank			
blew	came	flew	gave
grew	made	sang	took
wore			

Example: Dad will <u>make</u> a cake tonight.   _____ made _____

1. I will probably grow another inch this year.   _____

2. I will blow out the candles.   _____

3. Everyone will give me presents.   _____

4. I will wear my favorite red shirt.   _____

5. My cousins will come from out of town.   _____

6. It will take them four hours.   _____

7. My Aunt Betty will fly in from Cleveland.   _____

8. She will sing me a song.   _____

Irregular Verbs

There are some verbs that you do not change to past tense by simply adding **ed**. These verbs are spelled differently. They are called **irregular verbs**.

Examples:	**present:**	fly, sing, run, swim, begin, eat, buy, bring, take
	past:	flew, sang, ran, swam, began, ate, bought, brought, took

Directions: Read each sentence. Underline all the irregular verbs.

1. Jeremy climbed to the top of the mountain and sang.

2. Moisha ran into town.

3. After breakfast, Tony and Cara went into town and bought books.

4. Jennifer found a stable, rented a horse, and rode on a trail by the river.

5. I put on my bathing suit and swam in the river.

6. Dr. Dexterous flew a helicopter over the forest.

7. Yolanda went exploring and found an arrowhead.

8. Carl found the best Mexican restaurant where he ate tacos and burritos.

Name _____

Irregular Verbs

Past tense tells about what happened in the past. To make a regular verb past tense, add **d** or **ed** to the verb. Irregular verbs do not form the past tense by adding **d** or **ed**.

Examples: **regular verbs:** paint = painted   try = tried
               irregular verbs: fly = flew   eat = ate

Directions: Rewrite each sentence below in the past tense.

1. First, Aunt Betty picks out the paint for the shutters.

   _____

   _____

2. Then, Aunt Betty and Jenny make food for the picnic.

   _____

   _____

3. Next, they stop to get gas for the car.

   _____

   _____

4. After they shop, Aunt Betty begins to wash the car.

   _____

   _____

5. Finally, Aunt Betty's sisters arrive to have dinner.

   _____

   _____

Irregular Verbs

Directions: Circle the verb that completes each sentence.

1. Scientists will try to (find, found) the cure.

2. Eric (brings, brought) his lunch to school yesterday.

3. Every day, Betsy (sings, sang) all the way home.

4. Jason (breaks, broke) the vase last night.

5. The ice had (freezes, frozen) in the tray.

6. Mitzi has (swims, swum) in that pool before.

7. Now I (choose, chose) to exercise daily.

8. The teacher has (rings, rung) the bell.

9. The boss (speaks, spoke) to us yesterday.

10. She (says, said) it twice already.

Name _____

Irregular Verbs

Verbs that do not become past tense when you add **ed** are called **irregular verbs**. The spellings of these verbs change.

Example: **present**   **past**

begin, begins   began
eat, eats   ate

Directions: Finish each sentence with the past tense of the irregular verb.

1. Sam almost _____ (fall) when he tripped over the curb.

2. Diana made sure she _____ (take) bug spray on her hike.

3. Dave _____ (run) over to his friend's house.

4. Tim _____ (break) off a long piece of grass to put in his mouth.

5. Eve _____ (know) the path along the river well.

6. The clouds _____ (begin) to turn gray.

7. Kathy _____ (throw) a small piece of bread to the ducks.

8. Everyone _____ (eat) a very nutritious meal after the long adventure.

9. We all _____ (sleep) very well that night.

Name _____

The Irregular Verb "to Do"

It is important to use the correct form of **to do** whenever you speak or write.

Examples: Tara and Nan **do** stretching exercises.
Sara **did** the most sit-ups.

Directions: Circle the correct form of **to do** in each sentence.

1. Our soccer team (did, done) a great job last year.

2. They will (did, do) very well this year.

3. John (do, does) thirty sit-ups every morning.

4. Tara and Nan (do, does) laps in the afternoon.

5. Sara (do, does) the most practicing each day.

6. Our team (does, do) have a lot of spirit.

7. We (does, do) not ever get tired.

8. Mary (does, do) not always stop the ball.

9. Our coach (did, do) compliment us for our efforts.

10. Playing soccer well (do, does) require long hours of practice.

Name _____

The Irregular Verb "Be"

The verb **be** is different from all other verbs. The present-tense forms of **be** are **am**, **is**, and **are**. The past-tense forms of **be** are **was** and **were**. The verb **to be** is written in the following ways:

singular: I am, you are, he is, she is, it is
plural: we are, you are, they are

Directions: Finish each sentence with the correct form of **be** from the Word Bank.

Word Bank				
are	am	is	was	were

Example: I ___am___ feeling good at this moment.

1. My sister _____ a good singer.

2. You _____ going to the store with me.

3. Sandy _____ at the movies last week.

4. Rick and Tom _____ best friends.

5. He _____ happy about the surprise.

6. The cat _____ hungry.

7. I _____ going to the ball game.

8. They _____ silly.

9. I _____ glad to help my mother.

Name _____

The Irregular Verb "Be"

Be is an irregular verb. The present-tense forms of be are **be**, **am**, **is**, and **are**. The past-tense forms of be are **was** and **were**.

Directions: Write the correct form of **be** in the blanks.

Example: I ____am____ so happy for you!

1. Jared _____ unfriendly yesterday.

2. English can _____ a lot of fun to learn.

3. They _____ among the nicest people I know.

4. They _____ late yesterday.

5. She promises she _____ going to arrive on time.

6. I _____ nervous right now about the test.

7. If you _____ happy now, then so am I.

8. He _____ as nice to me last week as I had hoped.

9. He can _____ very nice.

10. Would you _____ mad if I moved your desk?

11. He _____ waiting at the door for me yesterday.

Name _____

Past-Tense Verbs

Present-tense verbs tell what is happening now. **Past-tense verbs** tell what happened in the past.

To change most action verbs to past tense, add **ed**.

Example: jump = jumped

To change the form of the verb **be** to past tense, follow these rules:

Examples: am = was   are = were   is = was

Directions: Read each sentence. Underline the verb. Then, rewrite each sentence and change the verb to past tense.

1. It is raining.

_____

2. Justin and Kendra splash in puddles.

_____

3. Paola plays in the rain.

_____

4. Lynda bakes cookies for a snack.

_____

5. Pan and Arthur watch movies on television.

_____

6. Carlos and Keith are at the library.

_____

7. I dash to the barn.

_____

8. I am soaking wet.

_____

Name _____

The Past-Tense Verb "Be"

Directions: Write sentences that tell about each picture using the words **is**, **are**, **was**, and **were**. Use words from the Word Bank as either nouns or verbs.

Word Bank					
pound	spill	toast	list	load	search

Name _____

Irregular Verbs: Past-Tense

Irregular verbs change completely in the past tense. Unlike regular verbs, past-tense forms of irregular verbs are not formed by adding **ed**.

Example: The past tense of **go** is **went**.
The past tense of **break** is **broke**.

A **helping verb** helps to tell about the past. **Has, have**, and **had** are helping verbs that you can use with action verbs to show that the action happened in the past. The past-tense form of the irregular verb sometimes changes when a helping verb is added.

Present Tense Irregular Verb	Past Tense Irregular Verb	Past Tense Irregular Verb With Helper	
go	went	have/has/had gone	
see	saw	have/has/had seen	
do	did	have/has/had done	
bring	brought	have/has/had brought	
sing	sang	have/has/had sung	
drive	drove	have/has/had driven	
swim	swam	have/has/had swum	
sleep	slept	have/has/had slept	

Directions: Choose four verbs from the chart. For each verb, write one sentence using the past-tense form without a helping verb. Then, write one sentence using the past-tense form with a helping verb.

1. _____

2. _____

3. _____

4. _____

Name _____

Irregular Verbs With Helpers

Past-tense verbs that do not have an **ed** or **d** ending are called **irregular verbs**.

present	past	past participle
ring	rang	has rung, have rung
see	saw	has seen, have seen

Directions: Fill in the missing verbs in the chart.

Present	Past	Past-Tense Irregular Verb With Helper
do, does		has or have done
go, goes	went	has or have
know, knows		has or have known
fall, falls		has or have fallen
speak, speaks	spoke	has or have
stand, stands		has or have stood
write, writes		has or have written
draw, draws	drew	has or have

Directions: Circle the correct verb form in the parentheses.

1. Dad and I (went, gone) on a walk in the park one morning.

2. More than six inches of snow had (fall, fallen).

3. Yesterday, the tall trees (stand, stood) silently in their white overcoats.

4. A rabbit (ran, run) away as we approached it.

5. We (heard, hears) a cardinal's call from the oak tree.

6. A squirrel's next (sat, sitted) in a tree overhead.

7. It (took, taken) us nearly an hour to make it back home.

Name _____

Regular and Irregular Verbs

Verbs that show action happening now are in the **present** tense. Verbs that show action happening in the past are in the **past** tense.

Examples: **present:**   The fire department **puts** out fires.
              past: The fire department **put** out fires yesterday.

Directions: Circle the verb (present or past) that finishes each sentence.

1. The police department (chases, chased) criminals every day.

2. Two days ago, our team (won, wins) the town trophy.

3. My teacher always (wears, wore) glasses.

4. The mailman (delivers, delivered) the wrong mail yesterday.

5. At last night's game, the mayor's daughter (sing, sang) the "Star-Spangled Banner."

6. A fire truck (races, raced) down the street this morning.

7. The bank (opens, opened) at 8 a.m. on Mondays.

8. When the score was (tie, tied), the pitcher threw a curve ball.

9. I (worked, work) at the library last week.

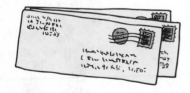

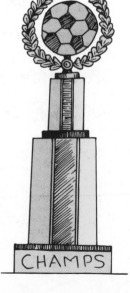

Name _____

Verb Tense

Directions: Use verbs to complete the story below.

Last week, Amy and I _____ a contest. We were supposed to make a card to give to a child in a hospital. First, we _____ a big sheet of white paper in half to make the card. Then, we _____ to draw a rainbow on the front.

Amy started coloring the rainbow all by herself. "Wait!" I said. "We both _____ the contest. Let me help!"

"Okay," Amy said. "We can _____ . You _____ a color, and then I'll _____ a color." It was more fun when we _____ . When we finished making the rainbow, we _____ to _____ a sun to the picture. I cut the sun out of yellow paper. Then, Amy _____ it just above the rainbow. Well, our card didn't win the contest, but it did make a little boy with a broken leg smile. Amy and I felt so happy! We _____ to go right home and make some more cards!

69

Name _____

Verb Forms

Directions: Finish each sentence with the correct verb form.

1. Before the wheel, people _____ heavy loads.   **drag, dragged**

2. No one knows who _____ the wheel.   **invented, invent**

3. The Sumerians _____ some of the first people to use the wheel.   **were, are**

4. They _____ the first wheels out of wood and stone.   **make, made**

5. The wheels _____ very heavy.   **be, were**

6. Then, people _____ of spokes.   **think, thought**

7. Spokes helped the wheels _____ more easily.   **turn, turned**

8. Soon, people were _____ roads.   **built, building**

9. I _____ glad that the wheel was invented.   **is, am**

10. There _____ many things that move on wheels.   **is, are**

11. Cars and trucks _____ wheels.   **has, have**

12. A potter_____ pots on a wheel.   **make, made**

13. A wool maker_____ wool on a spinning wheel.   **spin, spun**

14. Amusement park rides_____ wheels.   **have, has**

15. My favorite set of wheels _____ on my bike.   **is, am**

Name _____

Future-Tense Verbs

The **future tense** of a verb tells about something that will happen in the future. **Will** or **shall** are the helping verbs that are usually used with future tense.

Directions: Change the verb tense in each sentence to future tense.

Example: She cooks dinner.
                She will cook dinner.

1. He plays baseball.

   _____

2. She walks to school.

   _____

3. Bobby talks to the teacher.

   _____

4. I remember to vote.

   _____

5. Jack mows the lawn every week.

   _____

6. We go on vacation soon.

   _____

Name _____

Future-Tense Verbs

To change a verb to the future tense, you usually add the helping verb **will**.

Example: He **will** work.

Directions: Circle each verb that is in the future tense.

In the Jungle

We will walk through the hot, dark jungle. Monkeys will swing from the trees and parrots will squawk as they fly around us. Tigers will growl and roar. We will eat our lunches under a giant fern. I hope a hungry gorilla will join us for lunch. We will share our bananas. After lunch, we will pick more papayas, bananas, and mangos.

When the sun begins to set, we will store our fruit in a tree and pitch our tent. We will build a fire. Around the fire, we will tell scary stories and then try to fall asleep.

Future-Tense Verbs

Verbs in the **future tense** tell what will happen in the future. The helping verb **will** is usually used with the action verb to make the future tense.

Example: We **will take** a trip to see the pyramids.

Directions: First, underline the verb in each sentence. Then, write the verb in future tense on the line after each sentence.

1. We ask questions about the pyramids. _____

2. The explorer answers our questions. _____

3. Explorers find pyramids in Central and South America

   and Egypt. _____

4. The explorers visit the pyramid of Cheops

   in Egypt. _____

5. The explorers study the history and architecture of

   the pyramids. _____

6. The explorers compare the pyramids in Egypt with the pyramids in

   Central and South America. _____

7. The explorers write about what they saw. _____

8. The photographer donates his pictures to

   the project. _____

Name _____

Future-Tense Verbs

Verb tense tells time in a sentence. The **future tense** tells about what will happen in the future. The helping verb **will** is usually used with the action verb to show future time.

Example: Tomorrow we **will go** to our aunt's house.

Directions: Write each sentence below in the future tense.

1. I pick up groceries at the store.

_____

_____

2. I call the painter to paint the shutters.

_____

_____

3. The neighborhood builds a float for the parade.

_____

_____

4. There is a picnic at City Hall.

_____

_____

5. Jenny comes to visit.

_____

_____

Name _____

Using "ing" Verbs

Use the helping verbs **is** and **are** when describing something happening right now. Use the helping verb **was** and **were** when describing something that already happened.

Directions: Finish each sentence by adding **ing** to the verb and using the helping verb **is**, **are**, **was**, or **were**.

Examples:

When it started to rain, we ___were raking___ the leaves.
                                    rake

When the soldiers marched up that hill, Captain Stevens

___was commanding___ them.
     command

1. Now, the police _____ them of stealing the money.
                                accuse

2. Look! The eggs_____.
                             hatch

3. A minute ago, the sky_____.
                               glow

4. My dad says he _____ us to ice cream!
                         treat

5. She_____ the whole time we were at the mall.
                 sneeze

6. While we were at recess, he _____ our tests.
                         grade

7. I hear something. Who _____?
                         talk

8. As I watched, the workers _____ the wood into little chips.
                     grind

Name _____

Using "ing" Verbs

Using **ing** verbs can make your writing more interesting to read. Compare these lists of verbs:

List A	List B
went	skipping
look	discovering
find	digging
sleep	snoring
run	slithering
drop	sailing
go	soaring

Now, compare the sentences below. Notice that the second sentence is much more descriptive.

The children left the school.
The children were flying out of the school doors.

Directions: Change each boldface verb to a more descriptive **ing** verb. Do not forget to add a helping verb (**am, is, are, was, were**).

1. The snake **went** among the rocks.

_____

2. Water **fell** over the cliff.

_____

3. The leaves **drop** to the ground.

_____

4. Snowflakes **fall** from the sky.

_____

5. At the library, she **looked** for a book.

_____

6. Her horse got loose and **ran** across the meadow.

_____

Name _____

Using "ing" Verbs

Directions: Using descriptive **ing** verbs, write five sentences about activities you do every day.

Example: Peter is scarfing down his breakfast so he will not miss the bus.

1. _____

   _____

2. _____

   _____

3. _____

   _____

4. _____

   _____

5. _____

   _____

Name _____

Verb Tense

Not only do verbs tell the action of a sentence, but they also tell when the action takes place. This is called the **verb tense**. There are three verb tenses: past, present, and future tense.

Present-tense verbs tell what is happening now.

Examples:　　Jane **spells** words with long vowel sounds.

　　　　　　　Stan **is standing** out in the rain.

Past-tense verbs tell about action that has already happened.

Examples:　　stay = stayed　　John **stayed** home yesterday.

　　　　　　　talk = was talking　　Sally **was talking** to her mom.

Future-tense verbs tell what will happen in the future. Future-tense verbs are made by putting the word **will** before the verb.

Example:　　paint = will paint　　Susie and Sherry **will paint** the house.

Directions: Look at each verb below. Write whether the verb tense is past, present, or future.

Example:　　watches ____present____

Verb	Tense	Verb	Tense
1. wanted	_____	7. writes	_____
2. will eat	_____	8. vaulted	_____
3. was squawking	_____	9. were sleeping	_____
4. yawns	_____	10. will sing	_____
5. crawled	_____	11. is speaking	_____
6. will hunt	_____	12. will cook	_____

Name _____

Verb Tense

Verbs can be in the **past**, **present**, or **future**.

Directions: Match each sentence with the correct verb tense.
(**Think:** When did each thing happen?)

It will rain tomorrow.   past

He played golf.   present

Molly is sleeping.   future

Jack is singing a song.   past

I will buy a kite.   present

Dad worked hard today.   future

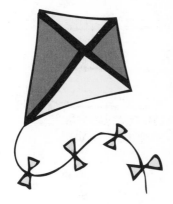

Directions: Rewrite each sentence and change the verb to the tense shown.

1. Jenny played with her new friend. (present)

   _____

2. Bobby is talking to him. (future)

   _____

3. Holly and Angie walk here. (past)

   _____

Past   Present   Future

Name _____

Verb Tense

Directions: Write **PRES** for present tense, **PAST** for past tense, or **FUT** for future tense.

1. _____ She will help him study.

2. _____ She helped him study.

3. _____ She helps him study.

4. _____ She promised she would help him study.

Directions: Write the past-tense form of each verb.

1. cry _____

2. sigh _____

3. hurry _____

4. pop _____

Directions: Write the correct form of **be**.

1. They _____ my closest neighbors.

2. I _____ very happy for you today.

3. He _____ there on time yesterday.

4. She _____ still the nicest girl I know.

Directions: Circle the correct verb.

1. He went/gone to my locker.

2. I went/gone to the beach many times.

3. Have you went/gone to this show before?

4. We went/gone all the way to the top!

VERBS

Verb Tense

Name _____

Directions: Read each sentence below. Underline the verbs. Above each verb, write whether it is past, present, or future tense.

past

Example: The crowd <u>was booing</u> the referee.

1. Sally will compete on the balance beam.

2. Matt marches with the band.

3. Nick is marching, too.

4. The geese swooped down to the pond.

5. Dad will fly home tomorrow.

6. They were looking for a new book.

7. Presently, they are going to the garden.

8. The children will pick the ripe vegetables.

9. Grandmother canned the green beans.

Directions: Write three sentences of your own using the correct verb tense.

Past tense:

_____

Present tense:

_____

Future tense:

_____

Name _____

Verbs: Present, Past, and Future Tense

The **present tense** of a verb tells what is happening now.

> Examples: I **am** happy. I **run** fast.

The **past tense** of a verb tells what has already happened.

> Examples: I **was** happy. I **ran** fast.

The **future tense** of a verb refers to what is going to happen. The word **will** usually comes before the future tense of a verb.

> Examples: I **will be** happy. I **will run** fast.

Directions: The sentences below are in the present tense. Rewrite each sentence using the past and future tenses of the verb.

> Example: I think of you as my best friend.
>
> I thought of you as my best friend.
>
> I will think of you as my best friend.

1. I hear you coming up the steps.

_____

_____

2. I rush every morning to get ready for school.

_____

_____

3. I bake brownies every Saturday.

_____

_____

VERBS

Name _____

Verbs: Present, Past, and Future Tense

Directions: Read each sentence below. Write **PRES** if the sentence is in the present tense. Write **PAST** if the sentence is in the past tense. Write **FUT** if the sentence is in the future tense.

Example: ___FUT___ I will be thrilled to accept the award.

1. _____ Will you go with me to the dentist?

2. _____ I thought he looked familiar!

3. _____ They ate every single slice of pizza.

4. _____ I run myself ragged sometimes.

5. _____ Do you think this project is worthwhile?

6. _____ No one has been able to repair the broken plate.

7. _____ Thoughtful gifts are always nice.

8. _____ I like the way he sang!

9. _____ With a voice like that, he will go a long way.

10. _____ I hope that they visit soon.

11. _____ I wanted that coat very much.

12. _____ She will be happy to take your place.

13. _____ Everyone thinks the test will be easy.

14. _____ Collecting stamps is her favorite hobby.

© 2006 School Specialty Publishing

Name _____

Adjectives

Adjectives are words that tell more about nouns, such as a **happy** child, a **cold** day, or a **hard** problem. Adjectives can tell **how many** (**one** airplane) or **which one** (**those** shoes).

Directions: The nouns are in bold letters. Circle the adjectives that describe the nouns.

Example: Some people have (unusual) **pets**.

1. Some people keep wild **animals**, like lions and bears.

2. These **pets** need special care.

3. These **animals** want to be free.

4. Even small **animals** can be difficult to care for if they are wild.

5. Raccoons and squirrels are not tame **pets**.

6. Never touch a wild **animal** that may be sick.

Directions: Finish the story below by writing your own adjectives. Use your imagination.

My Cat

My cat is a very _____ animal. She has _____

and _____ fur. Her favorite toy is a _____ ball.

She has _____ claws. She has a _____ tail. She

has a _____ face and _____ whiskers. I think she

is the _____ cat in the world!

Name _____

Describing Words: Adjectives

A word that **describes** a noun is called an **adjective**. Adjectives tell what something is like. Fill in each blank below using an adjective from the Word Bank.

Word Bank				
tiny	lumpy	pink	spotted	scary

Although the diamond was _____ , it sparkled like a huge spotlight.

"This bed is really uncomfortable. It is too _____ !" said Max.

The _____ monster in my living room was only a dream.

The _____ black and white dog is called a Dalmatian.

"_____ is my favorite color!" said the princess.

Name _____

Describing Words: Adjectives

A word that **describes** a noun is called an **adjective**.

Directions: Finish each sentence below using the adjectives from the Word Bank.

Word Bank
black ugly thousands soft expensive hairy

The _____ mattress was very

_____ to buy because it was

made of _____ of downy feathers.

The _____ , _____ spider

was so _____ that everybody was afraid

to look at it. All it really needed was a haircut!

Directions: Finish each sentence below using the adjectives from the Word Bank.

Word Bank
hungry delicate loud beautiful tall scary

Brown bears can be very _____ when they

are _____ . They stand up _____

and let out _____ growls.

Roses are _____ flowers and quite

_____ . Their petals feel like smooth velvet.

Name _____

Adjectives

Adjectives can tell the color, size, and number of the nouns they describe.

Directions: Look at the pictures. Then, complete the charts.

Example:

Noun	What Color?	What Size?	What Number?
flowers	red	small	two

Noun	What Color?	What Size?	What Number?

Noun	What Color?	What Size?	What Number?

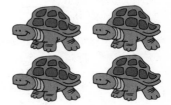

Noun	What Color?	What Size?	What Number?

Adjectives

Adjectives are describing words. They tell **how many**, **what kind**, or **which one**. When you use adjectives in your writing, you are making the sentences clearer and more interesting.

Example: The car speeds away.
The **sleek**, **red** car speeds away.

Directions: Use words from the Word Bank to make the story below more interesting.

Word Bank
beautiful   magical   pointy   fat   cruel   huge   wonderful   silly   fantastic
fun   blue   cold   funny   exciting   shy   rusty   strong   tiny   sweet

Once upon a time, there was a _____ princess who

wore a _____ hat. She lived in a _____

castle with her _____ cat. The princess was bored.

"There is nothing to do," the _____ princess complained.

She wandered off into the _____ garden in search of

adventure. "What is this I see?" she cried. There was a _____

box next to a _____ tree. The princess opened the lid

to find a _____ cloak. "This is a _____ cloak!"

she exclaimed. But when she slipped it on, the _____

princess vanished!

Name _____

Adjectives

Adjectives are words that describe nouns by telling **what kind**, **how many**, or **which one**.

Examples: **ten-thousand tiny**, **black** tarantulas
talented chefs
tall, **shiny** skyscrapers

Directions: Underline the adjectives that describe each noun listed below.

1. a bright, red fire engine

2. four awesome firemen

3. a tall, wooden ladder

4. two black-and-white

   dalmations

5. a soft bed

6. a skinny fire pole

7. a white gazebo

8. the ten members of the band

9. a red-and-white banner

10. magnificent fireworks

Name _____

Adjectives

Adjectives tell **which one**, **how many**, or **what kind**.

Example: **These three red** apples.

Directions: Underline the nouns in each sentence below. Circle the adjectives that describe the nouns. Then, write each adjective that you circled in the correct category.

1. The lovely, pink flower has five blossoms.

2. These white roses have a sweet fragrance.

3. Each flower has several dainty petals.

4. The refreshing aroma of the sweet-scented lavender filled the air.

5. These five yellow sunflowers are tall plants.

Which one?	What kind?	How many?
1. _____	_____	_____
_____	_____	_____
2. _____	_____	_____
_____	_____	_____
3. _____	_____	_____
_____	_____	_____
4. _____	_____	_____
_____	_____	_____
5. _____	_____	_____
_____	_____	_____

Adjectives

Name _____

Adjectives are words that describe nouns by telling **what kind**, **how many**, or **which one**.

Directions: Write three adjectives for each noun below. Do not use an adjective more than once. The first one is done for you.

book	foot	house
long		
good		
short		

car	chips	cloud

butterflies	shoes	flute

clown	flowers	pizza

Adjectives

Directions: Underline the adjectives in the story.

The Best Soup I Ever Had

I woke up one cold winter morning and decided to make a delicious pot of hot vegetable soup. First, I put sweet white onions in the big gray pot. Then, I added orange carrots and dark green broccoli. The broccoli looked just like tiny trees. I added fresh, juicy tomatoes and crisp potatoes next. I cooked the soup for a long, long time. This soup turned out to be the best soup I ever had.

Directions: Rewrite two of the sentences from the story. Substitute your own adjectives for the words that you underlined.

1. _____

_____

_____

2. _____

_____

_____

Adjectives

Adjectives tell more about nouns. Adjectives are describing words.

Examples: **scary** animals **bright** glow **wet** frog

Directions: Add at least two adjectives to each sentence below. Use your own words or words from the Word Bank.

Word Bank						
pale	soft	sticky	burning	furry	glistening	peaceful
faint	shivering	slippery	gleaming	gentle	foggy	tangled

Example: The stripe was blue.
The wide stripe was light blue.

1. The frog had eyes.

_____

2. The house was a sight.

_____

3. A boy heard a noise.

_____

4. The girl tripped over a toad.

_____

5. A tiger ran through the room.

_____

6. They saw a glow in the window.

_____

7. A pan was sitting on the stove.

_____

8. The boys were eating french fries.

_____

Name _____

Adjectives

Adjectives tell a noun's size, color, shape, texture, taste, brightness, darkness, personality, sound, and so on.

> **Examples: color** — red, yellow, green, black
> **size** — small, large, huge, tiny
> **shape** — round, square, rectangular, oval
> **texture** — rough, smooth, soft, scaly
> **brightness** — glistening, shimmering, dull, pale
> **personality** — gentle, grumpy, happy, sad

Directions: Follow the instructions below.

1. Look at an apple, orange, or other piece of fruit. Write adjectives that describe its size, color, shape, and texture.

   _____

2. Take a bite of fruit. Write adjectives that describe its taste, texture, and smell.

   _____

3. Use the adjectives from above to write a cinquain about your fruit. A **cinquain** is a five-line poem. See the form and sample poem below.

   Form: Line 1 — noun   **Example:**   Apple
   Line 2 — two adjectives   red, smooth
   Line 3 — three sounds   cracking, smacking, slurping
   Line 4 — four-word phrase   tastes sour and delicious
   Line 5 — noun   Apple

   _____

   _____ , _____

   _____ , _____ , _____

   _____ , _____

   _____

Adjectives

Directions: Finish each sentence below with the correct adjective from the Word Bank.

Word Bank					
polite	careless	neat	shy	selfish	thoughtful

1. Someone who is quiet and needs some time to make new friends

   is _____ .

2. A person who says "please" and "thank you" is _____ .

3. Someone who always puts all the toys away

   is _____ .

4. A person who will not share with others

   is _____ .

5. A person who leaves a bike out all night is _____ .

6. Someone who thinks of others is _____ .

Name _____

Adjectives: Explaining Sentences

Directions: Use a word from the Word Bank to tell about a person in each picture below. Then, write a sentence that explains why you chose that word.

Word Bank					
polite	neat	careless	shy	selfish	thoughtful

The word I picked: _____

I chose this word because . . .

_____

_____

The word I picked: _____

I chose this word because . . .

_____

_____

The word I picked: _____

I chose this word because . . .

_____

_____

Name _____

Adjectives

Directions: Look at each picture. Then, add adjectives to each sentence. Use colors, numbers, words from the Word Bank, and any other words you need to describe each picture.

Word Bank		
polite	neat	careless
shy	selfish	thoughtful

Example: The boy shared his pencil.

The polite boy shared his red pencil.
_____

The girl dropped her coat.

_____

The boy played with cars.

_____

The boy put books away.

_____

Name _____

Adjectives: Create a Word Puzzle

Directions: Make your own word puzzle! Write the words from the Word Bank in the puzzle below. Write some words across and others from top to bottom. Make some words cross each other. Fill the extra squares with other letters. See if someone else can find the words from the Word Bank in your puzzle!

Word Bank					
polite	neat	careless	shy	selfish	thoughtful

Example: Your puzzle will look like the one below. It has two of the words from the Word Bank in it. Can you find them?

l	a	e	n	x	f	y	h
c	a	r	e	l	e	s	s
y	u	a	a	r	n	m	z
g	w	i	t	b	i	v	s

Now, make your own puzzle!

Adjectives

Adjectives describe nouns. They tell **how many**, **what kind**, or **which one**.

Examples: **seven** children, **purple** flowers, **that** toy

Directions: Write three adjectives to describe each noun.

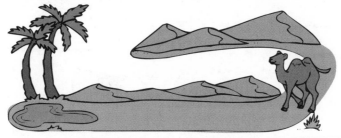

puppy	desert
storm	city
beetle	tulip
computer	snow

Name _____

Adjectives: Using the Five Senses

When you are writing, you can use your five senses to help you describe something. Think about what you might see, hear, smell, taste, and feel.

Example: **See:**   shiny, round

Taste: spicy, sweet

Hear: squeaky, roaring

Feel: sharp, prickly

Smell: rotten, smoky

Directions: Write two describing words for each noun. Use your five senses to help you.

1. strawberry   _____   _____
2. pony   _____   _____
3. sand   _____   _____
4. leather coat   _____   _____
5. golf ball   _____   _____
6. bicycle chain   _____   _____
7. paper   _____   _____

Directions: Now, use two of the nouns and describing words from above to write a descriptive sentence.

Name _____

Adjectives Plus "er"

The suffix **er** is often added to adjectives to compare two things.

    Examples: My feet are **large**.
                          Your feet are **larger** than my feet.

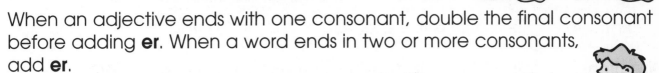

When an adjective ends with one consonant, double the final consonant before adding **er**. When a word ends in two or more consonants, add **er**.

    Examples: big = bigger (single consonant)
                          bold = bolder (two consonants)

When an adjective ends in **y**, change the **y** to **i** before adding **er**.

    Examples: easy = easier
                          greasy = greasier
                          breezy = breezier

Directions: Use the correct rule to add **er** to the words below.

    Example: fast   *faster* _____

1. thin _____
2. long _____
3. few _____
4. ugly _____
5. silly _____
6. busy _____
7. grand _____
8. lean _____
9. young _____

10. fat _____
11. poor _____
12. juicy _____
13. early _____
14. clean _____
15. thick _____
16. creamy _____
17. deep _____
18. lazy _____

Name _____

Adjectives: Making Comparisons

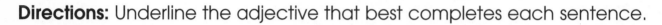

Adjectives that compare two things usually end in **er**.

   Example: Ants are **smaller** than ladybugs.

Adjectives that compare three or more things usually end in **est**.

   Example: February is the **shortest** month of the year.

Directions: Underline the adjective that best completes each sentence.

1. Margery is the (stronger, strongest) girl in third grade.

2. The blue sailboat is (faster, fastest) than the red sailboat.

3. July is usually (hotter, hottest) than January.

4. Which instrument is the (louder, loudest) one in the orchestra?

5. Turtles are (slower, slowest) than rabbits.

6. Travis is the (funnier, funniest) student in our class.

7. Your slice of cake is (thicker, thickest) than mine.

8. Frogs jump (higher, highest) than mice.

9. Mount Everest is the (taller, tallest) mountain in the world.

10. The summer solstice is the (longer, longest) day of the year.

Directions: Write a sentence for each adjective listed below. Use the adjective to compare two or more things.

1. short _____

2. bright _____

3. smart _____

4. cold _____

Name _____

Adding "er" and "est" to Adjectives

Directions: Circle the correct adjective for each sentence.

> **Example:** Of all the students in the gym, her voice was the (louder, (loudest)).

1. "I can tell you are (busier, busiest) than I am," he said to the librarian.

2. If you and Carl stand back to back, I can see which one is (taller, tallest).

3. She is the (kinder, kindest) teacher in the whole building.

4. Wow! That is the (bigger, biggest) pumpkin I have ever seen!

5. I believe your flashlight is (brighter, brightest) than mine.

6. "This is the (cleaner, cleanest) your room has been in a long time," Mother said.

7. The leaves on that plant are (prettier, prettiest) than the ones on the window sill.

Name _____

Adjectives That Compare

Add **er** to most **adjectives** when comparing two nouns. Add **est** to most adjectives when comparing three or more nouns.

Example: The forecaster said this winter is **colder** than last winter.
It is the **coldest** winter on record.

Directions: Finish each sentence with the correct form of the adjective.

1. The weather map showed that the _____ place of all was Marquette, Michigan.   (cold)

2. The _____ city of all was Phoenix, Arizona.
   (warm)

3. Does San Diego get_____ than
   San Francisco?   (hot)

4. The_____snow of all fell in the Twin Cities.
   (deep)

5. The snowfall was two inches_____
   than in Buffalo.   (deep)

6. The_____ place of all was Chicago,
   Illinois.   (windy)

7. The_____ winds of all blew there.
   (strong)

8. The_____city in the U.S. was Bangor,
   Maine. (foggy)

9. Seattle was the_____of all the cities.
   (rainy)

10. It is usually_____ in Seattle than
    in Portland.   (rainy)

Name _____

Adjectives Plus "est"

The ending **est** is often added to adjectives to compare more than two things.

> **Example:** My glass is **full**.
> Your glass is **fuller**.
> His glass is **fullest**.

When an adjective ends with one consonant, you usually double the final consonant before adding **est**.

> **Examples:** big = biggest (short vowel)
> steep = steepest (long vowel)

When an adjective ends in **y**, change the **y** to **i** before adding **est**.

> **Example:** easy = easiest

Directions: Use the correct rule to add **est** to the words below.

> **Example:** thin <u>thinnest</u>_____

1. skinny _____		10. big	_____
2. cheap _____		13. silly	_____
3. busy _____		14. tall	_____
4. loud _____		15. quick	_____
5. kind _____		16. red	_____
6. dreamy_____		17. happy	_____
7. ugly _____		18. high	_____
8. pretty _____		19. wet	_____
9. early _____		20. clean	_____

Name _____

Adjectives Plus "er" or "More"

Directions: Add the word or words needed in each sentence.

1. I thought the book was _____ than the movie. (interesting)

Black Beauty

2. Do you want to carry this box? It is _____ than the one you have now. (light)

3. I noticed you are moving _____ this morning. Does your ankle still bother you? (slow)

4. She stuck out her lower lip and said, "Your ice-cream

   cone is _____ than mine!" (big)

5. Mom said my room was _____ than it has been in a long time. (clean)

Name _____

Adjectives Preceded by "More"

The word **more** comes before most adjectives that have two or more syllables as a way to show comparison between two things.

Examples: **Correct**: intelligent = more intelligent
Incorrect: intelligenter

Correct: famous = more famous
Incorrect: famouser

Directions: Write **more** before the adjectives that fit the rule.
Write an **X** before the adjectives that do not fit the rule.

Examples: ____X____ cheap

     ___more___ beautiful

1. _____ quick

2. _____ terrible

3. _____ difficult

4. _____ interesting

5. _____ polite

6. _____ cute

7. _____ dark

8. _____ sad

9. _____ embarrassing

10. _____ nice

11. _____ often

12. _____ hard

13. _____ valuable

14. _____ close

15. _____ fast

16. _____ important

Name _____

Adjectives Plus "est" or "Most"

Directions: Add the word or words needed to complete each sentence.

Example: The star over there is the ____brightest____ of all!
(bright)

1. "I believe this is the _____ time I have ever had,"
said Mackenzie.   (delightful)

2. That game was the _____ one of the whole year!
(exciting)

3. I think this tree has the _____ leaves.
(green)

4. We will need the _____ knife you have.
(sharp)

5. Everyone agreed that your chocolate chip cookies

were the _____ of all.
(delicious)

ADJECTIVES

Adjectives Plus "Most"

The word **most** comes before most adjectives that have two or more syllables as a way to show comparison between more than two things.

Examples: **Correct:** intelligent = most intelligent
Incorrect: intelligentest

Correct: famous = most famous
Incorrect: famousest

Directions: Read the groups of sentences below. In the last sentence of each group, write the adjective with the word **most**.

Example: My uncle is intelligent.
My aunt is more intelligent.
My cousin is the _____ most intelligent _____.

1. I am thankful.
   My brother is more thankful.
   My parents are the _____.

2. Your sister is polite.
   Your brother is more polite.
   You are the _____.

3. The blouse was expensive.
   The sweater was more expensive.
   The coat was the _____.

4. The class was fortunate.
   The teacher was more fortunate.
   The principal was the _____.

5. The cookies were delicious.
   The cake was even more delicious.
   The brownies were the _____.

6. That painting is beautiful.
   The sculpture is more beautiful.
   The finger painting is the _____.

Name _____

Adjectives That Break the Rules

The adjectives **good** and **bad** do not follow the rules. Instead of using **er** and **est** or the words **more** and **most**, they use different spellings to compare two or more things.

good    better    best

Examples: **good** — This is a **good** book.
better — My book is **better** than your book.
best — This is the **best** book I've ever read.

bad — The weather is **bad** today.
worse — The weather is **worse** today than yesterday.
worst — Today's weather is the **worst** of the winter.

Directions: Circle the form of the adjective that finishes each sentence.

1. This is the (bad, worse, worst) pizza I have ever eaten.

2. My shoes are in (bad, worse, worst) condition than yours.

3. My grades are the (good, better, best) in the class.

4. Plastic cups make (good, better, best) paint containers.

5. This tool is the (good, better, best) one I have.

6. The bumpy drive was a (bad, worse, worst) one.

7. My brownies are (good, better, best) than yours.

8. This is a (bad, worse, worst) snowstorm.

9. This one looks even (good, better, best) than that one.

10. My brother's room looks (bad, worse, worst) than mine.

Name _____

Pronouns

Pronouns are words that are used in place of nouns.

Examples: he, she, it, they, him, them, her, him

Directions: Read each sentence. Write the pronoun that takes the place of each noun.

Example: The **monkey** dropped the banana. ___It___

1. **Dad** washed the car last night. _____

2. **Mary** and **David** took a walk in the park. _____

3. **Peggy** spent the night at her grandmother's house. _____

4. The **players** lost their game. _____

5. **Mike Van Meter** is a great soccer player. _____

6. The **parrot** can say five different words. _____

7. **Megan** wrote a story in class today. _____

8. They gave a party for **Teresa**. _____

9. Everyone in the class was happy for **Ted**. _____

10. The children petted the **giraffe**. _____

11. Linda put the **kittens** near the warm stove. _____

12. **Gina** made a chocolate cake for my birthday. _____

13. **Pete** and **Matt** played baseball on the same team. _____

14. Give the books to **Herbie**. _____

Pronouns

Singular Pronouns

I	me	my	mine
you	your	yours	
he	she	him	her
his	hers	it	its

Plural Pronouns

we	us	our
ours	you	your
yours	they	them
their	theirs	

Directions: Underline the pronouns in each sentence.

1. Mom told us to wash our hands.

2. Did you go to the store?

3. We should buy him a present.

4. I called you about their party.

5. Our house had damage on its roof.

6. They want to give you a prize at our party.

7. My cat ate my sandwich.

8. Your coat looks like his coat.

Name _____

Pronouns

A **pronoun** is a word that takes the place of a noun.

Example: Meg gave the ball to Dave.
He was glad to get **it**.

Directions: Read the sentences below. After each pronoun, write the word or words that the pronoun stands for.

Most penguins live near the South Pole. They (_____) spend most of their time underwater searching for food. Penguins surface for air and get enough of it (_____) to fill the air sacs throughout their bodies. These (_____) make it possible for them (_____) to stay underwater for long periods of time.

Although penguins have wings, they (_____) are not used for flying. Their wings are like flippers. They (_____) are used for swimming.

Penguins feel best in very cold water but leave it (_____) to nest and raise their young. A penguin's nest if very odd. It (_____) is simply a pile of stones on a rocky shore. The female lays one to three eggs. They (_____) are chalky white. After a time, the female passes her eggs to the male. He (_____) tucks them (_____) into a skin flap under his body to keep them (_____) warm. It (_____) is lined with thick, soft down. The parents take turns feeding the babies when they (_____) hatch.

Nouns and Pronouns

Pronouns can be substituted for nouns that are repeated.

Example: Mother made the beds.
Then, Mother started the laundry.

The noun **Mother** is used in both sentences.
The pronoun **she** could be used in place
of **Mother** the second time.

Directions: Cross out nouns when they appear a second and/or third time.
Write a pronoun that could be used instead.

Example:

_____we_____ My friends and I like to go ice skating in the winter. ~~My friends and I~~ usually fall down a lot, but ~~my friends and I~~ have fun!

1. _____ All the children in the fourth-grade class next to us must have been having a party. All the children were very loud. All the children were happy it was Friday.

2. _____ I try to help my father with work around the house on the weekends. My father works many hours during the week and would not be able to get everything done.

3. _____ Can I share my birthday treat with the secretary and the principal? The secretary and the principal could probably use a snack right now!

4. _____ I know Mr. Jones needs a copy of this history report. Please take it to Mr. Jones when you finish.

Name _____

Pronouns

A **pronoun** is a word that takes the place of a noun in a sentence.

Examples: I, my, mine, me
we, our, ours, us
you, your, yours
he, his, him
she, her, hers
it, its
they, their, theirs, them

I, ME, YOU.   WE!   HIM, HER, THEM.

Directions: Underline the pronouns in each sentence.

1. Bring them to us as soon as you are finished.

2. She has been my best friend for many years.

3. They should be here soon.

4. We enjoyed our trip to the Mustard Museum.

5. Would you be able to help us with the project on Saturday?

6. Our homeroom teacher will not be here tomorrow.

7. My uncle said that he will be leaving soon for Australia.

8. Hurry! Could you please open the door for him?

9. She dropped her gloves when she got off the bus.

10. I cannot figure out who the mystery writer is today.

Name _____

Nouns and Pronouns

Directions: Cross out nouns when they appear a second or third time. Write a pronoun that could be used instead.

1. _____ The merry-go-round is one of my favorite rides at the county fair. I ride the merry-go-round so many times that I sometimes get sick.

2. _____ My parents and I are planning a two-week vacation next year. My parents and I will be driving across the country to see the Grand Canyon. My parents and I hope to have a great time.

3. _____ The new art teacher brought many ideas from the city school where the new art teacher worked before.

4. _____ Green beans, corn, and potatoes are my favorite vegetables. I could eat green beans, corn, and potatoes for every meal. I especially like green beans, corn, and potatoes in stew.

5. _____ I think I left my pen at the library when I was looking for books earlier today. Did you find my pen when you cleaned?

6. _____ My grandmother makes very good apple pie. My grandmother said I could learn how to make one the next time we visit.

7. _____ My brothers and I could take care of your pets while you are away if you show my brothers and me what you want done.

Name _____

Pronoun Referents

A **pronoun referent** is the noun or nouns a pronoun refers to.

Example: **Green beans**, **corn**, and **potatoes** are my favorite vegetables. I could eat **them** for every meal.

The pronoun **them** refers to the nouns **green beans**, **corn**, and **potatoes**.

Directions: Find the pronoun in each sentence. Write it in the blank. Underline the word that the pronoun refers to.

Example: The fruit trees look so beautiful in the spring when they are covered with blossoms.

_____ they _____

1. Tori is a high school cheerleader. She spends many hours at practice.

   _____

2. The football must have been slippery because of the rain. The quarterback could not hold on to it.

   _____

3. Aunt Donna needs a babysitter for her three-year-old son tonight.

   _____

4. The art projects are on the table. Could you please put them on the top shelf along the wall?

   _____

Name _____

Pronoun Referents

Directions: Read each sentence carefully. Draw a line to connect each sentence to the correct pronoun.

1. All the teachers in our building said _____

   could use a day off!

   him

2. The whole cast spent a lot of time in rehearsals for the

   school play. _____ should go very well.

   it

3. Uncle Mike is driving around in a very old car. I know

   _____ would like to buy a new one.

   they

4. Mr. Barker is having some trouble programming that DVD

   player. Can you help _____?

   she

5. There are too many books on the shelf. I know I cannot fit

   all of _____ into this small box.

   them

6. Ms. Hart slipped on the bleachers at the football game.

   That is why _____ is using crutches.

   he

Name _____

Pronoun Referents

Directions: Find the pronoun in each sentence. Write it in the blank. Underline the word that the pronoun refers to.

1. Did Aaron see the movie *Titanic*? Jay thought it was a very good movie.

   _____

2. Maysie can help you with the spelling words now, Tasha.

   _____

3. The new tennis coach said to call him after 6:00 tonight.

   _____

4. Jim, John, and Jason called to say they would be later than planned.

   _____

5. Mrs. Burns enjoyed the cake her class made for the surprise party.

   _____

6. The children are waiting outside. Ask Josh to take the pinwheels out to them.

   _____

7. Mrs. Taylor said to go on ahead because she will be late.

   _____

8. The whole team must sit on the bus until the driver gives us permission to get off.

   _____

9. Dad said the umbrella did a poor job of keeping the rain off him.

   _____

10. The umbrella was blowing around too much. That is probably why it did not do a good job.

    _____

Name _____

Possessive Pronouns

Possessive pronouns show ownership.

    Example: **his** hat, **her** shoes, **our** dog

We can use the pronouns **my**, **our**, **you**, **his**, **her**, **its**, and **their** before a noun.

    Example: That is **my** bike.

We can use the pronouns **mine**, **yours**, **ours**, **his**, **hers**, **theirs**, and **its** without a noun.

    Example: That is mine.

Directions: Rewrite each sentence using a pronoun instead of the word or words in bold letters.

    Example: My **dog's** bowl is brown.   **Its** bowl is brown.

1. That is **Lisa's** book.

_____

2. This is **my pencil**.

_____

3. This hat is **your hat**.

_____

4. Fifi is **Kevin's** cat.

_____

5. That beautiful house is **our home**.

_____

6. **The gerbil's** cage is too small.

_____

Name _____

Possessive Pronouns

A **possessive pronoun** takes the place of a possessive noun.

Examples: Belinda's bicycle is red.   Shane and Bob's cat is gray.

Her bicycle is red.   **Their** cat is gray.

Possessive Pronouns						
my	your	her	his	its	our	their

Directions: Draw a line from each possessive noun to the correct possessive pronoun.

1. Leticia's   their

2. the boat's   our

3. the children's   their

4. the class'   his

5. my friends' and my   its

6. Matthew's   her

Directions: Write a sentence using each possessive pronoun.

1. _____

2. _____

3. _____

4. _____

5. _____

6. _____

7. _____

Name _____

Possessive Pronoun

A **possessive pronoun** shows ownership. It can replace a possessive noun. Some possessive pronouns can be used before a noun and some can be used alone.

Examples: Used before a noun: **my**, **your**, **its**, **her**, **his**, **our**, and **their**.
Used alone: **mine**, **yours**, **his**, **hers**, **yours**, and **theirs**.

Directions: Read each pair of sentences. If the correct possessive pronoun is used in the second sentence, circle **Right**. If it is not, circle **Wrong**.

1. An archaeologist studies people's remains.
   An archaeologist studies **their** remains.   **Right**   **Wrong**

2. The important discovery was the scientist's.
   The important discovery was **hers**.   **Right**   **Wrong**

3. She found part of a potter's wheel.
   She found part of **their** wheel.   **Right**   **Wrong**

4. Other treasures were found on the scientist's dig.
   Other treasures were found on **their** dig.   **Right**   **Wrong**

5. The pottery shards belonged to all of us on the crew.
   The pottery shards were **ours**.   **Right**   **Wrong**

6. Experts say the Pharoah's tomb took years to build.
   Experts say **their** tomb took years to build.   **Right**   **Wrong**

7. A Pharoah's tomb was said to be cursed.
   Its tomb was said to be cursed.   **Right**   **Wrong**

8. One theory about the mummy's curse is in the book.
   One theory about **its** curse is in the book.   **Right**   **Wrong**

9. The scientist's belief is that it is just superstition.
   Her belief is that it is just superstition.   **Right**   **Wrong**

Possessive Pronouns

Name _____

Possessive Pronouns show ownership. **My**, **mine**, **your**, **yours**, **his**, **her**, **hers**, **our**, **ours**, **their**, and **theirs** are possessive pronouns.

Example: **His** house was painted red and black.

Directions: Underline the possessive pronouns in each sentence of the story.

When I first saw this island, I knew it was as close to home as I could get. When the ten monks decided to join me, it became our home. Although we built all of these Chinese-looking buildings together, most were theirs. One hut was ours to share as a place to meditate and eat our meals. Their other buildings were used for living. One monk's hut was unusual. He had painted zebra stripes all along his walls. The monks kept their gardens around their living areas. My house was also built like the houses in China. Some of our other living quarters were more like the huts of African villages. We all lived together, sharing our food and sharing what was mine, theirs, and ours.

© 2006 School Specialty Publishing

Name _____

Possessive Pronouns

A **possessive pronoun** is a pronoun that shows ownership. Possessive pronouns include **my**, **mine**, **your**, **yours**, **his**, **her**, **hers**, **our**, **ours**, **its**, **their**, and **theirs**.

Example: **My** car runs faster than **yours**.
     Their friend went to the zoo.

Directions: Read the article. Underline each possessive pronoun.

There are many kinds of sharks, and their sizes vary greatly. They can be from six-inches to over forty-feet long. A shark does not have many bones in its body. Its body is quite different from your body. Much of its body is made of cartilage, which is similar to the material in your nose.

Our fear of sharks is well-founded. Their behavior is unpredictable. Many fishermen have had their catch eaten by sharks. For millions of years, the seas have been their domain. Their time on Earth began long before our species appeared here.

Directions: Substitute a possessive pronoun for the word or words in parentheses.

1. (A shark's) _____ hearing is very sharp.

2. Sharks can hear (divers') _____ sounds underwater.

3. (Dan's) _____ friend wrote a report about sharks.

4. (Janie's) _____ report gave us interesting facts.

5. the report used (Dan's and Tim's) _____ pictures.

6. (Janie's) _____ report was more interesting than

   (Jack's) _____ .

Name _____

Subject Pronouns

The subject of a sentence can be a noun or a **pronoun**. A pronoun can take the place of a noun. **Subject pronouns** include **I**, **you**, **he**, **she**, **it**, **we**, and **they**.

Examples: **The mayor** closed the office door.
He closed the office door.

Directions: Write the correct pronoun above the subject noun in each sentence.

1. Andrew is Mayor Sneak's administrative assistant.

2. Mayor Sneak has a huge computer.

3. The door to Mayor Sneak's office was closed.

4. The custodians swept the floor.

5. My class waited for a tour.

6. Mayor Sneak sneaked out.

7. Andrew met us instead.

8. Andrew and our class had a good time on our tour.

Name _____

Subject Pronouns

Subject Pronouns can take the place of the subject in a sentence. The **subject pronouns** are: **I**, **you**, **he**, **she**, **it**, **we**, **you**, and **they**.

Examples: **My brother** washed the car.
He washed the car.

Directions: Fill in the blanks with subject pronouns.

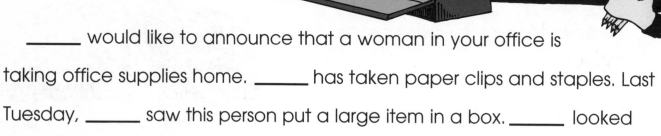

Dear Mayor Sneak,

_____ would like to announce that a woman in your office is

taking office supplies home. _____ has taken paper clips and staples. Last

Tuesday, _____ saw this person put a large item in a box. _____ looked

very heavy.

Later, when everything was dark and quiet, _____ heard a growl. A

female cat was growling as if _____ wanted to warn someone of an

intruder. The security guard was asleep in his chair by the door. _____ did

not see the thief escape with the large item in the box.

_____ may want to look into

this matter.

Sincerely,
A Silent Observer

Object Pronouns

Object pronouns take the place of the person, place, or thing that is the object of the sentence. Object pronouns include: **me**, **you**, **her**, **him**, **it**, **us**, and **them**.

    Example: He wanted to find **a dinosaur**.
                      He wanted to find **it**.

Directions: The objects in each sentence is underlined. Write the pronoun that can replace the object on the line following each sentence.

1. Henry turned the duty of standing guard over to <u>Maya</u>.

    _____

2. Everyone wanted to thank <u>Chuck</u> for making the dinner.

    _____

3. After we cleaned the dishes, we gathered around the fire to listen to <u>Hillary</u> sing.

    _____

4. We were just about ready for bed when we heard <u>a strange noise</u>.

    _____

5. Several of the crew raced to the river and saw <u>a large, furry shape</u>.

    _____

6. But the mysterious visitor was too quick for most of <u>the crew</u>.

    _____

7. Jason ran after <u>the mysterious creature</u>.

    _____

Name _____

Subject and Object Pronouns

A **pronoun** is a word that takes the place of a noun.

A **subject pronoun** takes the place of a noun in the subject of a sentence.

An **object pronoun** takes the place of a noun that follows a verb or a word like **to**, **from**, **of**, **at**, **with**, or **by**.

> **Subject Pronouns**
> I   you   he   she   it   we   they
>
> **Object Pronouns**
> me   you   him   her   it   us   you   them

Directions: The subject or object in each sentence is underlined. Rewrite each sentence, replacing the subject or object with the correct pronoun.

1. The <u>third-grade class</u> went on a class trip to the aquarium.

   _____

2. <u>The aquarium</u> was filled with interesting sea life.

   _____

3. Janice shrieked when <u>Janice</u> saw the shark tank.

   _____

4. "<u>The sharks</u> have really sharp teeth," Janice said.

   _____

5. David reassured Janice, "<u>The sharks</u> cannot hurt, Janice."

   _____

6. <u>The third-grade students</u> believed David because <u>David</u> was the tour guide.

   _____

Name _____

Subject and Object Pronouns

I and **we** are **subject pronouns**. **Me** and **us** are **object pronouns**.

Examples:	**subject pronoun:**	Mark and **I** are on our way to the park. **We** just love to launch rockets!
	object pronoun:	Will Sara come with **me**? Please feel welcome to join **us**.

Directions: Choose the correct pronoun to complete each sentence. Write it in the blank.

1. _____ plan to launch rockets in the park on Saturday.
   (we, us)

2. Joel bought _____ a two-stage rocket.
   (I, me)

3. Kate and _____ both brought fresh batteries for the launcher.
   (I, me)

4. Manuel plans to build _____ a rocket.
   (we, us)

5. Officer Bark wants _____ to attend the rocket safety course.
   (I, me)

6. _____ always paint the fins hot pink.
   (I, me)

7. Tim wants Janelle and _____ to chase after his rocket when it lands. (I, me)

8. Chin wants _____ to go to the launching site.
   (we, us)

Name _____

Subject and Object Pronouns

Pronouns are words that take the place of nouns in a sentence. Some pronouns take the place of subjects. Some take the place of objects.

Examples: **subject pronouns:**   I, you, he, she, it, we, you, they
object pronouns: me, you, him, her, it us, you, them

Directions: Write the correct subject or object pronoun above each underlined noun.

1. As <u>the boat</u> cruised along the shore, <u>the crew members</u> could see <u>surfers</u> riding huge waves.

2. When <u>the boat</u> docked, <u>hundreds of sailors</u> were on the wharf to greet the ship.

3. After <u>everyone</u> had left <u>the ship</u>, <u>the captain</u> received orders for another assignment.

4. <u>The message</u> asked that <u>the crew and the boat</u> be ready to depart for Mexico.

5. <u>The captain</u> knew where <u>the boat</u> was going next.

6. The trip had something to do with <u>whales</u>.

7. There are a lot of <u>whales</u> in the Gulf of Mexico because <u>the water</u> is warmer there.

Name _____

Adverbs

Adverbs are words that tell **when**, **where**, or **how**.

Adverbs of time tell when.

Example:
The train left **yesterday**.
Yesterday is an adverb of time. It tells when the train left.

Adverbs of place tell where.

Example:
The girl walked **away**.
Away is an adverb of place. It tells where the girl walked.

Adverbs of manner tell how.

Example:
The boy walked **quickly**.
Quickly is an adverb of manner. It tells how the boy walked.

Directions: Write the adverb from each sentence in the first column. In the second column, write whether it is an adverb of time, place, or manner.

Example:
The family ate downstairs.   _downstairs_   _place_

1. The relatives laughed loudly.   _____   _____

2. We will finish tomorrow.   _____   _____

3. The snowstorm will stop soon.   _____   _____

4. She sings beautifully!   _____   _____

5. The baby slept soundly.   _____   _____

6. The elevator stopped suddenly.   _____   _____

7. Does the plane leave today?   _____   _____

8. The phone call came yesterday.   _____   _____

Name _____

Adverbs of Time

Directions: Choose a word or group of words from the Word Bank that finishes each sentence.

Word Bank	
in 2 weeks	last winter
next week	at the end of the day
soon	right now
2 days ago	tonight

1. We had a surprise birthday party for him _____.

2. Our science projects are due _____.

3. My best friend will be moving _____.

4. Justin and Ronnie need our help _____!

5. We will find out who the winners are _____.

6. Can you take me to ball practice _____?

7. She said we will be getting a letter _____.

8. Diane made the quilt _____.

132

Name _____

Adverbs of Place

Directions: Choose one word from the Word Bank to finish each sentence. Make sure the adverb you choose makes sense with the rest of the sentence.

Word Bank			
inside	upstairs	below	everywhere
home	somewhere	outside	there

1. Each child took a new library book _____ .

2. We looked _____ for his jacket.

3. We will have recess _____ because it is raining.

4. From the top of the mountain, we could see the

   village far _____ .

5. My sister and I share a bedroom _____ .

6. The teacher warned the children, "You must play with the ball

   _____ ."

7. Mother said, "I know that recipe is _____

   in this file box!"

8. You can put the chair _____ .

Name _____

Adverbs of Manner

Directions: Choose a word from the Word Bank to finish each sentence. Make sure the adverb you choose makes sense with the rest of the sentence. You will use one word twice.

Word Bank					
quickly	carefully	loudly	easily	carelessly	slowly

1. The scouts crossed the old bridge _____.

2. We watched the turtle move _____ across the yard.

3. Everyone completed the math test _____.

4. The quarterback scampered _____ down the sideline.

5. The mother _____ cleaned the child's sore knee.

6. The fire was caused by someone

   _____ tossing a match.

7. The alarm rang _____ while we were eating.

Name _____

Adverbs

Like adjectives, **adverbs** are describing words. They describe verbs.
Adverbs tell **how**, **when**, or **where** action takes place.

Examples:	**How**	**When**	**Where**
	slowly	yesterday	here
	gracefully	today	there
	swiftly	tomorrow	everywhere
	quickly	soon	

Hint: To identify an adverb, first locate the
verb. Then, ask yourself if there are any
words that tell how, when, or where the
action takes place.

Directions: Read each sentence below. Underline the adverb.
Then, write whether it tells how, when, or where.

Example: At the end of the day, the children
ran <u>quickly</u> home from school.   ___how___

1. They will have a spelling test tomorrow.   _____

2. Slowly, the children filed to their seats.   _____

3. The teacher sat here at her desk.   _____

4. She will pass the tests back later.   _____

5. The students received their grades happily.   _____

Directions: Write four sentences of your own using any of the adverbs
above.

_____

_____

_____

_____

 **Adverbs**

Name _____

Adverbs

Adverbs are words that describe verbs. They tell **where**, **how**, or **when**.

Directions: Circle the adverb in each of the following sentences.

   Example: The doctor worked (carefully.)

1. The skater moved gracefully across the ice.

2. They returned their call quickly.

3. We easily learned the new words.

4. He did the work perfectly.

5. She lost her purse somewhere.

Directions: Finish each sentence below with your own adverb.

   Example: The bees worked _____busily_____.

1. The dog barked _____.

2. The baby smiled _____.

3. She wrote her name _____.

4. The horse ran _____.

Name _____

Adverbs

An **adverb** tells more about a verb. Adverbs can tell **how**, **when**, or **where** an action takes place.

Examples:	**how:**	Kallie drove the car **slowly**.
	when:	Kallie drove the car **then**.
	where:	Kallie drove the car **far**.

Directions: Circle the adverbs that tell how, when, or where something happened.

Our pilot landed the plane carefully in a valley near Mount Saint Helens. As we left the safety of the helicopter, we all looked up the valley to see the dome of the volcano. It looked far away, and it seemed long ago that it had last erupted. In 1980, the volcano totally destroyed many forests, cities, and farms. The violent eruption happened quickly. Tragically, 57 people died.

Mount Shasta stands quietly beneath its blanket of snow. It is one of the highest mountains in the Cascade Mountain Range. Only Mount Rainier is taller. As we hiked slowly toward the peak, we could still see some signs of its many eruptions. We could see where the magma had erupted quietly and flowed slowly from the vent.

Name _____

Adverbs

Adverbs describe verbs. They usually tell **how**, **when**, or **where** an action happened.

Examples: The horse walked **slowly**.
We went riding **yesterday**.

Directions: Finish each sentence with an adverb from the Word Bank.

Word Bank				
slowly	carefully	yesterday	recklessly	nearby
there	softly	later	happily	beautifully

1. Sandy _____ at her ice-cream cone.

2. Put your backpack _____.

3. Milo skated _____ and broke his wrist.

4. Tyler visited the museum _____.

5. When the baby is asleep, we must speak _____.

6. I have soccer practice _____.

7. The bear watched her cubs play _____.

8. Charlotte sings _____.

9. Mother decorated the cake _____.

10. The jellyfish swims _____.

Name _____

Adverbs

Directions: Read each sentence. Then, answer the questions.

Example: Charles ate hungrily.   **who?** _____Charles_____
                                                        (subject)

what? _____ate_____   **how?** _____hungrily_____
                (verb)   (adverb)

1. She dances slowly.   **who?** _____

   what? _____   **how?** _____

2. The girl spoke carefully.   **who?** _____

   what? _____   **how?** _____

3. My brother ran quickly.   **who?** _____

   what? _____   **how?** _____

4. Jean often walks home.   **who?** _____

   what? _____   **how?** _____

5. The children played loudly.   **who?** _____

   what? _____   **how?** _____

Adverbs

Adverbs tell **when**, **where**, or **how** about the verb in a sentence. Many adverbs end in **ly** when answering the question, "How?"

Examples: I celebrated my birthday **today**. (When?)
Children sat **near** me. (Where?)
I **excitedly** opened my gifts. (How?)

Directions: Underline the adverb in each sentence. Then, write **when**, **where**, or **how** on the line to tell which question it answers.

1. The children played quietly at home.

   _____

2. We went to the movie yesterday.

   _____

3. My friends came inside to play.

   _____

4. The child cut his meat carefully.

   _____

5. The girls ran upstairs to get their coats.

   _____

6. The play-off games start tomorrow.

   _____

7. The boys walked slowly.

   _____

8. The teacher said, "Write your name neatly."

   _____

Adverbs

Adverbs tell **when**, **where**, or **how** an action takes place.

Directions: Circle the adverbs that can tell about the verb.

study
later
well
often
math

painted
colorfully
joyfully
beautiful
oranges

laugh
happily
fun
today
loudly

listen
quietly
attentively
important
carefully

drive
everywhere
road
cautiously
there

plant
seeds
deep
sometimes
slowly

cried
yesterday
tears
sadly
silently

run
swiftly
fast
again
races

Name _____

Adverbs

Directions: Circle the 12 adverbs in the story. Then, write them in the correct spaces to show if they tell when, where, or how about the verb.

Robert and Tom went inside to dress for the movies. They planned to watch *Sonic Man* today.

"Hurry, or we will be late!" called Tom loudly.

They ran quickly to the bus stop and waited impatiently for the bus to arrive.

At the theater, the line wound outside. The boys worried they would have to return tomorrow.

The line moved slowly as the boys waited nervously. "I hope they have tickets left," moaned Robert quietly.

"Yes, we have seats left," said a ticket seller who stood nearby.

The movie began immediately as the boys settled in their seats.

HOW

1._____   2._____   3._____

4._____   5._____   6._____

WHEN

7._____   8._____   9._____

WHERE

10._____   11._____   12._____

Name _____

Adverbs

Directions: Finish each sentence with an adverb that tells how, when, or where about the verb.

Where?

1. Our team played _____. (when)

2. Brian writes _____. (how)

3. The cows move _____. (how)

4. Melissa will dance _____. (when)

5. My dog went _____. (where)

6. We ran _____. (how)

7. The choir sang _____. (how)

8. The cat purred _____. (where)

9. Hillary spoke _____. (how)

The monkeys are inside.

10. We will go on our vacation _____. (when)

11. The sign goes _____. (where)

12. Mother brought the groceries _____. (where)

13. David read the directions _____. (how)

14. We will be leaving _____. (when)

15. We have three bedrooms _____. (where)

16. We will arrive _____. (when)

17. The mother bird leaves the nest _____. (when)

18. Do not let the cat _____. (where)

Name _____

Adverbs

Adverbs are words that describe verbs. Adverbs tell **where**, **when**, or **how**. Most adverbs end in **ly**.

Directions: Finish each sentence with the correct part of speech.

Example:

Hank	wrote	here.
who? (noun)	what? (verb)	where? (adverb)

1. | _____ | was lost | _____ |
| who? (noun) | what? (verb) | where? (adverb) |

2. | _____ | _____ | quickly |
| who? (noun) | what? (verb) | how? (adverb) |

3. | _____ | felt | _____ |
| who? (noun) | what? (verb) | how? (adverb) |

4. | My brother | _____ | _____ |
| who? (noun) | what? (verb) | when? (adverb) |

5. | _____ | woke up | _____ |
| who? (noun) | what? (verb) | when? (adverb) |

6. | _____ | _____ | gladly |
| who? (noun) | what? (verb) | how? (adverb) |

Name _____

Adverbs

Adverbs show comparison by adding **er** or **est** to the end of the word. Add **er** when the adverb compares two actions. Add **est** when the adverb compares three or more actions.

Example: The clarinets played **louder** than the flutes.
The trumpets played the **loudest** of all the instruments.

Directions: Finish the following sentences by using a comparative form of the underlined adverb.

1. The airplane flew <u>high</u>.

   The airplane flew _____ than the bird.

   The jet flew _____ of all.

2. Jack's car raced <u>fast</u>.

   Jim's car raced _____ than Jack's car.

   Ted's car raced _____ of all.

You can also show comparison by adding the word **more**, **most**, **less**, or **least** in front of the adverb. These words are usually added to adverbs ending in **ly**.

Directions: Add **more**, **most**, **less**, or **least** to each adverb to show comparison.

1. Andrew travels overseas_____ frequently than Eric.

2. Vanessa travels overseas _____ often of all her friends.

3. Raquel drives her car _____ skillfully than Sara.

4. Dave drives _____ expertly of all.

5. Aaron uses his boat_____ often than Tim.

6. Tim sails _____ often than Aaron.

Name _____

Prepositions

Prepositions show relationships between the noun or pronoun and another noun in the sentence. The preposition comes before that noun.

Example: The book is on the table.

Common Prepositions

above	behind	by	near	over
across	below	in	off	through
around	beside	inside	on	under

Directions: Circle the prepositions in each sentence.

1. The dog ran fast around the house.

2. The plates in the cupboard were clean.

3. Put the card inside the envelope.

4. The towel on the sink was wet.

5. I planted flowers in my garden.

6. My kite flew high above the trees.

7. The chair near the counter was sticky.

8. Under the ground, worms lived in their homes.

9. I put the bow around the box.

10. Beside the pond, there was a playground.

Name _____

Prepositions

Prepositions are words that relate nouns to other words in a sentence. They show where a noun is going, how it might be going, or to whom it might be going. Some prepositions are: **in**, **on**, **under**, and **behind**.

Example: I sat **in the car**.

Directions: Underline the prepositions in the sentence below.

1. The tree fell behind the house.

2. I saw the movie with Sara.

3. I stepped out of the shower.

4. Do not play golf in the rain.

5. I put my book next to the T.V.

6. The painter climbed up the ladder.

7. We had recess in our classroom today.

8. The driver raced around the corner.

9. The pot fell off the table.

10. The cat was hiding under the bed.

Name _____

Prepositions

Prepositions relate one word in a sentence to another by location, direction, cause, or possession. A preposition, including the object and its modifiers, is called a **prepositional phrase**.

Example: I walked **beside the road**.

Directions: Circle each preposition in the sentences below. Then, underline the rest of the prepositional phrase.

1. I boarded the train at the whistle's blow.

2. I sat down by a woman in a purple dress and hat.

3. The conductor asked for my ticket.

4. We had to go to the club car for lunch.

5. For lunch, we had tomato soup, potato salad, and ham sandwiches.

6. After lunch, the conductor said, "Two hours to Littleville."

7. "I think I will take a short nap," said the woman in the purple dress.

8. My seat was by the window.

9. I spent the rest of the trip watching the world go by my window.

10. At three in the afternoon, we arrived in Littleville.

Name _____

Nouns and Verbs

A **noun** names a **person**, **place**, or **thing**. A **verb** tells what something does or what something is. Some words can be nouns and verbs, depending on how they are used.

Directions: Finish the sentences in each pair with a word from the Word Bank. The word will be a noun in the first sentence and a verb in the second sentence.

Word Bank			
mix	kiss	brush	crash

1. Did your dog ever give you a _____?
   (noun)

   I have a cold, so I cannot _____ you today.
   (verb)

2. I brought my comb and my _____ .
   (noun)

   I will _____ the leaves off your coat.
   (verb)

3. Was anyone hurt in the _____ ?
   (noun)

   If you are not careful, you will _____ into me.
   (verb)

4. We bought a cake _____ at the store.
   (noun)

   I will _____ the eggs together.
   (verb)

Name _____

Nouns and Verbs

Directions: Finish each sentence with a word from the Word Bank. Use each word once. Write **N** above the words that are used as nouns (people, places, and things). Write **V** above the words that are used as verbs (what something does or what something is).

                                   N   V

Example: I need a ____drink____ . I will ____drink____ milk.

Word Bank						
mix	beach	church	class	kiss	brush	crash

1. It is hot today, so we should go to the _____ .

2. The _____ was crowded.

3. I can't find my paint _____ .

4. Will you _____ my finger and make it stop hurting?

5. I will _____ the red and yellow paint to get orange.

6. The teacher asked our _____ to get in line.

7. If you move that bottom can, the rest will _____ to the floor.

Name _____

Nouns or Verbs?

Directions: Finish the sentences in each pair with a word from the Word Bank. Write **N** over the word if it is used as a noun and **V** if it is used as a verb. You may need to add **s, es, ing,** or **ed** to the verbs.

Example: The girl **sneezes**. Her **sneeze** scares the dog.

Word Bank						
sneeze	tape	claim	treat	grade	stream	date

1. I_____ around flowers.

   My_____ is louder than your_____.

2. Let's go buy a _____ at the store.

   Today, I will_____ you to a candy bar.

3. Sometimes we_____ our own papers.

   I always get a higher _____ than Josh.

4. The rain_____ down the window.

   The_____ behind our house is overflowing.

5. Please_____ that TV show for me.

   I will watch the_____ when I come home.

6. A boy in my class_____ I took his candy bar.

   I know his_____ is wrong.

7. My brother has a _____ tonight.

   He _____ the girl who lives next door.

Name _____

Nouns or Verbs?

Some words can be either **nouns** or **verbs**, depending on how they are used in a sentence.

Example: **noun:**   The **paint** on Aunt Betty's shutters is wet.
        verb: They will **paint** the shutters again later today.

Directions: In each sentence below, the noun or the verb is in bold. Write **N** if the word is a noun or **V** if the word is a verb.

1. _____ Aunt Betty said we need to look for a **ship**.

2. _____ We will **ship** the picnic basket to the island.

3. _____ There will be hardly any **light** in the forest.

4. _____ Aunt Betty will **light** the way with her trusty flashlight.

5. _____ We parked our car near the **water**.

6. _____ On the way, Aunt Betty stopped to **water** some flowers.

7. _____ Then, she picked some of the pink ones and put them in a **box**.

8. _____ "I will **box** these for my friend in Hawaii," Aunt Betty said.

9. _____ "It will be a **present** for my friend."

10. _____ "I hope to **present** it to her tomorrow."

11. _____ We will **play** all day on the island.

12. _____ At night, we will see a **play**.

154

Name _____

Adjectives and Nouns

Directions: Underline the adjective in each sentence below. Then, draw an arrow from the adjective to the noun it describes.

Example: A platypus is a <u>furry</u> animal that lives in Australia.

1. This animal likes to swim.

2. Its flat nose looks like a duck's bill.

3. It has a broad tail like a beaver.

4. Platypuses are great swimmers.

5. They have webbed feet that help them swim.

6. Their flat tails also help them move through the water.

7. The platypus is an unusual mammal because it lays eggs.

8. The platypus has reptile-like eggs.

9. Platypuses can lay three eggs at a time.

10. These babies do not leave their mothers for one year.

11. This animal spends most of its time hunting near streams.

155

Name _____

Nouns, Pronouns, and Adjectives

Directions: Circle the nouns that show ownership. Draw a box around the pronouns. Underline the adjectives.

Example: Tropical birds live in warm, wet lands.
        They live in dark forests and busy zoos.
        The birds' feathers are bright.

1. A canary is a small finch.

2. It is named for the Canary Islands.

3. Ben's birds are lovebirds.

4. He says they are small parrots that like to cuddle.

5. His parents gave him the lovebirds for his birthday.

6. Lisa's bird is a talking myna bird.

7. Her neighbors gave it to her when they moved.

8. She thanked them for the wonderful gift.

9. She says its feathers are dark with an orange mark on each wing.

10. Some children's myna birds can be very noisy.

11. Parakeets are this country's most popular tropical birds.

12. Parakeets' cages have ladders and swings.

13. A parakeet's diet is made up of seeds.

Name _____

Adjectives and Adverbs

Directions: Write **ADJ** on the line if the bold word is an adjective. Write **ADV** if the bold word is an adverb.

Example: _____ADV_____ That road leads **nowhere**.

1. _____ The squirrel was **nearby**.

2. _____ Her **delicious** cookies were all eaten.

3. _____ Everyone rushed **indoors**.

4. _____ He **quickly** zipped his jacket.

5. _____ She hummed a **popular** tune.

6. _____ Her **sunny** smile warmed my heart.

7. _____ I hung your coat **there**.

8. _____ Bring that **here** this minute!

9. _____ We all walked **back** to school.

10. _____ The **skinniest** boy ate the most food!

11. _____ She acts like a **famous** person.

12. _____ The **silliest** jokes always make me laugh.

13. _____ She must have parked her car **somewhere**!

14. _____ Did you take the test **today**?

Name _____

Adjectives and Adverbs

Directions: Finish each sentence by adding words that tell who, what, where, or when.

Example: They noticed a ___green___ glow ___behind___ the pine
trees.   (what)   (where)

1. _____ shifted across the room _____ .
   (who or what)   (when)

2. The shadow covered _____ _____ .
                        (what)   (where)

3. The door _____ opened _____ .
              (where)   (when)

4. _____ hurried _____ _____ .
   (who or what)   (where)   (when)

5. _____ stopped the _____ _____ .
   (who or what)   (what)   (when)

Adjectives and Adverbs

Directions: Read the story. Underline the adjectives. Circle the adverbs. Write the words in the correct column at the end of the story.

Surprise!

Emily and Elizabeth tiptoed quietly through the dark hallway. Even though none of the lights were lit, they knew the presents were there. Every year, the two sisters had gone to Mom and Dad's bedroom to wake them on Christmas morning. This year would be different, they decided.

Last night after supper, they had secretly plotted to look early in the morning before Mom and Dad were awake. The girls knew that Emily's red-and-green stocking and Elizabeth's striped stocking hung by the brick fireplace. They knew the beautiful tree was in the corner by the rocking chair.

"Won't Mom and Dad be surprised to awaken on their own?" asked Elizabeth quietly.

Emily whispered, "Click the overhead lights so we can see better."

"You don't have to whisper," said a voice.

There sat Mom and Dad as the Christmas-tree lights suddenly shone.

Dad said, "I guess the surprise is on you two!"

Adverbs	**Adjectives**
_____	_____
_____	_____
_____	_____
_____	_____
_____	_____
_____	_____
_____	_____

Name _____

Parts of Speech

Nouns name a person, place or thing.

Verbs tell what a person or thing does or is doing.

Pronouns take the place of nouns.

Adjectives describe nouns.

Adverbs tell when, where, or how about a verb.

Directions: Label the words in each sentence using the Word Key.

Word Key		
N — for noun	**Adj** — for adjective	**V** — for verb
P — for pronoun	**Adv** — for adverb	

	Adj	N	V	Adv
Example:	Talented	skaters	moved	gracefully.

1. Derek planted two maple trees yesterday.

2. Charles wrote them one letter.

3. They have several small dogs.

4. Plastic toys were everywhere.

5. Three children swam today.

6. Her tiny baby slept soundly.

7. They ate lunch quickly.

Name _____

Parts of Speech

Nouns, pronouns, verbs, adjectives, adverbs, and prepositions are all **parts of speech**.

Directions: Label each word in the sentence with the correct part of speech.

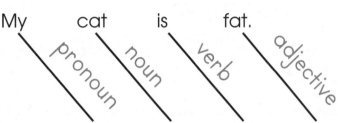

Example: My   cat   is   fat.
              pronoun noun verb adjective

1. My   cow   walks   in   this   barn

2. Red   flowers   grow   in   that   garden.

3. One   large   dog   was   excited.

Name _____

Parts of Speech

Directions: Ask a friend to give you a noun, verb, adjective, or pronoun to fill in each blank. Read the story to your friend when you finish.

The _____ Adventure
(adjective)

I went for a _____. I found a really big _____. It
(noun)   (noun)

was so _____ that I _____ all the way home. I put
(adjective)   (verb)

it in my _____. To my amazement, it began to
(noun)

_____. I _____. I took it to my _____.
(verb)   (past-tense verb)   (place)

I showed it to all my _____. I decided to _____ it
(plural noun)   (verb)

in a box and wrap it up with _____ paper. I gave it to
(adjective)

_____ for a present. When _____ opened it,
(person)   (pronoun)

_____ _____. _____ shouted,
(pronoun)   (past-tense verb)   (pronoun)

"Thank you! This is the best _____ I have ever had!"
(noun)

162

Name _____

Parts of Speech

Directions: Write the part of speech for each underlined word on the correct numbered line below.

①   ②
There <u>are</u> many <u>different</u> kinds of animals. Some animals live in the wild.

③
Some animals live in the <u>zoo</u>. And still others live in homes. The animals that

④
<u>live</u> in homes are called pets.

There are many types of pets. Some pets without fur are fish, turtles,

⑤   ⑥
snakes, and hermit crabs. Trained birds can fly <u>around</u> <u>your</u> house. Some

⑦
<u>furry</u> animals are cats, dogs, rabbits, ferrets, gerbils, and hamsters. Some

⑧   ⑨
animals can <u>successfully</u> learn tricks that <u>you</u> teach them. Animal can be

⑩
<u>special</u> friends!

1. _____   2. _____

3. _____   4. _____   5. _____   6. _____

7. _____   8. _____   9. _____   10. _____

Name _____

Review

Directions: Look at the word in bold in each sentence.
Write **N** if it is a noun, **P** if it is a pronoun, **V** if it is a verb,
ADJ if it is an adjective, or **ADV** if it is an adverb.

1. _____ She is the **tallest** one outside.

2. _____ **She** is the tallest one outside.

3. _____ She **is** the tallest one outside.

4. _____ She is the tallest one **outside**.

Directions: Look at the word in bold in each sentence.
Write **P** if it is an adverb of place, **T** if it is an adverb of time,
or **M** if it is an adverb of manner.

1. _____ Your shoes are **downstairs**.

2. _____ His response was **speedy**.

3. _____ **Here** is my homework.

Directions: Add **er** and **est** or **more** and **most** to each word below
to show comparison.

1. fat _____   _____

2. serious _____   _____

3. easy _____   _____

Directions: Look at the word in bold in each sentence. Write **ADV** if it is an
adverb or **ADJ** if it is an adjective.

1. _____ **Grumpy** people are not pleasant.

2. _____ Put the package **there**, please.

3. _____ **Upstairs** is where I sleep.

4. _____ **Warm** blankets feel toasty on cold nights.

Name _____

Sentences

A **sentence** has a **beginning** and an **ending**. A sentence tells a **complete thought**. When you write a sentence, make sure that all of it is there! Just a beginning or just an ending is not a complete sentence!

"I just don't feel complete."

Directions: Draw a line from each sentence's beginning to its correct ending.

Summer   has thorns on its stem.

My pet turtle   runs fast.

The cheetah   is Kim's favorite color.

A rose   is my favorite season.

Blue   eats a lot!

Name _____

Sentences

Every sentence must have two things: a **noun** or **pronoun** that tells who or what is doing something and a **verb** that tells what the noun is doing.

Directions: Add a **noun**, a **pronoun**, or a **verb** to complete each sentence. Be sure to begin your sentences with capital letters and end them with periods.

Example: reads after school

Brandy reads after school.

1. brushes her dog every day

_____

2. at the beach, we

_____

3. kisses me too much

_____

4. in the morning, our class

_____

5. stopped with a crash

_____

Name _____

Sentences

Directions: Write one sentence about each picture. Write **N** above the noun in each sentence. Write **V** above the verb in each sentence.

_____

_____

_____

_____

_____

_____

_____

_____

_____

_____

_____

_____

Name _____

Subjects

A **subject** is a **noun** or a **pronoun**. It tells who or what the sentence is about.

Directions: Underline the subject in each sentence below.

   Example: The zebra is a striped animal.

1. Zebras live in Africa.

2. Zebras are related to horses.

3. Horses have longer hair than zebras.

4. Zebras are good runners.

5. Their feet are protected by their hooves.

6. Some animals live in groups.

7. These groups are called herds.

8. Zebras live in herds with other grazing animals.

9. Grazing animals eat mostly grass.

10. They usually eat three times a day.

11. They often travel to water holes.

Name _____

Subjects

Directions: Finish each sentence below with a subject.

  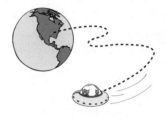

1. _____ landed in my backyard.

2. _____ rushed out of the house.

3. _____ had bright lights.

4. _____ were tall and green.

5. _____ talked to me.

6. _____ came outside with me.

7. _____ ran into the house.

8. _____ shook hands.

9. _____ said funny things.

10. _____ gave us a ride.

11. _____ flew away.

12. _____ will come back soon.

Name _____

Subjects

Directions: Circle the subject in each sentence. Change the subject to make a new sentence. The word or words you add must make sense with the rest of the sentence.

Example: (Twelve students) signed up for the student council elections.

Only one person in my class signed up for the student council elections.

1. Our whole family went to the science museum last week.

_____

_____

2. The funny story made us laugh.

_____

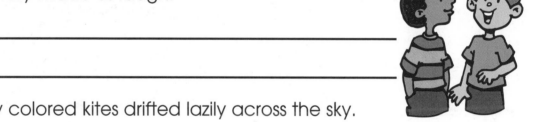

_____

3. The brightly colored kites drifted lazily across the sky.

_____

_____

4. My little brother and sister spent the whole day at the

amusement park.

_____

_____

5. The tiny sparrow made a tapping sound at my window.

_____

_____

Name _____

Predicates

A **predicate** always has a **verb**. It tells what the subject is doing, has done, or will do.

Directions: Underline the predicate in each sentence below.

Example: Woodpeckers <u>live in trees</u>.

1. They hunt for insects in the trees.

2. Woodpeckers have strong beaks.

3. They can peck through the bark.

4. You can hear the pecking sound from far away.

Directions: Circle each group of words that can be a predicate.

have long tongues   pick up insects

hole in bark   sticky substance

help it to climb trees   tree bark

Directions: Choose the correct predicate from above to finish each sentence below.

1. Woodpeckers _____.

2. They use their tongues to _____.

3. Its strong feet _____.

Name _____

Predicates

Directions: Write a predicate for each sentence below.

1. The swimming pool _____.

2. The water _____.

3. The sun _____.

4. I always _____.

5. My friends _____.

6. We always _____.

7. The lifeguard _____.

8. The rest periods _____.

9. The lunch _____.

10. My favorite food _____.

11. The diving board _____.

12. We never _____.

Name _____

Predicates

Directions: Circle the predicate in each sentence. Change the predicate to make a new sentence. The words you add must make sense with the rest of the sentence.

Example: Twelve students (signed up for the student council elections.)

Twelve students were absent from my class today!

1. Our whole family went to the science museum last week.

_____

_____

2. The funny story made us laugh.

_____

_____

3. The brightly colored kites drifted lazily across the sky.

_____

_____

4. My little brother and sister spent the whole day at the park.

_____

_____

5. The tiny sparrow made a tapping sound at my window.

_____

_____

Name _____

Subject-Verb Agreement

The verb and subject in a sentence must match in number. This is called **subject-verb agreement**.

Present tense tells what is happening right now. If the verb is present tense and the subject refers to only one thing, then add an **s** or **es** to the verb.

> **Examples:** The branch **sways** softly in the breeze.
> Hannah **munches** on carrot sticks

If the verb is present tense and the subject refers to more than one thing, then do not add an **s** or **es** to the verb.

> **Examples:** Gophers **live** underground.
> They **crush** plants.

Directions: Read each sentence. Underline the form of the verb that agrees with the subject.

1. Mary (receive, receives) a new bicycle on her birthday.

2. She (put, puts) on her helmet.

3. Tony and Jennifer (ride, rides) to Mary's house.

4. Mary (jump, jumps) on the shiny red bike.

5. She (spin, spins) around in the driveway.

6. The friends (laugh, laughs) as they ride.

7. They (race, races) down the sidewalk.

8. The streamers (fly, flies) in the wind.

9. Jennifer (reach, reaches) the finish line first.

10. Tony (finish, finishes) last.

11. Mary (enjoy, enjoys) her new bike.

12. They will all (meet, meets) tomorrow for another ride.

Name _____

Subject-Verb Agreement

In a sentence, the subjects and verbs must agree. When the subject is a single person, place, or thing, it is **singular**. You should match it to a **singular verb**. When the subject is more than one person, place, or thing, it is **plural**. You should match it to a **plural verb**.

Examples: **One** of my friends **is** going to see the Grand Canyon.
There **are** thirty-five **students** on the bus.

Directions: Finish each sentence, using the correct tense to make the subject and verb agree.

1. Thirty-five students _____ on their way to the Grand Canyon.
   (to be)

2. One of the students _____ a fear of heights and _____
   (to have)   (to be)
   scared of hiking down the narrow trails.

3. "There _____ one more stop before we get to the canyon," the
   (to be)
   bus driver said as he stopped the big bus.

4. When he stopped, there _____ thirty-five students who got off
   (to be)
   the bus and _____ to see the sands of the Painted Desert.
   (to go)

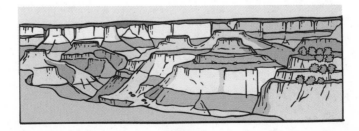

Name _____

Subject and Predicate

The **subject** of a sentence tells who or what the sentence is about. The subject can be a **noun** or a **pronoun**. The **predicate** of a sentence always has a **verb**. It tells what the subject is or does.

	subject	predicate
Example:	The sailboat	took us to the island.

Directions: In each sentence, underline the subject and double underline the predicate.

1. We all climbed aboard the boat for the trip to the island.

2. Aunt Betty took the tiller.

3. We pushed off from the shore.

4. The lake was very quiet.

5. A few ducks followed our boat.

6. I fed them crusts of bread from our sandwiches.

7. I became more and more excited.

8. Aunt Betty gave me some binoculars.

9. I saw a man with a long beard wearing

   a strange outfit on the dock.

Name _____

Subject and Predicate

The **subject** of a sentence tells whom or what the sentence is about. It is always a noun or pronoun. The subject can be one word or more than one word.

The **predicate** is the part of the sentence that tells what the subject is or does. It always has a verb. The predicate can be one word or more than one word.

Directions: Match each subject to the correct predicate. Write the letter of the predicate in the space before the correct subject.

Subjects

1. ____ Parker

2. ____ The ballerina

3. ____ My sister's parakeet

4. ____ Our teacher

5. ____ The amusement park ride

6. ____ That ice-cream sundae

7. ____ Emily

8. ____ The goalie

Predicates

a. was closed for repairs.

b. dove into the freezing-cold pool.

c. made the save.

d. assigned the class lots of homework.

e. likes to ride his skateboard.

f. flew out of the window.

g. twirled on her toes.

h. is almost too sweet to eat!

Name _____

Subjects and Predicates

Directions: Finish each sentence by filling in the subject.

1. _____ went to school last Wednesday.

2. _____ did not understand the joke.

3. _____ barked so loudly that no one could sleep a wink.

4. _____ felt unhappy when the ball game was rained out.

5. _____ wonder what happened at the end of the book.

6. _____ jumped for joy when she won the contest.

Directions: Finish each sentence by filling in the predicate.

1. Everyone _____.

2. Dogs _____.

3. I _____.

4. Justin _____.

5. Jokes _____.

6. Twelve people _____.

Subjects and Predicates

A **sentence** is a group of words that expresses a complete thought. It must have a subject and a predicate.

Examples: **Sentence:** John felt tired and went to bed early.
Not a sentence: Went to bed early.

Directions: Write **S** if the group of words is a complete sentence. Write **NS** if the group of words is not a sentence.

1. _____ Which one of you?

2. _____ We're happy for the family.

3. _____ We enjoyed the program very much.

4. _____ Felt left out and lonely afterwards.

5. _____ Everyone said it was the best party ever!

6. _____ No one knows better than I what the problem is.

7. _____ Seventeen of us!

8. _____ Quickly before they.

9. _____ Squirrels are lively animals.

10. _____ Not many people believe it really happened.

11. _____ Certainly, we enjoyed ourselves.

12. _____ Tuned her out.

Name _____

Subjects and Predicates

Directions: On page 179, some of the groups of words are not sentences. Rewrite them to make complete sentences.

1. _____

_____

2. _____

_____

3. _____

_____

4. _____

_____

5. _____

_____

Name _____

Compound Subjects

Compound subjects are two or more nouns that have the same predicate.

Directions: Combine the subjects to create one sentence with a compound subject.

Example: Jill can swing.

Whitney can swing.

Luke can swing.

Jill, Whitney, and Luke can swing.

1. Roses grow in the garden. Tulips grow in the garden.

_____

2. Apples are fruit. Oranges are fruit. Bananas are fruit.

_____

3. Bears live in the zoo. Monkeys live in the zoo.

_____

4. Jackets keep us warm. Sweaters keep us warm.

_____

Name _____

Compound Subjects

The **subject** of a sentence tells who or what the sentence is about. A **compound subject** is two or more simple subjects joined by the word **and**.

Examples: **Toads** are amphibians. **Frogs** are amphibians.
Toads and frogs are amphibians.

Directions: If the sentence has a compound subject, write **CS** on the line. If the sentence does not have a compound subject, write **NO**.

1. _____ An amphibian lives in the water and on land.

2. _____ Frogs and salamanders are amphibians.

3. _____ A salamander has a long body and a tail.

4. _____ Adult frogs and toads do not have tails.

5. _____ It is easy for them to move on land.

6. _____ Frogs use their strong legs for leaping.

7. _____ Toads have shorter legs and cannot jump as far.

8. _____ The eyes and nose of a frog are on the top of its head.

9. _____ Tree frogs are expert jumpers and can cling to things.

Directions: Combine each set of sentences to make one sentence with a compound subject. Write the new sentence on the line.

1. Toads lay their eggs in water. Frogs lay their eggs in water.

_____

2. Newts have tails. Salamanders have tails.

_____

3. Tree frogs are noisy. Bullfrogs are noisy.

_____

Name _____

Compound Subjects

Directions: Underline the simple subjects in each compound subject.

Example: Dogs and cats are good pets.

1. Blueberries and strawberries are fruit.

2. Jesse, Jake, and Hannah like school.

3. Cows, pigs, and sheep live on a farm.

4. Boys and girls ride the bus.

5. My family and I took a trip to Duluth.

6. Fruits and vegetables are good for you.

7. Katarina, Lexi, and Mandi like to go swimming.

8. Petunias, impatiens, snapdragons, and geraniums are all flowers.

9. Coffee, tea, and milk are beverages.

10. Dave, Karla, and Tami worked on the project together.

Name _____

Compound Predicates

Compound predicates have two or more verbs that have the same subject.

Directions: Combine the predicates to create one sentence with a compound predicate.

Example: We went to the zoo. We watched the monkeys.

We went to the zoo and watched the monkeys.
_____

1. Students read their books. Students do their work.

_____

2. Dogs can bark loudly. Dogs can do tricks.

_____

3. The football player caught the ball. The football player ran.

_____

4. My dad sawed wood. My dad stacked wood.

_____

5. My teddy bear is soft. My teddy bear has big brown eyes.

_____

Name _____

Compound Predicate

The **predicate** of a sentence tells who the subject is or what the subject is doing. A **compound predicate** is two or more simple predicates joined by the word **and**.

> **Example:**   Dad **picks up** Troy. Dad **drives** to the dentist.
> Dad **picks up** Troy **and drives** to the dentist.

Directions: If the sentence has a compound predicate, write **CP** on the line. If the sentence does not have a compound predicate, write **NO**.

1. _____ Dad and Troy park the car and go inside.

2. _____ Troy reads and watches T.V. while waiting for the dentist.

3. _____ Dad talks to another patient.

4. _____ The hygienist comes into the waiting room and gets Troy.

5. _____ The hygienist cleans, polishes, and X-rays Troy's teeth.

6. _____ The dentist examines Troy's teeth and checks the X-rays.

7. _____ The dentist gives Troy a toothbrush to take home.

8. _____ Troy thanks the dentist.

9. _____ Dad pays the dentist.

Directions: Combine each set of sentences to make one sentence with a compound predicate. Write the new sentence on the line.

1. Troy wiggles his tooth. Troy pulls it loose.

_____

2. Troy smiles. Troy shows Dad the empty space in his mouth.

_____

3. Dad laughs. Dad hugs Troy.

_____

Name _____

Compound Predicates

Directions: Underline the verbs in each compound predicate.

    Example: The fans <u>clapped</u> and <u>cheered</u> at the game.

1. The coach talks and encourages the team.

2. The cheerleaders jump and yell.

3. The basketball players dribble and shoot the ball.

4. The basketball bounces and hits the backboard.

5. The ball rolls around the rim and goes into the basket.

6. Everyone leaps up and cheers.

7. The team scores and wins!

Name _____

Simple and Complete Subjects

The **simple subject** of a sentence tells who or what the sentence is about. It does not contain any adjectives or articles.

Example: The **surface** of the ocean sometimes looks angry in a storm.

The **complete subject** of a sentence is all the words in the part of the sentence that tells about the subject. It can contain adjectives and articles.

Example: **The top of the ocean** sometimes looks angry in a storm.

Directions: Underline the simple subject and circle the complete subject in each sentence below.

1. The killer whale is found in all oceans.

2. Killer whales, or orcas, travel in groups or pods.

3. Pods can have from two to dozens of whales.

4. Each pod "talks" with its own set of

   underwater sounds.

5. Most of the crew members had seen orcas before.

6. The killer whale has teeth, unlike some other whales.

7. These whales feed on salmon and other fish.

8. They do not usually attack people.

Name _____

Simple and Complete Subjects

The **simple subject** is who or what the sentence is about. It does not include any adjectives or articles.

Example: The flying cactus **critter** was huge.

The **complete subject** is the simple subject plus any adjectives or articles.

Examples: **The flying cactus critter** was huge.

Directions: Underline the simple subject and circle the complete subject in each sentence below.

1. Many deserts receive little rainfall.

2. About one-fifth of the earth's land consists of deserts.

3. The largest desert in the world is the Sahara.

4. Most towns and cities in desert regions must

   get water from wells or nearby rivers.

5. People in desert regions must protect themselves

   from the intense heat.

6. Deserts can consist of sand, gravel, and rocky hills and mountains.

7. Many desert soils are rich in minerals.

8. An oasis is an unusually wet area in a desert where many

   plants can grow.

9. Most deserts receive less than 10 inches of rainfall per year.

10. Most desert animals eat at night to avoid high

    daytime temperatures.

Name _____

Simple Predicates

A **simple predicate** is the main verb or verbs in the complete predicate.

Directions: Draw a line between the complete subject and the complete predicate. Circle the simple predicate.

Example: The ripe apples | (fell) to the ground.

1. The farmer scattered feed for the chickens.

2. The horses galloped wildly around the corral.

3. The baby chicks stayed warm by the light.

4. The tractor bailed hay.

5. The silo was full of grain.

6. The cows waited to be milked.

7. The milk truck drove up to the barn.

8. The rooster woke up everyone.

Name _____

Simple and Complete Predicates

The **simple predicate** tells what the subject is or does.

Example: I **created** a flying critter.

The **complete predicate** includes all of the words in the predicate (including adjectives, articles, and verbs).

Example: I **created a flying critter**.

Directions: Underline the simple predicate and circle the complete predicate in each sentence below.

1. All birds have wings and feathers.

2. There is no other animal on earth that can travel faster than a bird.

3. Some birds cannot fly.

4. Ostriches and penguins use their wings for balance or to swim.

5. Many birds have vibrantly colored wings.

6. People have used birds as symbols on flags and in crests.

7. The smallest bird is the bee hummingbird.

8. The largest bird, the ostrich, may grow to be 8 feet tall.

9. Birds live all over the world.

10. Some birds even live in the Arctic and Antarctic.

Direct Objects

A **direct object** is the word or words that answer the question **whom** or **what** about the verb.

Examples: Aaron wrote a **letter**.
Letter is the direct object. It tells what Aaron wrote.

We heard **Tom**.
Tom is the direct object. It tells whom we heard.

Directions: Identify the direct object in each sentence. Write it in the blank.

1. _____ My mother called me.

2. _____ The baby dropped it.

3. _____ I met the mayor.

4. _____ I like you!

5. _____ No one visited them.

6. _____ We all heard the cat.

7. _____ Jessica saw the stars.

8. _____ She needs a nap.

9. _____ The dog chewed the bone.

10. _____ He hugged the doll.

11. _____ I sold the radio.

12. _____ Douglas ate the banana.

13. _____ We finally found the house.

Name _____

Direct Objects

Directions: Finish each sentence by writing a direct object.

1. Eric sang _____.

2. Our class rode _____.

3. Jordan made _____.

4. Keesha baked _____.

5. All the children got _____.

6. Our new principal read _____.

7. My brother wrote _____.

8. Sheree gave _____.

9. The girls played _____.

10. I bought _____.

11. Mrs. Bernhard typed _____.

12. Barb and Valerie traded _____.

13. We all raked _____.

14. Jennifer climbed _____.

Name _____

Indirect Objects

An **indirect object** is the word or words that receive the action of the verb. An indirect objects tells **to whom** or **what** or **for whom** or **what** something is done.

Examples: He read **me** a funny story.

Me is the indirect object. It tells to whom something (reading a story) was done.

Directions: Identify the indirect object in each sentence. Write it in the blank.

1. The coach gave Bill a trophy.   _____

2. He cooked me a wonderful meal.   _____

3. She told Maria her secret.   _____

4. Someone gave my mother a gift.   _____

5. The class gave the principal a new flag for the cafeteria. _____

6. The restaurant pays the waiter a good salary.   _____

7. You should tell your dad the truth.   _____

8. She sent her son a plane ticket.   _____

9. The waiter served the patron a salad.   _____

10. Grandma gave the baby a kiss.   _____

11. I sold Steve some cookies.   _____

12. He told us six jokes.   _____

13. She brought the boy a sucker.   _____

Name _____

Indirect Objects

Directions: Finish each sentence below with the correct indirect object from the Word Bank. Write the letter of the indirect object in the blank.

Word Bank

a. the librarian   **b.** the coach   **c.** all the teachers   **d.** the class

e. Mom   **f.** the waiter   **g.** all of us   **h.** our parents

---

Example: __c__ The principal gave ___ the notice about the meeting.

1. _____ My sister told ___ the truth.

2. _____ Our teacher told ___ the homework assignment.

3. _____ Dad bought ___ a delicious treat.

4. _____ She gave ___ her overdue books.

5. _____ We helped ___ clean the house.

6. _____ The customer gave ___ a good tip.

7. _____ Michael told ___ about his sore leg.

Direct and Indirect Objects

Sentences can have direct and indirect objects. A **direct object** answers the question **what** or **whom** about the verb.

    Example: Sharon told a story.

Told is the verb. If you ask, **what did Sharon tell**, you can figure out the direct object. Sharon told a story, so **story** is the direct object.

An **indirect object** receives the action of the verb. It answers the question **to what** or **to whom** is something done.

    Example: Sharon told Jennifer a story.

If you ask, **to whom did sharon tell a story**, you can figure out the indirect object. Sharon told Jennifer a story, so **Jennifer** is the indirect object.

Directions: Circle the direct object and underline the indirect object in each sentence.

1. The teacher gave the class a test.

2. Josh brought Elizabeth the book.

3. Someone left the cat a present.

4. The poet read David all his poems.

5. My big brother handed me the ticket.

6. Luke told everyone the secret.

7. Jason handed his dad the newspaper.

8. Mother bought Jack a suitcase.

9. They cooked us an excellent dinner.

10. I loaned Jonathan my bike.

11. She threw him a curve ball.

Name _____

Direct and Indirect Objects

Directions: Finish each sentence by adding a direct object and an indirect object. Circle the direct object and underline the indirect object.

1. The happy clown gave _____.

2. The smiling politician offered _____.

3. My big brother handed _____.

4. His uncle Seth works _____.

5. The friendly waiter gave _____.

6. Elizabeth told _____.

7. My mother brought _____.

8. He served _____.

9. Jane should tell _____.

10. Someone threw _____.

11. The bookstore sent _____.

12. The salesclerk gave _____.

13. The magician brought _____.

14. Her father cooked _____.

15. Her boss pays. _____.

Name _____

Direct and Indirect Objects

Directions: Circle the direct object and underline the indirect object in each sentence. Then, write the direct and indirect objects in the correct columns.

Example: All the girls wrote (letters) to their friends.

1. Each child brought the teacher an apple.

2. My Dad gave my Mom flowers on their anniversary.

3. Christopher gave the class a book report .

4. The bus drivers gave the children oranges.

5. We showed Mom the prizes.

6. My brother gave Mom and Dad his report card.

Example:

Direct Objects	Indirect Objects
letters	friends

1. _____   _____

2. _____   _____

3. _____   _____

4. _____   _____

5. _____   _____

6. _____   _____

Sentence Fragments

A **sentence** tells a complete thought. It has a **subject**—what or who the sentence is about. And it has a **predicate**—what happened to the subject or what the subject did.

A **sentence fragment** is **not a complete thought**.

Example:	**Sentences:**	The museum was open.
		The movie starts at three o'clock.
		Mr. Tillbury is coming for dinner.
	Fragments:	Because Mr. Tillbury.
		The museum.
		Starts at three o'clock.

Directions: Write **sentence** on the line before each complete sentence. Write **fragment** on the line before each fragment.

1. _____ Because I like chocolate.

2. _____ Paris is in France.

3. _____ Nina likes fritters.

4. _____ Washington, D.C., the capital of the USA.

5. _____ The ancient ruins of the Incas.

Directions: Rewrite each fragment below so that it is a complete sentence.

1. _____ Likes to cook.

2. _____ Mr. Tillbury.

3. _____ Because fritters taste good.

4. _____ To bring to dinner.

Name _____

Sentence Fragments

A **sentence** is a group of words that expresses a complete thought. It contains a subject and a predicate.

Example: Miranda eats pizza every day.

A **fragment** does not express a complete thought. It may be missing either the subject or the predicate.

Example: Pepperoni and cheese on it.

Directions: Decide if it is a sentence or fragment. Circle **S** if the group of words is a sentence. Circle **F** if the group of words is a fragment.

1. Pizza tastes delicious.   **S**   **F**

2. Let the dough rise before spreading it out.   **S**   **F**

3. Dough in the air.   **S**   **F**

4. Anthony pours tomato sauce on the crust.   **S**   **F**

5. Mom arranges the toppings on the sauce.   **S**   **F**

6. Mario sprinkles the pizza with red pepper.   **S**   **F**

7. More cheese.   **S**   **F**

8. We baked the pizza in the oven for 10 minutes.   **S**   **F**

Directions: Write four sentences of your own about pizza. Each sentence needs a subject and a predicate.

1. _____

2. _____

3. _____

4. _____

Name _____

Sentence Fragments

A **sentence fragment** is only a part of a sentence. It does not express a complete thought.

Example: **fragment:** If I pass the test.
            sentence: If I pass the test, I will graduate.

Directions: Write **S** if the group of words is a complete sentence. Write **F** if the group of words is a fragment.

1. ____ The cactus looks just like Mom's pincushion for sewing.

2. ____ Prickly pear cactus and hedgehog cactus.

3. ____ Sucks up water when it rains.

4. ____ Spines help.

5. ____ The agave and ocotillo thrive in the desert.

Directions: Connect the fragments to make complete sentences.

All cactuses	Cactuses
do not need a lot of water to live.	can be white, yellow, red, or orange.
Cactus flowers	Animals
cannot eat cactuses because of the spines.	stores water for dry spells.
The stem of the cactus	have roots close to the top of the sand.

Word Order

Each sentence needs a **subject** and a **predicate** to be complete. Usually, the subject comes before the predicate. If the parts are not in order, the sentence may not make sense.

Example: **Incorrect:** Rode my bike to town I.
 Correct: I rode my bike to town.

Directions: Draw a line to match the subject to the correct predicate. Then, write each complete sentence on the lines below to form a story.

goes along Waddle Lake.   It

                    Horses   will sing songs and have hayfights.

will be available after the ride.   will drink cider and eat pumpkin pie.

                The townsfolk   will pull the wagons.

    The hungry party-goers   Food

will be a wonderful night.   The hayride

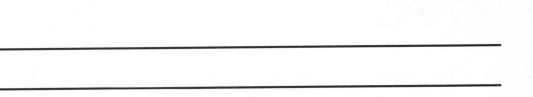

_____

_____

_____

_____

_____

Name _____

Word Order

The words in a sentence must be in a certain **order** for the sentence to make sense. If you change the order of the words in a sentence, you will change the meaning of the sentence as well.

Example: The ball hit the wall.
                 The wall hit the ball.

Directions: Rewrite each sentence below so that the words are in the correct order.

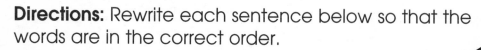

1. Mayor Sneak called the order to meeting.

2. Was first on the agenda the escape of the circus animals.

3. Spoke about the escape Mrs. Greenshoes.

4. Suggested that all animals should be in cages an officer.

5. With Officer Bark all the members of the council agreed.

6. To the Gambezi Brothers the secretary wrote a letter.

1. _____

2. _____

3. _____

4. _____

5. _____

6. _____

Word Order

Word order is the logical order of words in sentences.

Directions: Put the words in order so that each sentence tells a complete idea.

 Example: outside put cat the

Put the cat outside.

1. mouse the ate snake the

_____

2. dog John his walk took a for

_____

3. birthday Maria the present wrapped

_____

4. escaped parrot the cage its from

_____

5. to soup quarts water three of add the

_____

6. bird the bushes into the chased cat the

_____

Name _____

Run-On Sentences

When you join together two or more sentences without punctuation, you have created a **run-on sentence**.

Examples:

Run-on sentence: I lost my way once did you?
Correct punctuation: I lost my way once. Did you?

Run-on sentence: I found the recipe it was not hard to follow.
Correct punctuation: I found the recipe. It was not hard to follow.

Directions: Rewrite each run-on sentence so that it becomes two or more sentences.

Example: Did you take my umbrella I cannot find it anywhere!

Did you take my umbrella? I cannot find it anywhere!

1. How can you stand that noise I cannot!

_____

2. The cookies are gone I see only crumbs.

_____

3. The dogs were barking they were hungry.

_____

4. She is quite ill please call a doctor immediately!

_____

5. The clouds piled up we knew the storm would hit soon.

_____

Name _____

Run-On Sentences

A **run-on sentence** is made up of two or more complete sentences that are joined together without the correct punctuation.

> **Example:** **Run-On:** I am a desert creature I love the heat
> **Correct:** I am a desert creature. I love the heat.

Directions: Rewrite each run-on sentence so that it becomes two or more complete sentences.

I am a nocturnal animal I shed my skin and I eat rodents, lizards, and even birds. I can inject my poison through my fangs I have a rattle at the tip of my tail it tells when I may attack.

_____

_____

_____

_____

I am cold-blooded my body temperature is the same as the air around me I am a tiny animal that looks like the giant dinosaurs that lived a long time ago.

_____

_____

_____

_____

Name _____

Run-On Sentences

A **run-on sentence** is two or more sentences that run together. You can use punctuation and capitalization to make complete sentences.

Examples: **Run-On:**   Katelyn's garden is in the backyard she works there each day.

Correct: Katelyn's garden is in the backyard. She works there each day.

Directions: Rewrite each run-on sentence correctly. Write two or more shorter sentences.

1. Katelyn cleared the garden she raked the leaves and collected rocks.

_____

2. Katelyn planted seeds she planted beans and pumpkins.

_____

3. the seeds grow quickly they like warm sunshine.

_____

4. Water helps the plants grow Katelyn waters them every day.

_____

5. Insects visit Katelyn's garden some bugs are good.

_____

6. Pulling weeds is not very fun it is an important job.

_____

7. Pumpkins grow very large beans grow very tall.

_____

8. Katelyn harvests the vegetables they taste good.

_____

Conjunctions

Name _____

Words that join sentences or combine ideas, such as **and**, **but**, **or**, **because**, **when**, **after**, and **so**, are called conjunctions.

Examples:

I played the drums, **and** Sue played the clarinet.
She likes bananas, **but** I do not.
We could play music **or** just enjoy the silence.
I needed the book **because** I had to write a book report.
He gave me the book **when** I asked for it.
I asked her to eat lunch **after** she finished the test.
You wanted my bike **so** you could ride it.

Conjunctions can affect the meaning of a sentence.

Example: He gave me the book **when** I asked for it.
He gave me the book **after** I asked for it.

Directions: Choose the best conjunction to combine each pair of sentences.

Example: I like my hair curly. Mom likes my hair straight.

I like my hair curly, but Mom likes it straight.
_____

1. I can remember what she looks like. I cannot remember her name.

_____

2. We will have to wash the dishes. We will not have clean plates for dinner.

_____

3. The yellow flowers are blooming. The red flowers are not.

_____

4. I like banana cream pie. I like chocolate donuts.

_____

Name _____

Conjunctions

Directions: Use a conjunction from the Word Bank to combine the pairs of sentences.

Word Bank							
and	but	or	because	when	after	so	

1. I like Leah. I like Ben.

_____

2. Should I eat the orange? Should I eat the apple?

_____

3. You will get a reward. You turned in the lost item.

_____

4. I really mean what I say! You had better listen!

_____

5. I like you. You are nice, friendly, helpful, and kind.

_____

6. You can have dessert. You ate all your peas.

_____

7. I like your shirt better. You should decide for yourself.

_____

8. We walked out of the building. We heard the fire alarm.

_____

9. I like to sing folk songs. I like to play the guitar.

_____

Name _____

"And," "But," "Or"

Directions: Write **and**, **but**, or **or** to finish each sentence.

1. I want to try that new hamburger place, _____ Mom wants to eat at the Spaghetti Shop.

2. We could stay home, _____ would you rather go to the game?

3. She went right home after school, _____ he stopped at the store.

4. Mother held the piece of paneling, _____ Father nailed it in place.

5. She babysat last weekend, _____ her big sister went with her.

6. She likes raisins in her oatmeal, _____ I prefer brown sugar.

7. She was planning on coming over tomorrow, _____ I asked her if she could wait until the weekend.

8. Tomato soup with crackers sounds good to me, _____ would you rather have vegetable beef soup?

Name _____

"And" or "But"

We can use **and** or **but** to make one longer sentence from two short ones.

Directions: Use **and** or **but** to make two short sentences into a longer, more interesting one.

Example: The skunk has black fur. The skunk has a white stripe.
The skunk has black fur and a white stripe.

1. The skunk has a small head. The skunk has small ears.

   _____

2. Skunks have short legs. Skunks can move quickly.

   _____

3. Skunks sleep in hollow trees. Skunks sleep underground.

   _____

4. Larger animals may try to chase a skunk. Skunks do not run away.

   _____

5. Skunks sleep during the day. Skunks hunt at night.

   _____

Name _____

"When" or "After"

Directions: Write **when** or **after** to finish each sentence.

1. I knew we were in trouble_____ I heard the thunder in the distance.

2. We carried the baskets of cherries to the car_____ we were finished picking them.

3. Mother took off her apron_____ I reminded her that our dinner guests would be here any minute.

4. I wondered if we would have school tomorrow_____ I noticed the snow begin to fall.

5. The boys and girls all clapped _____ the magician pulled the colored scarves out of his sleeve.

6. I was startled _____ the phone rang so late last night.

7. You will need to get the film developed _____ you have taken all the pictures.

8. The children began to run _____ the snake started to move!

Name _____

"Because" or "So"

Directions: Write **because** or **so** to finish each sentence.

1. She cleaned the paint brushes _____ they would be ready in the morning.

2. Father called home complaining of a sore throat _____ Mom stopped by the pharmacy.

3. His bus will be running late _____ it has a flat tire.

4. We all worked together _____ we could get the job done sooner.

5. We took a variety of sandwiches on the picnic _____ we knew not everyone liked cheese and olives with mayonnaise.

6. All the school children were sent home _____ the electricity went off at school.

7. My brother wants us to meet his girlfriend _____ she will be coming to dinner with us on Friday.

8. He forgot to take his umbrella along this morning _____ now his clothes are very wet.

Name _____

Joining Sentences

Directions: Use **because**, **after**, or **when** to join each set of sentences into one longer sentence.

1. I pack my own lunch. I do not like the school's food.

   _____

   _____

2. I decided to be a zoo keeper. We visited the zoo.

   _____

   _____

3. I am surprised there is such a crowd. It costs so much to get in.

   _____

   _____

4. I beat the eggs for two minutes. The recipe called for egg yolk.

   _____

   _____

213

Name _____

Combining Sentences

Some simple sentences can be easily combined into one sentence.

Examples:

Simple sentences: The bird sang. The bird was tiny.
The bird was in the tree.

Combined sentence: The tiny bird sang in the tree.

Directions: Combine each set of simple sentences into one sentence.

Example:

The older girls laughed. They were friendly. They helped the little girls.
The older, friendly girls laughed as they helped the little girls.

1. The dog was hungry. The dog whimpered. The dog looked at its bowl.

_____

2. Be quiet now. I want you to listen. You listen to my joke!

_____

3. I lost my pencil. My pencil was stubby. I lost it on the bus.

_____

4. I see my mother. My mother is walking. My mother is walking down the street.

_____

5. Do you like ice cream? Do you like hot dogs? Do you like mustard?

_____

6. Tell me you will do it! Tell me you will! Tell me right now.

Name _____

Using Fewer Words

Writing can be more interesting when you use fewer words. Combining sentences is easy when the subjects are the same. Notice how the comma is used.

Example: Sally woke up. Sally ate breakfast. Sally brushed her teeth.
Sally woke up, ate breakfast, and brushed her teeth.

Combining sentences with more than one subject is a little more complicated. Notice how commas are used to "set off" information.

Examples: Jane went to the store. Jane is Sally's sister.
Jane went to the store with Sally, her sister.

Eddy Eddie likes to play with cars. Eddie is my younger brother.
Eddie, my younger brother, likes to play with cars.

Directions: Write each pair of sentences as one sentence.

1. Jerry played soccer after school. He played with his best friend, Tom.

   _____

2. Spot likes to chase cats. Spot is my dog.

   _____

3. Lori and Janice both love ice cream. Janice is Lori's cousin.

   _____

4. Jayna is my cousin. Jayna helped me move into my new apartment.

   _____

5. Romeo is a big tomcat. Romeo loves to hunt mice.

   _____

Name _____

Putting Ideas Together

Directions: Make each pair of sentences into one sentence. (You may have to change the verbs for some sentences—from **is** to **are**, for example.)

Example: Our house was flooded. Our car was flooded.
Our house and car were flooded.

1. Kenny sees a glow. Carrie sees a glow.

   _____

2. Our new stove came today. Our new refrigerator came today.

   _____

3. The pond is full of toads. The field is full of toads.

   _____

4. Stripes are on the flag. Stars are on the flag.

   _____

5. The ducks took flight. The geese took flight.

   _____

6. Joe reads stories. Dana reads stories.

   _____

7. French fries taste good. Milkshakes taste good.

   _____

8. Justine heard someone groan. Kevin heard someone groan.

   _____

Name _____

Putting Ideas Together

Directions: Write each pair of sentences as one sentence.

Example:
Jim will deal the cards one at a time.
Jim will give four cards to everyone.
Jim will deal the cards one at a time and give four cards to everyone.

1. Amy won the contest. Amy claimed the prize.

   _____

2. We need to find the scissors. We need to buy some tape.

   _____

3. The stream runs through the woods. The stream empties into the East River.

   _____

4. Katie tripped on the steps. Katie has a pain in her left foot.

   _____

5. Grandpa took me to the store. Grandpa bought me a treat.

   _____

6. Charity ran two miles. She walked one mile to cool down afterward.

   _____

Statements

A **statement** is a sentence that tells something.

Directions: Finish each statement using a word from the Word Bank.

Word Bank					
glue	decide	add	share	enter	fold

1. It took ten minutes for Mike to _____ the numbers.

2. Ben wants to _____ his cookies with me.

3. "I cannot _____ which color to choose," said Rocky.

4. You can use _____ to make things stick together.

5. "This is how you _____ your paper in half," said Mrs. Green.

6. The opposite of leave is _____.

Directions: Write your own statement on the line below.

_____

Questions

Questions are asking sentences. They begin with a capital letter and end with a question mark. Many questions begin with the word **who**, **what**, **why**, **when**, **where**, or **how**.

Directions: Write six questions using the question words below. Make sure to end each sentence with a question mark.

1. Who _____

_____

2. What _____

_____

3. Why _____

_____

4. When _____

_____

5. Where _____

_____

6. How _____

_____

Name _____

Writing Question Sentences

Directions: Rewrite each sentence to make it a question. In some cases, you will need to change the form of the verb.

Example: She slept soundly all day.
Did she sleep soundly all day?

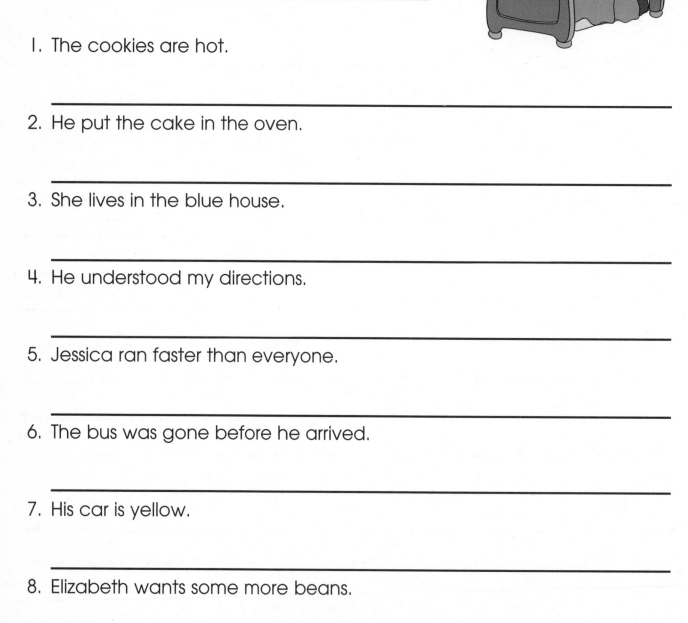

1. The cookies are hot.

_____

2. He put the cake in the oven.

_____

3. She lives in the blue house.

_____

4. He understood my directions.

_____

5. Jessica ran faster than everyone.

_____

6. The bus was gone before he arrived.

_____

7. His car is yellow.

_____

8. Elizabeth wants some more beans.

_____

Statements and Questions

A **statement** tells some kind of information. It is followed by a period (.).

    Examples: It is a rainy day.
                    We are going to the beach next summer.

A **question** asks for a specific piece of information. It is followed by a question mark (?).

    Examples: What is the weather like today?
                    When are you going to the beach?

Directions: Write whether each sentence is a statement or question.

    Example: Jamie went for a walk at the zoo.   _____statement_____

1. The leaves turn bright colors in the fall. _____

2. When does the Easter Bunny arrive? _____

3. Madeleine went to the new art school. _____

4. Is school over at 3:30? _____

5. Grandma and Grandpa are moving. _____

6. Anthony went home. _____

7. Did Mary go to Amy's house? _____

8. Who went to work late? _____

Directions: Write two statements and two questions below.

Statements:

_____

_____

Questions:

_____

_____

221

Name _____

Commands

A **command** is a sentence that tells someone or something to do something.

Directions: Finish each command with a word from the Word Bank.

Word Bank					
glue	decide	add	share	enter	fold

1. _____ a cup of flour to the cake batter.

2. _____ how much paper you will need to write your story.

3. Please _____ the picture of the apple onto the paper.

4. _____ through this door and leave through the other door.

5. Please _____ the letter and put it into an envelope.

6. _____ your toys with your sister.

Directions: Write four commands on the lines below.

_____

_____

_____

SENTENCES

Directions

A **direction** is a sentence written as a command.

Directions: Write the missing directions for these pictures. Begin each direction with one of the verbs from the Word Bank.

Word Bank					
glue	decide	add	share	enter	fold

How To Make a Peanut Butter and Jelly Sandwich:

1. Spread peanut butter on the bread.

2. _____

3. Cut the sandwich in half.

4. _____

How To Make a Valentine:

1. _____

2. Draw half of a heart.

3. Cut along the line you drew.

4. _____

Name _____

Exclamations

Exclamation points end sentences or phrases that express strong feelings.

Example: **Wait!**
Don't forget to call!

Directions: Add an exclamation point at the end of each sentence that expresses strong feelings. Add a period at the end of each statement.

1. My parents and I watched television__

2. The snow began falling around noon__

3. Wow__

4. The snow was really coming down__

5. We turned the television off and looked out the window__

6. The snow looked like a white blanket__

7. How beautiful__

8. We decided to put on our coats and go outside__

9. Hurry__

10. Get your sled__

11. All the people on the street came out to see the snow__

12. How wonderful__

13. The children began making a snowman__

14. What a great day__

Name _____

Commands and Exclamations

A command tells someone to do something. It is followed by a period (.).

   Examples: Get your math book. Do your homework.

An exclamation shows strong feeling or excitement.
It is followed by an exclamation mark (!).

   Examples: Watch out for that car!
                   There's a snake!

Directions: Write whether each sentence is a command or an exclamation.

   Examples:

   Please clean your room.   command

   Wow! Those fireworks are beautiful!   exclamation

   1. Come to dinner now.   _____

   2. Color the sky and water blue. _____

   3. Trim the paper carefully.   _____

   4. Here comes the bus!   _____

   5. That is a lovely picture!   _____

   6. Stop playing and clean up.   _____

   7. Brush your teeth before bedtime. _____

Directions: Write two commands and two exclamations below.

Commands:

_____

_____

Exclamations:

_____

_____

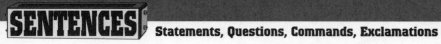

Name _____

Four Kinds of Sentences

Directions: Write **S** if the sentence is a statement, **Q** if the sentence is a question, **C** if the sentence is a command, or **E** if the sentence is an exclamation. End each sentence with a period, question mark, or exclamation mark.

Example: __E__ Oh my gosh!

_____ 1. My little brother insists on coming with us__

_____ 2. Tell him movies are bad for his health__

_____ 3. He says he is fond of movies__

_____ 4. Does he know there are monsters in this movie__

_____ 5. He says he needs facts for his science report__

_____ 6. He is writing about something that hatched from an old egg__

_____ 7. Could he go to the library__

_____ 8. Could we dress him like us so he will blend in__

_____ 9. You must be kidding__

_____ 10. Would he sit by himself at the movie__

_____ 11. That would be too dangerous__

_____ 12. Mom said she would give us money for candy if we took him with us__

_____ 13. That is awesome__

_____ 14. Get your brother and go__

SENTENCES

Name _____

Four Kinds of Sentences

exclamation
question
command
statement

Directions: For each pair of words, write two kinds of sentences (any combination of questions, commands, statements, or exclamations). Use one or both of the words in each sentence. Name each kind of sentence that you wrote.

Example:

pump   crop

_____Question_____ : _What kind of crops did you plant?_____

_____Command_____ : _Pump the water as fast as you can._____

1. pinch   health

   _____ : _____

   _____ : _____

2. fond   fact

   _____ : _____

   _____ : _____

3. insist   hatch

   _____ : _____

   _____ : _____

exclamation   command   statement   question

Name _____

Punctuation

A **sentence** is a group of words that tells a complete thought.

A sentence that tells something ends with a period (**.**).
A sentence that asks a question ends with a question mark (**?**).
A sentence that shows strong feeling ends with an exclamation point (**!**).
A sentence that gives a command ends with a period (**.**).

Directions: Read each sentence. Write the correct punctuation mark to end the sentence.

1. Do you want to go to the movies on Saturday__

2. We are going to the theater at the mall__

3. I am going to buy a large popcorn and a bag of candy__

4. What do you like to eat at the movies__

5. This movie is great__

6. Meet me outside__

Directions: Write four sentences about a move you have seen. Try to include at least two different kinds of sentences.

_____

_____

_____

_____

CAPITALIZATION AND PUNCTUATION

Name _____

Capitalization

The first word in a sentence should begin with a capital letter.

Directions: Read each sentence. Underline with three short lines the first letter of each word that needs a capital letter. Rewrite the word correctly.

Example: ___Today___ today is the first day of school.

1. _____ sam takes the bus to school.

2. _____ the children play soccer at recess.

3. _____ everyone has fun reading a story.

4. _____ when will we do a science experiment?

5. _____ lunch is served in the cafeteria.

6. _____ our principal came to visit our class.

7. _____ students should be quiet in the library.

8. _____ the teacher writes the homework on the board.

9. _____ clean your desk before you go home.

10. _____ have a great day!

Name _____

Punctuation and Capitalization

Directions: In the paragraphs below, use periods, question marks, or exclamation points to show where one sentence ends and the next begins. Circle the first letter of each new sentence to show the capitalization.

Example: ⓜy sister accused me of not helping her rake the leaves. Ⓣhat is silly! Ⓘhelped at least a hundred times.

1. I toss out my fishing line when it moves up and down, I know a fish is there after waiting a minute or two, I pull up the fish it is fun

2. I tried putting lemon juice on my freckles to make them go away did you ever do that it did not work my skin just got sticky now, I am slowly getting used to my freckles

3. once, I had an accident on my bike I was on my way home from school what do you think happened my wheel slipped in the loose dirt at the side of the road my bike slid into the road

4. one night, I dreamed I lived in a castle in my dream, I was the king or maybe the queen everyone listened to my commands then, Mom woke me up for school I tried commanding her to let me sleep it did not work

5. my dad does exercises every night to make his stomach flat he says he does not want to grow old I think it is too late do not tell him I said that

CAPITALIZATION AND PUNCTUATION

Name _____

Punctuation and Capitalization

Directions: In the paragraphs below, use periods, question marks, and exclamation points to show where one sentence ends and the next begins. Circle the first letter of each new sentence to show the capitalization.

1. It was Christmas Eve Santa and the elves were loading the toys onto his sleigh the deer keepers were harnessing the reindeer and walking them toward the sleigh

2. the reindeer were prancing with anxious anticipation of their midnight flight soon, the sleigh was overflowing with its load, and Santa was ready to travel crack went his whip the reindeer pulled and tugged against their harnesses the sleigh inched forward, slowly at first, then it climbed swiftly into the holiday night sky

3. everything was going smoothly Santa and the reindeer made excellent time traveling from house to house and city to city at each home, of course, the children had left snacks of cookies and milk for Santa

4. around 2 o'clock in the morning, Santa felt his red suit begin to get tight around his middle "hmm," he said to himself "I have been eating too many snacks" he decided that he would have to cut back on his cookie calories

5. the reindeer team guided Santa to his next stop he hopped out of his sleigh, grabbed his bundle of toys, and jogged to the chimney he climbed up to the chimney's opening and started down to the fireplace oops something awful happened Santa got stuck oh, no *what do we do now* wondered the reindeer

Name _____

Capitalization

A **proper noun** names a special person, place, or thing. Capitalize the first letter in each word of a proper noun.

Examples: california cafe = California Cafe
malibu = Malibu

Directions: In the post card, underline with three short lines the first letter of each word that needs a capital letter.

Dear trudy,
My family and I are in los angeles, california. We have been to hollywood, santa monica beach, and rodeo drive in beverly hills. Tomorrow, we are going to visit disney land. I hope I will get to meet mickey mouse. Wish you were here!
Your friend, roberta

Trudy Little
3501 Courtland
Garden City, KS
67846

Directions: Rewrite Roberta's postcard with the correct capitalization.

_____

_____

_____

CAPITALIZATION AND PUNCTUATION

Name _____

Capitalization

A person's name begins with a capital letter. The pronoun **I** is written as a capital letter.

Directions: Read each sentence. Underline with three short lines the first letter of each word that needs a capital letter. Write each sentence correctly.

Example:

The librarian helped tracy find a book about susan b. anthony.

The librarian helped Tracy find a book about Susan B. Anthony.

1. i learned that george washington was the first president.

_____

2. matthew and amelia are doing a project about thomas jefferson.

_____

3. elisa and i are studying about abraham lincoln.

_____

4. harriet tubman helped rescue many people from slavery.

_____

5. Many people admire helen keller's courage and intelligence.

_____

6. Can i write a report about jackie robinson?

_____

Name _____

Capitalization

Capitalize the first letter of each word in the names of holidays and special events.

Directions: Read each sentence. Underline with three short lines the first letter of each word that needs a capital letter. Rewrite each sentence correctly.

1. Did you watch the rose parade on new year's day?

   _____

   _____

2. The librarian helps us choose books during national book week.

   _____

3. My family eats turkey and potatoes on thanksgiving day.

   _____

4. The class planted a tree on arbor day.

   _____

5. Our christmas tree is decorated with lights and ornaments.

   _____

6. We watched fireworks at the park on independence day.

   _____

CAPITALIZATION AND PUNCTUATION

Name _____

Capitalization

Capitalize the first letter of each word in geographical names and historical periods of time.

Examples: pacific ocean = Pacific Ocean
renaissance = Renaissance

Directions: Read each word. If the word should begin with a capital letter, rewrite it correctly on the line.

1. rocky mountains _____

2. lake superior _____

3. ocean _____

4. kenya _____

5. country _____

6. middle ages _____

7. dinosaur _____

8. north pole _____

9. stone age _____

10. river _____

11. jurassic period _____

12. nile river _____

13. europe _____

14. state _____

15. atlantic ocean _____

Name _____

Abbreviations

An **abbreviation** is the shortened form of a word. Most abbreviations begin with a capital letter and end with a period.

Mr. = Mister	A.M. = Before Noon	St. = Street
Mrs. = Missus	P.M. = After Noon	Ave. = Avenue
Dr. = Doctor		Blvd. = Boulevard
		Rd. = Road

Weekdays: Sun. Mon. Tues. Wed. Thurs. Fri. Sat.

Months: Jan. Feb. Mar. Apr. Aug. Sept. Oct. Nov. Dec.

Directions: Write the abbreviation for each word.

Street _____   Doctor _____   Tuesday _____

Road _____   Mister _____   Avenue _____

Missus _____   October _____   Friday _____

Before Noon _____   March _____   August _____

Directions: Rewrite each sentence using abbreviations.

1. On Monday at 9:00 before noon, Mister Jones had a meeting.

_____

2. In December, Doctor Carlson saw Missus Zuckerman.

_____

3. One Tuesday in August, Mister Wood went to the park.

_____

CAPITALIZATION AND PUNCTUATION

Name _____

Abbreviations

Use a **period** after an **abbreviation**.

Example: Monday = Mon.   December = Dec.

Do not use abbreviations in sentences.

Example: I like to skate on Mondays in December.

Directions: Fill in each blank with the correct abbreviation from the Word Bank.

1. Wednesday ———	7. Rural Route ———
2. January ———	8. Thursday ———
3. Street ———	9. Avenue ———
4. Boulevard ———	10. Road ———
5. February ———	11. April ———
6. Saturday ———	12. Post Office ———

Word Bank

Blvd.	St.
Jan.	Sat.
Wed.	Feb.
P.O.	R.R.
Rd.	Apr.
Ave.	Thurs.

Directions: Rewrite each sentence correctly on the lines below.

1. Every Mon. in Jan., they shovel driveways for the elderly.

   _____

   _____

2. Their meetings are held each Tues. at Julie's house on Webster St.

   _____

   _____

3. During Feb., they visited nursing homes every Sun. evening.

   _____

   _____

Name _____

Capitalization

A **title** tells what a person is or does. It begins with a capital letter and ends with a period. An **initial** is the first letter of a person's first, middle, or last name.

Examples: **Mr. Rogers**
                Dr. B.J. Honeycut

Directions: Write each name and title correctly.

1. dr seuss _____

2. gen g patton _____

3. mr rogers _____

4. mrs e roosevelt _____

5. miss gloria steinem _____

6. capt james t kirk _____

7. mr m twain _____

8. dr s freud _____

9. miss louisa m alcott _____

10. mr maurice sendak _____

11. dr l pasteur _____

12. gen e braddock _____

Capitalization

Capitalize the first letter in each month of the year, in each day of the week, in a title of respect, and when abbreviating a title of respect.

Examples: january = January   tuesday = Tuesday

doctor jones = Doctor Jones   mrs. clark = Mrs. Clark

Directions: Read the story below. Underline with three short lines the first letter of each word that needs a capital letter. Rewrite the story correctly.

My baby brother, Nicholas, was born on sunday, september 8, 2002.

On saturday, my mom went to see doctor nelson at the hospital. Our

neighbors, mr. and mrs. Bigelow, let me sleep over at their house. My mom

and Nicholas came home on monday.

_____

_____

_____

_____

_____

_____

Name _____

Capitalization

A specific name of a **person, place,** and **pet,** a **day of the week,** a **month of the year,** and a **holiday** each begins with a capital letter.

Directions: Read the words in the Word Bank. Write the words in the correct columns with the correct letters capitalized.

Word Bank			
ron polsky	tuesday	march	april
presidents' day	saturday	woofy	october
blackie	portland, oregon	corning, new york	molly yoder
valentine's day	fluffy	harold edwards	arbor day
bozeman, montana	sunday		

People

_____

_____

_____

Places

_____

_____

_____

Pets

_____

_____

_____

Days

_____

_____

_____

Months

_____

_____

_____

Holidays

_____

_____

_____

Name _____

Book Titles

Capitalize the first and last words in a book's title. Capitalize all other words in a book's title except short prepositions, such as **of**, **at**, and **in**, conjunctions, such as **and**, **or**, and **but**, and articles, such as **a**, **an**, and **the**.

Examples:

Have you read <u>War and Peace</u>?
Pippi Longstocking in Moscow is her favorite book.

Directions: Underline the book titles. Circle the words that should be capitalized.

Example: ⟨murder⟩ in the ⟨blue room⟩ by Elliot Roosevelt

1. growing up in a divided society by Sandra Burnham

2. the corn king and the spring queen by Naomi Mitchison

3. new kids on the block by Grace Catalano

4. best friends don't tell lies by Linda Barr

5. turn your kid into a computer genius by Carole Gerber

6. amy the dancing bear by Carly Simon

7. garfield goes to waist by Jim Davis

8. the hunt for red october by Tom Clancy

9. fall into darkness by Christopher Pike

10. oh the places you'll go! by Dr. Seuss

Name _____

Book Titles

All words in the title of a book are underlined or italicized.

Examples: <u>The Hunt for Red October</u> was a best-seller!
Have you read *Lost in Space*?

Directions: Underline the book titles in these sentences.

Example: <u>The Dinosaur Poster Book</u> is for
eight-year-old children.

1. Have you read Lion Dancer by Kate Waters?

2. Baby Dinosaurs and Giant Dinosaurs were both written by Peter Dodson.

3. Have you heard of the book That's What Friends Are For by Carol Adorjan?

4. J.B. Stamper wrote a book called The Totally Terrific Valentine Party Book.

5. The teacher read Almost Ten and a Half aloud to our class.

6. Marrying Off Mom is about a girl who tries to get her widowed mother to start dating.

7. The Snow and The Fire are the second and third books by author Caroline Cooney.

8. The title sounds silly, but Goofbang Value Daze really is the name of a book!

9. A book about space exploration is The Day We Walked on the Moon by George Sullivan.

10. Alice and the Birthday Giant tells about a giant who came to a girl's birthday party.

Name _____

Titles

Titles of books are underlined when you write them by hand. When they are typed, titles of books are underlined or in italics.

> **Examples:**   <u>James and the Giant Peach</u>
> *James and the Giant Peach*

Titles of stories, poems, and songs are always in quotation marks.

> **Examples:**   "Sleeping Beauty" (story)
> "Paul Revere's Ride" (poem)
> "Blue Suede Shoes" (song)

Directions: Read each sentence. Underline the title of a book. Put quotation marks around the title of a story, poem, or song.

1. Luis read Number the Stars for his book report.

2. Stanley the Fierce is a poem by Judith Viorst.

3. Laura Ingalls Wilder wrote Little House in the Big Woods.

4. Our class sang America the Beautiful for the veterans.

5. The Gift of the Magi is a good story.

6. Do you know how to play Happy Birthday on the piano?

7. A Girl's Garden is a poem by Robert Frost.

8. Last week, I checked out Because of Winn-Dixie from the library.

9. My dad read us the story Tom Thumb before we went to sleep.

10. Our class is reading Sarah, Plain and Tall this month.

Name _____

Commas

Commas are used to separate words in a series of three or more.

   Example: My favorite fruits are apples, bananas, and oranges.

Directions: Put commas where they are needed in each sentence.

1. Please buy milk eggs bread and cheese.

2. I need paper pencils and a folder for school.

3. Some good pets are cats dogs gerbils fish and rabbits.

4. Aaron Mike and Matt went to the baseball game.

5. Major forms of transportation are planes trains and automobiles.

Name _____

Commas

Use a comma to separate words in a series. A comma is used after each word in a series but is not needed before the last word. Both ways are correct. In your own writing, be consistent about which style you use.

Examples: We ate apples, oranges, and pears.
We ate apples, oranges and pears.

Always use a comma between the name of a city and a state.

Example: She lives in Fresno, California.
He lives in Wilmington, Delaware.

Directions: Write **C** if the sentence is punctuated correctly. Write **X** if the sentence is not punctuated correctly.

Example: __X__ She ordered shoes, dresses and shirts to be sent to her home in Oakland California.

1. _____ No one knew her pets' names were Fido, Spot and Tiger.

2. _____ He likes green beans lima beans, and corn on the cob.

3. _____ Typing paper, pens and pencils are all needed for school.

4. _____ Send your letters to her in College Park, Maryland.

5. _____ Orlando Florida is the home of Disney World.

6. _____ Mickey, Minnie, Goofy and Daisy are all favorites of mine.

7. _____ Send your letter to her in Reno, Nevada.

8. _____ Before he lived in New York, City he lived in San Diego, California.

9. _____ She mailed postcards, and letters to him in Lexington, Kentucky.

10. _____ Teacups, saucers, napkins, and silverware were piled high.

11. _____ Can someone give me a ride to Indianapolis, Indiana?

12. _____ He took a train a car, then a boat to visit his old friend.

Name _____

Commas

Commas separate words in a list or series.

Examples: We will need to take a train, a helicopter, a bus, and a boat to get to the island.

Directions: Put commas where they belong in the story below.

We are on an expedition to visit these volcanoes: Mount Saint Helens Mount Etna Mount Pinatubo Mount Pelee and Mount Vesuvius. The members of our team are geologists botanists and volcanologists. They will help us study these volcanoes and learn more about the formation the craters the types of volcanoes the types of eruptions and the environmental impact. Violent explosions or blasts from the volcano can produce lava rock fragments and gas. We will also look at the natural resources these volcanoes provide. The energy from volcanoes is used to heat homes in Iceland and greenhouses that grow vegetables and fruits. Geothermal steam produces electricity in Italy New Zealand the United States and Mexico.

Name _____

Commas

Commas separate words or groups of words to help make the meaning of a sentence clear.

Use commas in a series of items.

Example: I love eating yogurt, toast, and cucumbers for breakfast!

Use commas when talking to people.

Example: Do you know where my shirt is, Andrew?

Directions: Write **C** if the sentence is punctuated correctly. Write **X** if the sentence is not punctuated correctly.

1. _____ Bob is Sam going to the grocery store?

2. _____ Sam is supposed to buy grapes, bananas, and apples.

3. _____ Can you go with Sam, Bob?

4. _____ Make sure to buckle your seatbelt drive safely and be careful in the parking lot.

5. _____ Sam are you ready?

Name _____

Commas

Use a **comma** to set apart the name of someone who is being addressed.
Use a comma to set apart introductory words, such as **yes**, **no**, and **well**.

Examples: **Kate**, do you think that butterflies are graceful?
Yes, they are very graceful and colorful.
I agree with you, **Jamal**, that we need more butterflies.

Directions: Add commas where they belong in each sentence below.

1. Monica have you seen any butterflies fluttering around your yard?

2. Well yesterday I saw one but just for a second.

3. When was the last time you saw butterflies in your garden Betsy?

4. Meredith can you name the four stages of the butterfly life cycle?

5. Yes I can. They are the egg, larva, chrysalis, and adult butterfly.

6. Jeff do you know the name of the butterfly's long feeding tube?

7. Yes it is called the proboscis. The butterfly uses it to drink nectar.

8. Heather did you know that Queen Alexandra's birdwing butterfly is the largest butterfly in the world?

9. No I did not know that.

10. Well did you know that butterflies are insects?

11. Yes I knew that Alyson.

12. Did you know Dave that butterflies like to warm up out in the sun?

13. No but that must be because they are cold-blooded.

14. Yes they cannot become more active until their bodies warm up.

Name _____

Commas

Use commas to separate the day from the year.

Example: May 13, 1950

Directions: Rewrite each date, putting the comma in the correct place. Capitalize the name of each month.

Example: Jack and Dave were born on february 22 1982.
February 22, 1982
_____

1. My father's birthday is may 19 1948.

_____

2. My sister was fourteen on december 13 1994.

_____

3. Lauren's seventh birthday was on november 30 1998.

_____

4. october 13 1996 was the last day I saw my lost cat.

_____

5. On april 17 1997, we saw the Grand Canyon.

_____

6. Our vacation lasted from april 2 1998 to april 26 1998.

_____

7. Molly's baby sister was born on august 14 1991.

_____

8. My mother was born on june 22 1959.

_____

Name _____

Commas

Use a comma to separate the day of the month and the year. Do not use a comma to separate the month and the year if no day is given.

Examples: June 14, 1999
June 1999

Use a comma after **yes** or **no** when it is the first word in a sentence.

Examples: Yes, I will do it right now.
No, I do not want any.

Directions: Write **C** if the sentence is punctuated correctly. Write **X** if the sentence is not punctuated correctly.

Example: ___C___ No, I do not plan to attend.

1. _____ Yes, I told them I would go.

2. _____ Her birthday is March 13, 1995.

3. _____ He was born in May, 2003.

4. _____ Yes, of course I like you!

5. _____ No I will not be there.

6. _____ They left for vacation on February, 14.

7. _____ No, today is Monday.

8. _____ The program began on August 12, 1991.

9. _____ In September, 2007 how old will you be?

10. _____ He turned 12 years old on November, 13.

11. _____ No, I will not go to the party!

12. _____ Yes, she is a friend of mine.

13. _____ His birthday is June 12, 1992.

14. _____ No I would not like more dessert.

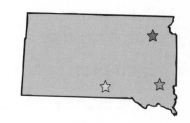

Name _____

Commas

Capitalize the first letter in the name of a city and a state. Use a comma to separate the name of a city and a state.

Directions: Use capital letters and commas to write the names of the cities and states correctly.

Example: sioux falls south dakota _Sioux Falls, South Dakota_

1. plymouth massachusetts _____

2. boston massachusetts _____

3. philadelphia pennsylvania _____

4. white plains new york _____

5. newport rhode island _____

6. yorktown virginia _____

7. nashville tennessee _____

8. portland oregon _____

9. mansfield ohio _____

Name _____

Commas

Use a **comma** after the day in a date. Do not put a comma after the month if no day is given.

Examples: May 12, 2002 or May 2002

Use a comma after each part of an address.

Example: 123 Main Street, Seattle, Washington

Use a comma between the city name and the state name when they are used together.

Example: Seattle, Washington

Directions: Rewrite the story putting the commas in the correct places.

My grandpa had a very interesting life! He was born on, August, 20 1943. He grew up in, Boston Massachusetts. In January, 1963, he moved to, Los Angeles California. My grandpa lived at 349, James Street Los Angeles California. On June, 8, 1964, he married my grandma at a church in, San Francisco California. My dad was born on, February 1 1966.

_____

_____

_____

_____

_____

_____

_____

_____

Name _____

Commas

Use a **comma** after the greeting and closing in a friendly letter.

Examples: **Greeting:** **Closing:**
Dear Teresa, Your friend,
Samantha

Directions: Put commas where they belong in the letter below.

Dear Donovan

    I can hardly wait to get to your house this weekend. My dad will be dropping me off on Saturday afternoon. We will have fun sleeping in your tree house. Can we build a campfire?

    Your friend
    Simon

Directions: Write your own letter to a friend.

_____

_____

_____

_____

_____

_____

_____

Commas

Use a **comma** in the greeting and closing of a letter. Also use a comma between the day and the year of a date. Use a comma to separate a city from its state.

Examples: **heading:** Dear Grandma,
closing: Love, Megan
date: October 27, 2002
address: Tempe, Arizona

Directions: Put commas where they belong in each letter below.

Sunday, August, 22 1999

Aunt Betty
The Little White House
Littleville California

Dear Aunt Betty

    I am so excited to visit you. Did you get our Model T fixed yet? Remember how it scared everyone at the 4th of July parade? I will see you in two weeks.

    Love
    Jennifer

Wednesday, August 25, 1999

Jennifer
Big Brown Cottage
Bear Town Washington

Dear Jenny

    I am also excited about your visit. Yes, my old car is fixed. We can drive to town to see my sisters. See you soon!

    Love
    Aunt Betty

Commas

Use a **comma** to set apart an introductory clause to make your meaning clear.

Example: Apart from his uncle, Abner is the strangest
in the family.

Directions: Add commas where they belong in each sentence below.

1. At first I thought I won the race.

2. In the gym I saw a basketball game.

3. According to Billy Molly and Jim were up late last night
trying to find apples, cheese, and desserts.

4. Looking back at her younger brother Molly stuck out her tongue!

5. After she left her aunt Susan started to cry.

Name _____

Quotation Marks

Quotation marks show that someone is speaking. The opening quotation mark is used just before the first word, which begins with a capital letter. The closing quotation mark is used after the final punctuation mark. Make sure you use a comma to set apart quotations.

Example: "Follow me," he said.
                 She replied, "I'll be right there."

Directions: Put quotation marks and the correct punctuation in each sentence below.

1. Wow! This is beautiful Sean said

2. Ling said I cannot see anything yet

3. Do you have any extra water

   Sean asked

4. Ling said Yes, it is in my backpack

5. Good. It is going to be a hot day Sean said.

6. Stop Ling shouted

7. Why Sean asked

8. I think I saw a bear up ahead Ling answered.

   It is coming this way

9. Climb Sean yelled as he started up a tree

Name _____

Quotation Marks

Quotation marks are punctuation marks that tell what a person says out loud. Quotation marks go before the first word and after the punctuation mark. The first word in a quotation begins with a capital letter if the quote is a complete sentence.

   Example: Katie said, "Never go in the water without a friend."

Directions: Put quotation marks where they belong in each sentence below.

   Example: "Wait for me, please," said Laura.

1. John, would you like to visit a jungle? asked his uncle.

2. The police officer said, Do not worry. We will help you.

3. James shouted, Hit a home run!

4. My friend Carol said, I really do not like cheeseburgers.

Directions: Answer each question below. Be sure to put quotation marks around your words.

1. What would you say if you saw a dinosaur?

   _____

   _____

2. What would your best friend say if your hair turned purple?

   _____

   _____

Name _____

Punctuation: Quotation Marks

Use **quotation marks** before and after words that a person speaks out loud.

Examples: I asked Aunt Martha, "How do you feel?"
            "I feel awful," Aunt Martha replied.

Do not put quotation marks around words that are a summary of what a person said out loud.

Examples: I asked Aunt Martha how she felt.
            Aunt Martha said she felt awful.

Directions: Write **C** if the sentence is punctuated correctly. Write **X** if the sentence is not punctuated correctly.

Example: _C_ "I want it right now!" she demanded angrily.

1. ____ "Do you want it now? I asked."

2. ____ She said "she felt better" now.

3. ____ Her exact words were, "I feel much better now!"

4. ____ "I am so thrilled to be here!" he shouted.

5. ____ "Yes, I will attend," she replied.

6. ____ Elizabeth said "she was unhappy."

7. ____ "I'm unhappy," Elizabeth reported.

8. ____ "Did you know her mother?" I asked.

9. ____ I asked "whether you knew her mother."

10. ____ I asked, "What will dessert be?"

11. ____ "Which will it be, salt or pepper?" the waiter asked.

12. ____ "No, I don't know the answer!" he snapped.

13. ____ He said "yes he'd take her on the trip.

14. ____ Be patient, he said. "it will soon be over."

Name _____

Quotation Marks

Directions: Rewrite each sentence, putting quotation marks around the correct words.

1. Can we go for a bike ride? asked Katrina.

   _____

2. Yes, said Mom.

   _____

3. We should go to the park, said Mike.

   _____

4. Great idea! said Mom.

   _____

5. How long until we get there? asked Katrina.

   _____

6. Soon, said Mike.

   _____

7. Here we are! exclaimed Mom.

   _____

Name _____

Quotation Marks

Use quotation marks to set off a direct quotation. Also use quotation marks around the titles of poems, stories, T.V. shows, and reports.

    Examples: The teacher said, "Kate, you got a 100 percent on your test."

                      Todd read the poem "The Owl and the Pussycat."

Directions: In each sentence below, put quotation marks where they belong.

1. Mr. Fry asked, Sara, are you going to the park?

2. Mom read me the poem Who Has Seen the Wind?

3. The Magic School Bus is one of my favorite T.V. shows.

4. Are you going to the game? Raquel asked.

5. Anna gave a report called Tribes of the Northwest.

6. My brother can read the story Little Red Riding Hood.

7. Maria remarked, It is very cold today.

8. Terrence wrote a report titled Inside the Super Computer.

9. We Should get together tomorrow, said Laura.

10. Have you read the poem called Dancers' Delight?

11. Monica said, Raquel, we should play after school.

12. Jenny's report was titled Great Modern Painters.

Name _____

Quotation Marks

Use quotation marks around the titles of songs and poems.

Examples: Have you heard the song "Still Cruising" by the Beach Boys?

"Ode to a Nightingale" is a famous poem.

Directions: Write **C** if the sentence is punctuated correctly. Write **X** if the sentence is not punctuated correctly.

Example: _C_   Do you know "My Bonnie Lies Over the Ocean"?

1. ____ We sang The Stars and Stripes Forever" at school.

2. ____ Her favorite song is "The Eensy Weensy Spider."

3. ____ Turn up the music when "A Hard Day's "Night comes on!

4. ____ "Yesterday" was one of Paul McCartney's most famous songs.

5. ____ "Mary Had a Little Lamb" is a very silly poem!

6. ____ A song everyone knows is "Happy Birthday."

7. ____ "Swing Low, Sweet Chariot" was first sung by slaves.

8. ____ Do you know the words to Home on "the Range"?

9. ____ "Hiawatha" is a poem many people had to memorize.

10. ____ "Happy Days Are Here Again! is an upbeat tune.

11. ____ Frankie Valli and the Four Seasons sang "Sherry."

12. ____ The words to "Rain, Rain" Go Away are easy to learn.

13. ____ A slow song I know is called "Summertime."

261

Name _____

Apostrophes

An **apostrophe** shows where letters are missing in a contraction. A **contraction** is a shortened form of two words.

Example: Was not = wasn't

By adding an apostrophe and the letter **s** to the end of a person, place, or thing, you are showing that person, place, or thing to have ownership of something.

Example: Mary's cat

Directions: Write the apostrophe in each contraction below.

Example: We shouldn't be going to their house so late at night.

1. We didn t think that the ice cream would melt so fast.

2. They re never around when we re ready to go.

3. Didn t you need to make a phone call?

4. Who s going to help you paint the bicycle red?

Directions: Add an apostrophe and an **s** to each word below that shows ownership.

Example: Jill's bike is broken.

1. That is Holly   flower garden.

2. Mark   new skates are black and green.

3. Mom threw away Dad   old shoes.

4. Buster   food dish was lost in the snowstorm.

Name _____

Contractions

A **contraction** is a shortened form of two words. Apostrophes show where letters are missing.

Example: It is = it's

  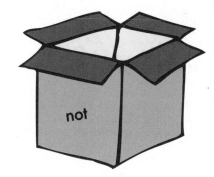

Directions: Write the words that make up each contraction.

we're _____ + _____   they'll _____ + _____

you'll _____ + _____   aren't _____ + _____

I'm _____ + _____   isn't _____ + _____

Directions: Write the contraction for each set of words.

you have _____   have not _____

had not _____   we will _____

they are _____   he is _____

she had _____   it will _____

I am _____   is not _____

Name _____

Contractions and Apostrophes

A **contraction** is two words made into one word by replacing one or more letters with an **apostrophe**.

Examples: I + am = I'm
we + will = we'll

Directions: Above each pair of underlined words, write the correct contraction.

We <u>are not</u> happy about the move. The moving trucks are waiting.

Our friends said they <u>would not</u> help us load our things because they

<u>did not</u> want us to leave.

"<u>We are</u> all packed. <u>We will</u> even load the trucks ourselves," Mom

said. On the way to our new home, we talked about our old friends and

all of the new friends <u>we would</u> meet at our new school.

Name _____

Contractions and Apostrophes

Contractions are two words that are shortened and put together to make one word. An **apostrophe** replaces the missing letters.

Examples: does not = doesn't
                       cannot = can't

Directions: Draw a line from each pair of words to its matching contraction.

1. is not	weren't
2. are not	wasn't
3. was not	aren't
4. were not	isn't
5. have not	didn't
6. can not	haven't
7. do not	couldn't
8. did not	can't
9. could not	shouldn't
10. should not	don't

Do not use a contraction that ends in **n't** with another negative like **no**, **nothing**, **no one**, and **never**.

Examples: **Incorrect:** I didn't get no milk.
                       Correct: I didn't get any milk.

Directions: Rewrite each sentence correctly.

1. Molly doesn't have no tennis shoes.

_____

2. We aren't doing nothing on Saturday.

_____

APOSTROPHES AND CONTRACTIONS

Name _____

Contractions and Apostrophes

Contractions are made by putting together two words.
An **apostrophe** replaces the letters that are dropped.

Examples: we + will = we'll
I + would = I'd

Directions: Write the correct contraction on the line to
replace the two bold words.

1. **We would** _____ take the trails up and down the hill.

2. At the top **we will** _____ stop to look at the view.

3. Do you see the buildings? **You would** _____ see houses like those in China.

4. I **was not** _____ the only person to build this island.

5. You **would have** _____ seen monks here two years ago.

6. Since you **were not** _____ here then, **I will** _____ tell you about them.

7. **They had** _____ built great houses and gardens.

8. **They have** _____ left their mark here.

APOSTROPHES AND CONTRACTIONS

Name _____

Contractions and Apostrophes

Directions: Circle the two words in each sentence that are not spelled correctly. Then, write the words correctly.

1. Arn't you going to shere your cookie with me?

_____   _____

2. We planed a long time, but we still wern't ready.

_____   _____

3. My pensil hassn't broken yet today.

_____   _____

4. We arn't going because we don't have the correct adress.

_____   _____

5. Youve stired the soup too much.

_____   _____

6. Weave tried to be as neet as possible.

_____   _____

7. She hasnt seen us in this darknes.

_____   _____

Name _____

Capitalization and Punctuation Review

Directions: The following sentences have errors in punctuation, capitalization, or both. The number in parentheses **( )** tells you how many errors the sentence contains. Rewrite each sentence correctly.

1. I saw mr. Johnson reading <u>War And Peace</u> to his class. (2)

   _____

2. Do you like to sing "Take me Out to The Ballgame"? (2)

   _____

3. He recited Hiawatha to Miss. Simpson's class. (2)

   _____

4. Bananas and oranges are among Dr smiths favorite fruits. (4)

   _____

5. "Daisy, daisy is a song about a bicycle built for two. (2)

   _____

6. Good Morning, Granny Rose is a story about a woman and her dog. (1)

   _____

7. Garfield goes to waist isnt a very funny book. (4)

   _____

8. Peanut butter, jelly, and bread are Miss. Lees favorite treats. (2)

   _____

HOMOPHONES AND MISUSED WORDS

Name _____

Homophones

Homophones are words that sound the same but are spelled differently and have different meanings.

Example:

sew   **sow**    **so**

So what do I do now?

Directions: Read the sentences and write the correct word in the blanks.

Example: blue   blew   She has <u>blue</u> eyes.

The wind <u>blew</u> the barn down.

1. He hurt his left _____ playing ball.   **eye   I**

   _____ like to learn new things.

2. Can you _____ the winning runner from here?   **see   sea**

   He goes diving for pearls under the _____ .

3. The baby _____ the banana.   **eight   ate**

   Jane was _____ years old last year.

4. Jill _____ first prize at the science fair.   **one   won**

   I am the only _____ in my family with red hair.

5. Jenny cried when a _____ stung her.   **be   bee**

   I have to _____ in bed every night at eight o'clock.

6. My father likes _____ play tennis.   **two   to   too**

   I like to play, _____ .

   It takes at least _____ people to play.

Name _____

Homophones and Commonly Misused Words

Homophones are words that sound the same but are spelled differently and have different meanings.

Directions: Answer each riddle below with a homophone from the Word Bank.

Word Bank				
main	meat	peace	dear	to
mane	meet	piece	deer	too

1. Which word has the word **pie** in it? _____

2. Which word rhymes with **ear** and is an animal? _____

3. Which word rhymes with **shoe** and means **also**? _____

4. Which word has the word **eat** in it and is something you might eat? _____

5. Which word has the same letters as the word **read** but in a different order? _____

6. Which word rhymes with **train** and is something on a pony? _____

7. Which word, if it began with a capital letter, might be the name of an important street? _____

8. Which word sounds like a number but has only two letters? _____

9. Which word rhymes with **greet** and is a synonym for **greet**? _____

10. Which word rhymes with cease and can mean quiet? _____

HOMOPHONES AND MISUSED WORDS

Name _____

Common Corrections

Some words look and sound very much alike but have very different meanings.

Directions: Finish each sentence below with the correct word from the Word Bank.

Word Bank		
series	lose	bear
serious	loose	bare

1. I love collecting an entire

   _____ of comic books.

2. The power button on my television is

   _____ .

3. The tree will _____

   luscious fruit.

4. We need to have a _____ talk.

5. I will never _____

   this journal.

6. The _____ wall

   really needs some pictures.

Name _____

Common Corrections

Some words look and sound very much alike but have very different meanings.

Directions: Look at the words and their meanings below. Then, write the correct word to complete each sentence.

their: pronoun that shows possession or ownership

there: at or in that place

angel: a figure with halo and wings

angle: two lines that connect at a single point

accept: to say yes

except: not including or otherwise

intend: to plan

attend: to be present at

1. I want to visit _____ house.

2. I _____ your invitation to go _____ .

3. I think _____ house is beautiful _____ for

   the olive-green kitchen wallpaper.

4. The photographer took pictures from two different _____ (s).

   The little girl in the picture looked like an _____ .

5. I _____ to _____ _____ party.

HOMOPHONES AND MISUSED WORDS

Name _____

Common Corrections

Some words look and sound very much alike but have very different meanings.

Directions: Finish each sentence below using the correct word from the Word Bank.

Word Bank		
united	whether	now
untied	weather	know

1. Nine children _____ to form
   a new baseball team.

2. The _____ is lovely during the summer.

3. I _____ many facts from reading

   the encyclopedia!

4. Careful, your shoe is _____!

5. I am not sure _____ I should go or not.

6. We are late! We need to go _____!

Name _____

Common Corrections

Some words look and sound very much alike but have very different meanings.

Directions: Look at the words and meanings below. Write the correct word to finish each sentence.

thorough: complete

through: in one side and out the other

then: at that time

than: a comparison

mere: a tiny bit

mirror: a reflective surface

1. I am taller _____ you by five inches!

2. Please do a _____ job when you sweep the floor.

3. There was a _____ drop of ketchup left in the bottle!

4. The ball went _____ the glass window!

6. Do your homework and _____ we will go play.

7. Do you have a _____ I could use so that I can fix my hair?

Name _____

"Good" or "Well"

Use the word **good** to describe a noun. **Good** is an adjective.

> **Example:** She is a **good** teacher.

Use the word **well** to tell or ask how something is done or to describe someone's health. **Well** is an adverb. It describes a verb.

> **Example:** She is not feeling **well**.

Directions: Write **good** or **well** to finish each sentence correctly.

> **Example:** _____good_____ Our team could use a good/well captain.

1. _____ The puny kitten does not look good/well.

2. _____ He did his job so good/well that everyone praised him.

3. _____ Whining is not a good/well habit.

4. _____ I might just as good/well do it myself.

5. _____ She was one of the most well-/good- liked girls at school.

6. _____ I did the book report as good/well as I could.

7. _____ The television works very good/well.

8. _____ You did a good/well job repairing the TV!

9. _____ Thanks for a job good/well done!

10. _____ You did a good/well job fixing the computer.

11. _____ You had better treat your friends good/well.

12. _____ Can your grandmother hear good/well?

13. _____ Your brother will be well/good soon.

Name _____

"Your" or "You're"

The word **your** shows possession.

    Examples: Is that **your** book?
                      I visited **your** class.

The word **you're** is a contraction for **you are**.
A **contraction** is two words joined together as one.
An **apostrophe** shows where letters have been left out.

    Examples: **You're** doing well on that painting.
                      If **you're** going to pass the test, you should study.

Directions: Write **your** or **you're** to finish each sentence correctly.

    Example: ___You're___ Your/You're the best friend I have!

1. _____ Your/You're going to drop that!

2. _____ Your/You're brother came to see me.

3. _____ Is that your/you're cat?

4. _____ If your/you're going, you'd better hurry!

5. _____ Why are your/you're fingers so red?

6. _____ It's none of your/you're business!

7. _____ Your/You're bike's front tire is low.

8. _____ Your/You're kidding!

9. _____ Have it your/you're way.

10. _____ I thought your/you're report was great!

11. _____ He thinks your/you're wonderful!

12. _____ What is your/you're first choice?

13. _____ What's your/you're opinion?

14. _____ If your/you're going, so am I!

15. _____ Your/You're welcome.

Name _____

"Good" or "Well" and "Your" or "You're"

Directions: Finish each sentence with the correct word: **good, well, your** or **you're**.

1. Are you sure you can see _____ enough to read with the lighting you have?

2. _____ going to need a paint smock when you go to art class tomorrow afternoon.

3. I can see _____ having some trouble. Can I help with that?

4. The music department needs to buy a speaker system that has _____ quality sound.

5. The principal asked, "Where is _____ hall pass?"

6. You must do your job _____ if you expect to keep it.

7. The traffic policeman said, "May I please see _____ driver's license?"

8. The story you wrote for English class was done quite_____.

9. That radio station you listen to is a _____ one.

10. Let us know if _____ unable to attend the meeting on Saturday.

Name _____

"Its" or "It's"

The word **its** shows ownership.

Examples: **Its** leaves have all turned green.
Its paw was injured.

The word **it's** is a contraction for **it is**.

Examples: **It's** better to be early than late.
It's not fair!

Directions: Write **its** or **it's** to finish each sentence correctly.

Example: ___It's___ Its/It's never too late for ice cream!

1. _____ Its/It's eyes are already open.

2. _____ Its/It's your turn to wash the dishes!

3. _____ Its/It's cage was left open.

4. _____ Its/It's engine was beyond repair.

5. _____ Its/It's teeth were long and pointed.

6. _____ Did you see its/it's hind legs?

7. _____ Why do you think its/it's mine?

8. _____ Do you think its/it's the right color?

9. _____ Don't pet its/it's fur too hard!

10. _____ Its/It's from Uncle Harry.

11. _____ Can you tell its/it's a surprise?

12. _____ Is its/it's stall always this clean?

13. _____ Its/It's not time to eat yet.

14. _____ She says its/it's working now.

Name _____

"Can" or "May"

The word **can** means **am able** to or to be able to.

    Examples: I can do that for you.
                            Can you do that for me?

The word **may** means **be allowed** to or **permitted to**. May is used to ask or give permission. **May** can also mean **might** or **perhaps**.

    Examples: May I be excused?
                            You may sit here.

Directions: Write **can** or **may** to finish each sentence correctly.

    Example: _____May_____ Can/May I help you?

1. _____ He is smart. He can/may do it himself.

2. _____ When can/may I have my dessert?

3. _____ He can/may speak French fluently.

4. _____ You can/may use my pencil.

5. _____ I can/may be allowed to attend the concert.

6. _____ It is bright. I can/may see you!

7. _____ Can/May my friend stay for dinner?

8. _____ You can/may leave when your report is finished.

9. _____ I can/may see your point!

10. _____ She can/may dance well.

11. _____ Can/May you hear the dog barking?

12. _____ Can/May you help me button this sweater?

13. _____ Mother, can/may I go to the movies?

Name _____

"Its" or "It's" and "Can" or "May"

Directions: Finish each sentence with the correct word: **its**, **it's**, **can**, or **may**.

1. "It looks as though your arms are full, Diane. _____ I help you

   with some of those things?" asked Michele.

2. The squirrel _____ climb up the tree quickly with his mouth

   full of acorns.

3. She has had her school jacket so long that it is beginning to lose

   _____ color.

4. How many laps around the track _____ you do?

5. Sometimes you can tell what a story is going to be about by looking at

   _____ title.

6. Our house _____ need to be painted again in two or three years.

7. Mother asked, "Jon, _____ you open the door for your father?"

8. _____ going to be a while until your birthday,

   but do you know what you want?

9. I can feel in the air that _____ going to snow soon.

10. If I am careful with it, _____ I borrow your CD player?

Name _____

"Sit" or "Set"

The word **sit** means to rest.

    Examples: Please **sit** here!
                       Will you **sit** by me?

The word **set** means to put or place something.

    Examples: **Set** your purse there.
                       Set the dishes on the table.

Directions: Write **sit** or **set** to finish each sentence correctly.

    Example: _____sit_____ Would you please sit/set down here?

1. _____ You can sit/set the groceries there.

2. _____ She sit/set her suitcase in the closet.

3. _____ He sit/set his watch for half past three.

4. _____ She is a person who cannot sit/set still.

5. _____ Sit/set the baby on the couch beside me.

6. _____ Where did you sit/set your new shoes?

7. _____ They decided to sit/set together during the movie.

8. _____ Let me sit/set you straight on that!

9. _____ Instead of swimming, he decided to sit/set in the water.

10. _____ He sit/set the greasy pan in the sink.

11. _____ She sit/set the file folder on her desk.

12. _____ Do not ever sit/set on the refrigerator!

13. _____ She sit/set the candles on the cake.

14. _____ Get ready! Get sit/set! Go!

Name _____

"They're," "Their," "There"

The word **they're** is a contraction for **they are**.

> **Examples:** **They're** our very best friends!
> Ask them if **they're** coming.

The word **their** shows ownership.

> **Examples:** **Their** dog is friendly.
> It's **their** bicycle.

The word **there** shows place or direction.

> **Examples:** Look over **there**.
> **There** it is.

Directions: Write **they're**, **their**, or **there** to finish each sentence correctly.

Example: ____There____ They're/Their/There is the sweater I want!

1. _____ Do you believe they're/their/there stories?

2. _____ Be they're/their/there by one o'clock.

3. _____ Were you they're/their/there last night?

4. _____ I know they're/their/there going to attend.

5. _____ Have you met they're/their/there mother?

6. _____ I can go they're/their/there with you.

7. _____ Do you like they're/their/there new car?

8. _____ They're/Their/There friendly to everyone.

9. _____ Did she say they're/their/there ready to go?

10. _____ She said she would walk by they're/their/there house.

11. _____ Is anyone they're/their/there?

12. _____ I put it right over they're/their/there!

282

HOMOPHONES AND MISUSED WORDS

Name _____

"Sit" or "Set" and "They're," "There," or "Their"

Directions: Finish each sentence with the correct word: **sit, set, they're, there,** or **their.**

1. Her muscles became tense as she heard the gym teacher say,

   "Get ready, get _____, go!"

2. When we choose our seats on the bus, will you _____ with me?

3. _____ is my library book! I wondered where I had left it!

4. My little brother and his friend said _____ not going to the ball

   game with us.

5. Before the test, the teacher wants the students

   to sharpen _____ pencils.

6. She blew the whistle and shouted, "Everyone _____ down on

   the floor!"

7. All the books for the fourth graders belong over _____ on the

   top shelf.

8. The little kittens are beginning to open _____ eyes.

9. I'm going to _____ the dishes on the table.

10. _____ going to be fine by themselves for a few minutes.

Name _____

"This" or "These"

The word **this** is an adjective that refers to a specific thing. **This** always describes a singular noun. Singular means **one**.

Example: I'll buy **this** coat.
(Coat is singular.)

The word **these** is also an adjective that refers to specific things. **These** always describes a plural noun. Plural means **more than one**.

Example: I will buy **these** flowers.
(Flowers is a plural noun.)

Directions: Write **this** or **these** to finish each sentence correctly.

Example: ____these____ I will take this/these cookies with me.

1. _____ Do you want this/these seeds?

2. _____ Did you try this/these nuts?

3. _____ Do it this/these way!

4. _____ What do you know about this/these situation?

5. _____ Did you open this/these doors?

6. _____ Did you open this/these window?

7. _____ What is the meaning of this/these letters?

8. _____ Will you carry this/these books for me?

9. _____ This/These pans are hot!

10. _____ Do you think this/these light is too bright?

11. _____ Are this/these boots yours?

12. _____ Do you like this/these rainy weather?

Name _____

Double Negatives

Only use one **negative word** in a sentence. **Not**, **no**, **never**, and **none** are some negative words.

Examples:
   Incorrect: No one nowhere was sad when it started to snow.
   Correct: No one anywhere was sad when it started to snow.

Directions: Circle the word in parentheses that makes each sentence correct.

1. There wasn't (no, any) snow on our grass this morning.

2. I couldn't find (no one, anyone) who wanted to build a snowman.

3. We couldn't believe that (no one, anyone) wanted to stay inside.

4. We shouldn't ask (anyone, no one) to go ice skating with us.

5. None of the students could think of (nothing, anything) to do at recess except to play in the new-fallen snow.

6. No one (never, ever) thinks it is a waste of time to go ice skating on the pond.

Directions: Write the correct word on each line to replace the negative word in parentheses.

1. You shouldn't (never) _____ play catch with a snowball unless you want to be covered in snow.

2. Isn't (no one) _____ else going to eat icicles?

3. There wasn't (nothing) _____ wrong with using fresh snow to make our fruit drinks.

4. The snowman outside isn't (nowhere) _____ as large as the statue in front of our school.

5. Falling snow isn't (no) _____ fun if you cannot go out and play in it.

Name _____

Word Usage Review

Directions: Finish each sentence by writing the correct word in the blank.

1. _____ You have a good/well attitude.

2. _____ The teacher was not feeling good/well.

3. _____ She sang extremely good/well.

4. _____ Everyone said Josh was a good/well boy.

5. _____ Your/You're going to be sorry for that!

6. _____ Tell her your/you're serious.

7. _____ Your/You're report was wonderful!

8. _____ Your/You're the best person for the job.

9. _____ Do you think its/it's going to have babies?

10. _____ Its/It's back paw had a thorn in it.

11. _____ Its/It's fun to make new friends.

12. _____ Is its/it's mother always nearby?

13. _____ How can/may I help you?

14. _____ You can/may come in now.

15. _____ Can/May you lift this for me?

16. _____ She can/may sing soprano.

17. _____ I will wait for you to sit/set down first.

18. _____ We sit/set our dirty boots outside.

19. _____ It is they're/their/there turn to choose.

20. _____ They're/Their/There is your answer!

21. _____ They say they're/their/there coming.

22. _____ I must have this/these one!

23. _____ I saw this/these gloves at the store.

24. _____ He said this/these were his.

Proofreading

Directions: Proofread the sentences. Write **C** if the sentence has no errors. Write **X** if the sentence contains errors.

Example: ___C___ The new Ship Wreck Museum in Key West is exciting!

1. ____ Another thing I liked was the litehouse.

2. ____ Do you remember Hemingways address in Key West?

3. ____ The Key West Cemetery is on 21 acres of ground.

4. ____ Ponce de leon discovered Key West Florida.

5. ____ The cemetery in key west is on francis street.

6. ____ My favorete tombstone was the sailor's.

7. ____ His wife wrote the words.

8. ____ The words said, at least I know where to find him now!

9. ____ The sailor must have been away at sea.

10. ____ The trolley ride around Key West isnt boring.

11. ____ Do you why it is called Key West?

12. ____ Can you imagine a lighthouse in the middle of your town?

13. ____ It is interesting that Key West is the more southern city.

14. ____ Besides Harry Truman and Hemingway did other famous people live there?

Name _____

Proofreading: Capitalization

When you are reviewing your own or another student's writing, it helps to use proofreading marks to show where corrections are needed.

To show where a capital letter should be, write three short lines below the letter that needs to be capitalized.

Example: the mosleys took a trip to maryland.

Directions: Read the paragraph below. Write three short lines under letters that should be capitalized.

the white house was the first official building

in washington, d.c. construction began on october

13, 1792. it is located at 1600 pennsylvania

avenue in washington, d.c. it is the home of the

president of the united states. the president and

his family live in one section of the house. every

american president except george washington

has lived in the white house. the other section is

used for the president's office. the white house is

a beautiful building.

Name _____

Proofreading: Inserting Words and Punctuation

When you are reviewing your own or another student's writing, it helps to use proofreading marks to show where corrections are needed. Show where a punctuation mark or word is needed by using a carat (∧).

Example: Mary Jo Patty and Serena splashed in the lake

Directions: Use the proofreading mark to insert punctuation marks where they are needed in the paragraph and letter below.

"A picnic at the lake is a wonderful idea" exclaimed Mary Jo "I will bring cherry pie ham sandwiches and potato chips"

Patty replied "Great I will bring a blanket an umbrella and lemonade"

Can I come" Serena asked "I could bring toys and games"

"Sure you can come" Patty said "We will have lots of fun"

1543 Treetop Lane

Forrester Illinois 56284

July 23 2002

Dear Mary Jo

Thank you for inviting me to the picnic at the lake It was really fun I enjoyed splashing in the lake and riding in the boat Your ham sandwiches tasted terrific I hope we can go to the lake again

Your friend

Serena

Name _____

Proofreading

Proofreading means searching for and correcting errors by carefully reading and rereading what has been written. Use the proofreading marks below when correcting someone's writing, including your own.

To insert a word or a punctuation mark that has been left out, use a carat (^).

went
Example: We^to the dance together.

To show that a letter should be capitalized, put three lines under it.

Example: Mrs. jones drove us to school.

To show that a capital letter should be lower case, draw a diagonal line through it.

Example: Mrs. Jones Drove us to school.

To show that a word is spelled incorrectly, draw a horizontal line through it and write the correct spelling above it.

walrus
Example: The wolres is an amazing animal.

Directions: Proofread the two paragraphs below using proofreading marks.

The Modern ark

My book report is on <u>the modern ark</u> by Cecilia Fitzsimmons. The book tells abut 80 of worlds endangered animals. The book also an ark and animals inside for kids put together.

Their House

<u>there house</u> is a Great book! The arthur's name is Mary Towne. <u>they're house</u> tells about a girl name Molly. Molly's Family bys an old house from some people named warren. Then there big problems begin!

Name _____

Proofreading

Proofreading marks help us to revise our writing. These marks show where changes should be made.

¶   Indent a paragraph

∧   Insert something

℘   Take something out

≡   Capitalize

/   Make lowercase

Directions: Edit the paragraph below. Use proofreading marks.

Margaret Thatcher was the first female prime minister in Great Britain. A prime minister is like a president. Mrs. Thatcher was born in a town called grantham in 1925. She went to school at the University of oxford. She became chemist Later, she married a man named denis. After passing the bar examination, She became a tax lawyer. Mrs. Thatcher got involved in politics in 1959. She became the prime minister of Great Britain in 1979.

Name _____

Proofreading

Directions: Proofread the paragraphs using proofreading marks. There are seven capitalization errors, three missing words, and eleven errors in spelling or word usage.

Key West

key West has been tropical paradise ever since Ponce de Leon first saw the set of islands called the keys in 1513. Two famus streets in Key West are named duval and whitehead. You will find the city semetery on Francis Street. The tombstones are funny!

The message on one is, "I told you I was sick!" On sailor's tombston is this mesage his widow: "At lease I no where to find him now."

The cemetery is on 21 akres in the midle of town. The most famous home in key west is that of the authur Ernest Hemingway. Heminway's home was at 907 whitehead Street. He lived their for 30 years.

Name _____

Proofreading

Directions: Proofread and correct the errors in the description below. There are eight errors in capitalization, seven misspelled words, a missing comma, and three missing words.

More About Key West

a good way to lern more about key West is to ride the trolley. Key West has a great troley system. The trolley will take on a tour of the salt ponds. You can also three red brick forts. The troley tour goes by a 110-foot-high lighthouse. It is rite in the middle of the city. Key west is the only city with a Lighthouse in the midle of it! It is also the southernmost city in the United States.

If you have time, the new Ship Wreck Museum. Key west was also the hom of former president Harry truman. During his presidency, Trueman spent many vacations on key west.

Name _____

Paragraphs

A **paragraph** is a group of sentences that tell about one main idea. It begins with a **topic sentence**. **Supporting sentences** tell more about the topic. The paragraph ends with a **concluding sentence**.

Example: **Topic Sentence:** States the main idea.

Supporting Sentences: Give more detail about the main idea.

Concluding Sentence: Rephrases the topic sentence and summarizes the main idea.

Directions: Underline the topic sentence in this paragraph. Number each of the supporting sentences. Circle the concluding sentence.

My dog is the smartest dog in the world. ☐ Her name is Lulu. ☐ She

can fetch the newspaper when Dad asks her to. ☐ When Mom is sad,

Lulu cheers her up by licking her face. ☐ I really like it when Lulu helps

me find my lost tennis shoe. Lulu is the best dog!

Paragraphs

A **paragraph** is a group of sentences that tell about one main idea. The **topic sentence** tells the main idea of the paragraph. The **supporting sentences** tell more about the main idea. The **concluding sentence** rephrases the main idea or connects it to the next paragraph.

Directions: Write a concluding sentence for each paragraph.

1. It looks like rain. Heavy gray clouds are collecting in the sky. The icy wind is blowing through my sweater. Drops splatter the sidewalk and my glasses.

   _____

   _____

2. The flowers bloom in brilliant colors. Daffodils smile with their yellow faces. Purple irises complement the pink tulips. Many people cut the white daisies to put in vases.

   _____

   _____

3. Birds build nests to prepare a home for their eggs. First, they find a safe place for a nest. Then, they collect twigs, branches, and leaves. Finally, the birds arrange the nest.

   _____

   _____

Name _____

Paragraphs

A **paragraph** is a group of sentences that tell about one main idea. It begins with a topic sentence. The **topic sentence** tells the main idea of the paragraph. The rest of the paragraph relates to the main idea.

Directions: Write a topic sentence for each paragraph.

_____First, I put on my helmet. Next, I practiced balancing on the bike. My mom gave me a little push, and I was on my way. I pedaled as fast as I could. I steered carefully. I was riding by myself!

_____We go outside and eat our snacks. When the teacher excuses us, we race out to the field. Some kids play on the jungle gym and others swing on the swing set. A game of soccer is organized. Everyone has fun at recess.

_____We use computers to help us write reports. We use them to surf the web and learn new things. Computers ring up our purchases at the store. They can even make phone calls for us. The computer is a wonderful invention.

_____He spills milk on the table at snack time. He talks when the teacher is talking and gets sent to the principal's office. He fools around in line for the bus. Bradley Johnson is always in trouble.

Name _____

Paragraphs

A **paragraph** is a group of sentences that tell about one main idea. The **topic sentence** tells the main idea of the paragraph. The **supporting sentences** tell more about the main idea.

Directions: Write three supporting sentences for each topic sentence.

Police officers are very helpful.

_____

_____

_____

I was really scared during the thunderstorm.

_____

_____

_____

My favorite amusement park ride is the bumper cars.

_____

_____

_____

Saturday is the best day of the week.

_____

_____

_____

Name _____

Write Your Own Paragraph

My Topic: _____

Topic sentence

_____

_____

Supporting Sentence 1

_____

_____

Supporting Sentence 2

_____

_____

Supporting Sentence 3

_____

_____

Concluding Sentence

_____

_____

Proofreading: Paragraphs

When you are reviewing your own or another student's writing, it helps to use proofreading marks to show where corrections are needed. Use this symbol (¶) to show where a new paragraph should begin.

A **paragraph** is a group of sentences that tell about one main idea. It begins with a topic sentence. Supporting sentences tell more about the topic. The paragraph ends with a concluding sentence.

Directions: Insert a proofreading mark (¶) where each new paragraph should begin in the report below.

Birds are unique animals. Birds hatch out of eggs, and many are born without feathers. Birds have bills instead of mouths, but they do not have teeth. They can cool their bodies while flying through the air or panting at rest. These features make birds special animals. There are different kinds of birds. Ostrich are the largest birds. They can be almost 8 feet tall. Bee hummingbirds are the smallest birds and are no more than $2^{1}/_{2}$ inches tall. Hummingbirds are the only birds that are capable of flying backward. Penguins use their wings as oars when swimming through water. Woodpeckers drum on trees to create nesting holes and to communicate with other woodpeckers. Bird feathers have many different uses. The bright colors can attract mates or scare away other birds. Feathers can act as camouflage to protect birds. They help protect birds from cold weather. They are water-repellent on swimming birds. Feathers are important to birds' survival.

Name _____

Proofreading Checklists

Use these checklists when editing your own or someone else's writing.

Mechanics Checklist

Name _____

___ Every sentence begins with a capital letter and ends with the correct punctuation mark.

___ Commas are in the right places.

___ Words that need capital letters begin with capital letters.

___ All words are spelled correctly.

___ Each sentence is one complete thought.

___ There are no fragments or run-ons.

___ The beginning of each paragraph is indented.

Checked by _____

Style Checklist

Name _____

___ Verbs are interesting and exciting.

___ Adjectives describe with detail. No boring words are used.

___ Sentences show, not tell.

___ Story has a beginning, a middle, and an end.

___ Paragraphs have a topic sentence, supporting sentences, and a concluding sentence.

___ Each sentence does not begin with the same word.

Checked by _____

Glossary

Abbreviations: A shortened form of a word. Most abbreviations begin with a capital letter and end with with a period. Example: **Doctor = Dr.**

Adjectives: Words that tell more about a person, place, or thing. Example: **sad**.

Adverbs: Words that describe verbs. Adverbs tell where, how, or when. Examples: **quickly**, **now**.

Apostrophes: Punctuation that is used with contractions in place of the missing letter or used to show ownership. Examples: **don't, Susan's**.

Articles: Small words that help us better understand nouns. Examples: **a, an**.

Capitalization: Letters that are used at the beginning of names of people, places, days, months, and holidays. Capital letters are also used at the beginning of sentences.

Commas: Punctuation marks that are used to separate words or phrases. They are also used to separate dates from years, cities from states, etc.

Common Nouns: Nouns that name any member of a group of people, any place, or any thing, rather than a specific person, place, or thing. Example: **person**.

Compound Predicates: Two or more verbs that have the same subject.

Compound Sentences: Two complete ideas that are joined together into one sentence by a **conjunction**, such as **and**, **but**, **or**, **so**, etc.

Compound Subjects: Two or more nouns that have the same predicate.

Concluding Sentences: Sentences at the end of paragraphs that tie the story together.

Contractions: A short way to write two words together. Example: **it is = it's**.

Exclamations: Sentences that express strong feelings. Exclamations often end with an exclamation point. These sentences can be short or long and can be a command. Example: **Look at that!**

Future-Tense Verbs: A verb that tells about something that has not happened yet but will happen in the future. **Will** or **shall** are usually used with future tense. Example: We **will eat** soon.

Helping Verbs: A word used with an action verb. Example: They **are** helping.

Homophones: Words that sound the same but are spelled differently and mean different things. Example: **blue** and **blew**.

Irregular verbs: Verbs that do not change from the present tense to the past tense in the regular way with **d** or **ed**. Example: **run, ran**.

Linking Verbs: Verbs that connect the noun to a descriptive word. Linking verbs are always a form of "to be." Example: I **am** tired.

Nouns: Words that name a person, place, or thing.

Paragraph: A group of sentences that all tell about the same thing.

Past-Tense Verbs: A verb that tells about something that has already happened. A **d** or **ed** is usually added to the end of the word. Example: **walked**.

Plural Nouns: Nouns that name more than one person, place, or thing.

Possessive Nouns: Nouns that tell who or what is the owner of something. Example: the **dog's** ball.

Possessive Pronouns: Pronouns that show ownership. Example: **his** dish.

Predicates: The verb in the sentence that tells the main action. It tells what the subject is doing, had done, or will do.

Prepositions: Words that show the relationship between a noun or pronoun and another word in the sentence. Example: The boy is **behind** the chair.

Present-Tense Verbs: A verb that tells about something that is happening now, happens often, or is about to happen. An **s** or **ing** is usually added to the verb. Examples: **sings, singing**.

Pronouns: Words that can be used in place of nouns. Example: **It**.

Proper Nouns: Names of specific people, places, or things. Example: **Iowa**.

Questions: Sentences that ask. They begin with a capital letter and end with a question mark.

Quotation Marks: Punctuation marks that tell what is said by a person. Quotation marks go before and after a direct quote. Example: She said, **"Here I am!"**

Sentences: Sentences tell a complete idea with a noun and a verb. They begin with a capital letter and have end punctuation (a period, question mark, or exclamation point).

Supporting Sentences: Sentences that support the topic sentence in a paragraph.

Nouns

A **noun** names a person, place, or thing.

Examples:

person — sister, uncle, boy, woman

place — building, city, park, street

thing — workbook, cat, candle, bed

Directions: Circle the nouns in each sentence.

Example: The (dog) ran into the (street).

1. Please take this (book) to the (librarian).
2. The red (apples) are in the (kitchen).
3. That (scarf) belongs to the bus (driver).
4. Get some blue (paper) from the (office) to make a (card).
5. Look at the (parachute)!
6. Autumn (leaves) are beautiful.
7. The (lion) roared loudly at the (visitors).

Directions: Write each noun you circled in the correct group.

People	Places	Things	
librarian	street	dog	paper
driver	kitchen	book	card
visitors	office	apples	parachute
		scarf	leaves
		lion	

Page 6

Nouns

Directions: Write nouns that name people.

1. Could you please give this report to my _____?
2. The _____ works many long hours to plant crops.
3. I had to help my little _____ when he wrecked his bike yesterday.

Directions: Write nouns that name places.

1. I always keep my library books on top of the _____ so I _____

2. We _____

ANSWERS WILL VARY

3. Dad built a nice fire in the _____ to keep us warm.

Directions: Write nouns that name things.

1. The little _____ purred softly as I held it.
2. Wouldn't you think a _____ would get tired of carrying its house around all day?
3. The _____ scurried into its hole with the piece of cheese.
4. I can tell by the writing that this _____ is mine.
5. Look at the _____ I made in art class.
6. His _____ blew away because of the strong wind.

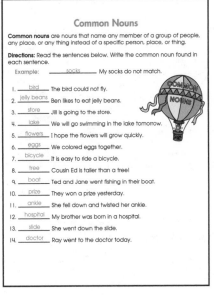

Page 7

Nouns

A **noun** is a word that names a person, place, or thing.

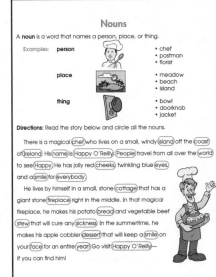

Examples:	person	• chef
		• postman
		• florist
	place	• meadow
		• beach
		• island
	thing	• bowl
		• doorknob
		• jacket

Directions: Read the story below and circle all the nouns.

There is a magical (chef) who lives on a small, windy (island) off the (coast) of (Ireland). His (name) is Happy O'Reilly. (People) travel from all over the (world) to see (Happy). He has jolly red (cheeks), twinkling blue (eyes), and a (smile) for (everybody).

He lives by himself in a small, stone (cottage) that has a giant stone (fireplace) right in the middle. In that magical fireplace, he makes his potato (bread) and vegetable beef (stew) that will cure any (sickness). In the summertime, he makes his apple cobbler (dessert) that will keep a (smile) on your (face) for an entire (year)! Go visit (Happy O'Reilly)— if you can find him!

Page 8

Idea Nouns

Nouns can also name ideas. **Ideas** are things we cannot see or touch, such as bravery, beauty, or honesty.

Directions: Underline the "idea" nouns in each sentence.

1. <u>Respect</u> is something that you must earn.
2. <u>Truth</u> and justice are two things that people value.
3. The <u>beauty</u> of the flower garden was breathtaking.
4. You must learn new <u>skills</u> in order to master new things.
5. His <u>courage</u> impressed everyone.
6. She finds <u>peace</u> out in the woods.
7. Their <u>friendship</u> was amazing.
8. The man's <u>honesty</u> in the face of such hardship was refreshing.
9. The dog showed its <u>loyalty</u> toward its owner.
10. <u>Trouble</u> is brewing.
11. The policeman's <u>kindness</u> calmed the the scared child.
12. The boy had a <u>fear</u> of the dark.

Page 9

Common Nouns

Common nouns are nouns that name any member of a group of people, any place, or any thing instead of a specific person, place, or thing.

Directions: Read the sentences below. Write the common noun found in each sentence.

Example: _____socks_____ My socks do not match.

1. _____bird_____ The bird could not fly.
2. _____jelly beans_____ Ben likes to eat jelly beans.
3. _____store_____ Jill is going to the store.
4. _____lake_____ We will go swimming in the lake tomorrow.
5. _____flowers_____ I hope the flowers will grow quickly.
6. _____eggs_____ We colored eggs together.
7. _____bicycle_____ It is easy to ride a bicycle.
8. _____tree_____ Cousin Ed is taller than a tree!
9. _____boat_____ Ted and Jane went fishing in their boat.
10. _____prize_____ They won a prize yesterday.
11. _____ankle_____ She fell down and twisted her ankle.
12. _____hospital_____ My brother was born in a hospital.
13. _____slide_____ She went down the slide.
14. _____doctor_____ Ray went to the doctor today.

Page 10

Proper Nouns

Proper nouns are names of specific people, places, or things. A proper noun begins with a capital letter.

Directions: Read the sentences below. Circle the proper nouns in each sentence.

Example: (Aunt Frances) gave me a puppy for my birthday.

1. We lived on (Jackson Street) before we moved to our new house.
2. (Angela's) birthday party is tomorrow night.
3. We drove through (Cheyenne, Wyoming) on our way home.
4. (Dr. Charles) always gives me a treat for not crying.
5. (George Washington) was our first president.
6. Our class took a field trip to the (Johnson Flower Farm).
7. (Uncle Jack) lives in (New York City).
8. (Amy) and (Elizabeth) are best friends.
9. We buy doughnuts at the (Grayson Bakery).
10. My favorite movie is (E.T.)
11. We flew to (Miami, Florida) in a plane.
12. We go to the (Great American Ballpark) to watch the baseball games.
13. (Mr. Fields) is a wonderful music teacher.
14. My best friend is (Tom Dunlap).

Page 11

Proper Nouns

Directions: Write about you! Write a proper noun for each category below. Capitalize the first letter of each proper noun.

1. Your first name: **ANSWERS WILL VARY**

2. Your last name: _____

3. Your street: _____

4. Your city: _____

5. Your state: _____

6. Your school: _____

7. Your best friend's name: _____

8. Your teacher: _____

9. Your favorite book character: _____

10. Your favorite vacation place: _____

Page 12

Common and Proper Nouns

A **common noun** does not begin with a capital letter unless it is the first word in a sentence. A **common noun** names any person, place, or thing.

Examples: skater, ice

A **proper noun** begins with a capital letter. A **proper noun** names a specific person, place, or thing.

Examples: Peggy Fleming, Michelle Kwan

Directions: Read the story. Circle each common noun and underline each proper noun.

Peggy Fleming

Peggy Fleming is a famous iceskater. She was born in California and began skating when she was nine years old. She won many iceskating competitions as a child. In 1964, Peggy competed in the Winter Olympics in Austria. She came in sixth place.

Peggy took ballet classes to become a better iceskater. This helped her win a gold medal in the 1968 Winter Olympics in France.

After the Olympics, Peggy became a professional skater and toured the country doing ice shows. After her skating career, Peggy became a commentator for television.

Page 13

Common and Proper Nouns

Common nouns are nouns that name any person, place, or thing. **Proper nouns** are nouns that name specific people, places, or things. A proper noun always starts with a capital letter.

Examples: **common:** boy
proper: Robert

Directions: Underline the common nouns and circle the proper nouns in the story below.

Crafty Critters Give Police the Slip

When the Gambezi Brothers' Circus passed the town library, Jeremiah Clank blew his trumpet loudly. The noise scared Ellie the Elephant, Harriet the Hyena, and Grumbles the Tiger. A stampede followed.

An emergency police call from Captain Courageous went out over the radio and television: "Emergency! Alert! Everyone should be on the lookout for the circus animals that have escaped from the Gambezi Brothers' Circus."

Thankfully, the police were able to capture all the circus animals and no one was injured. Jeremy Clank will spend the week cleaning the cages of the animals that he scared.

Page 14

Singular and Plural Nouns

A **noun** names a person, place, or thing.

A **singular noun** names one person, place, or thing.

A **plural noun** names more than one person, place, or thing.

Add **s** to change most singular nouns to plural nouns.

Example: dog = dogs

Add **es** to singular nouns that end in **sh, ch, s, x,** or **z** to make them plural.

Example: wish = wishes

Directions: Circle the correct spelling of the plural noun.

1. elephant — (elephants) — elephantes
2. box — (boxes) — boxs
3. drum — drumes — (drums)
4. clown — clownes — (clowns)
5. swing — (swings) — swinges
6. horse — (horses) — horsees
7. tent — tentes — (tents)
8. ticket — (tickets) — ticketes
9. costume — costumees — (costumes)
10. bicycle — (bicycles) — bicyclees
11. flash — flashs — (flashes)
12. announcer — announceres — (announcers)
13. trampoline — (trampolines) — trampolinees
14. punch — (punches) — punchs
15. cannon — cannones — (cannons)

Page 15

Singular and Plural Nouns

A **singular noun** names one person, place, or thing.

Example: **The class** went on a **field trip** to the **forest.**

A **plural noun** names more than one person, place, or thing.

Example: **The classes** went on field **trips** to the **forests.**

Directions: Draw one line under each singular noun. Draw two lines under each plural noun.

1. One girl saw three foxes run across the field.
2. Squirrels were running up and down the sides of the trees.
3. A bunny scurried under a bush.
4. As the child watched, some bluebirds flew overhead.
5. Pictures in books helped the students identify many animals.

Directions: Write a sentence for each of these singular or plural nouns.

(apples) _____

(town) _____

(trees) **ANSWERS WILL VARY**

(boys) _____

(girls) _____

(cake) _____

Page 16

Plural Nouns

A **plural** form of most nouns is formed by adding the letter **s.** Some plural nouns are formed by:

- adding **s** to nouns ending in a **vowel** and a **y.**
- adding **es** to nouns ending in **s, x, z, ch,** and **sh.**
- changing **y** to an **i** and adding **es** if the noun ends with a consonant and a **y.**

Examples: boy = boys
fox = foxes
family = families

Directions: Write the plural form above each underlined noun.

1. Aunt Betty took the box of gold fruit and carefully put them in the box for the boy and girl.
   boxes   fruits   boys   girls

2. Aunt Betty wrapped the box of toy with bow and ribbon.
   toys   bows   ribbons

3. On one of the box, Aunt Betty drew some red fox.
   boxes   foxes

4. On the box for the baby, Aunt Betty put pink and blue ribbon.
   babies   ribbons

5. In the box with the dish, she put lots and lots of tissue.
   dishes   tissues

6. In one of the boxes she put watercolor paint and paintbrush.
   paints   paintbrushes

7. Then, in each of the picnic basket, she packed four peanut butter and jelly sandwich.
   baskets   sandwiches

8. She also packed several book and two small peach.
   books   peaches

Page 17

Plural Nouns

Directions: Write the plural of each noun to complete the sentences below. Remember to change the **y** to **ie** before you add **s**!

1. I am going to two birthday _____parties_____ this week.
   (party)

2. Sandy picked some _____cherries_____ for Mom's pie.
   (cherry)

3. At the store, we saw lots of _____bunnies_____ .
   (bunny)

4. My change at the candy store was three _____pennies_____ .
   (penny)

5. All the _____ladies_____ baked cookies for the bake sale.
   (lady)

6. Thanksgiving is a special time for _____families_____ to gather together.
   (family)

7. Boston and New York are very large _____cities_____ .
   (city)

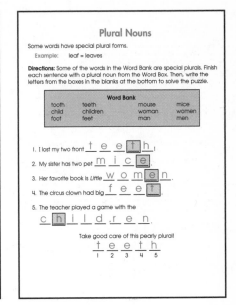

Page 18

Plural Nouns

To make **plural nouns**:

Add **s** to a singular noun ending in a vowel and an **o**.

   Example: rodeo = rodeos

Add **es** to a singular noun ending in a consonant and an **o**.

   Example: tomato = tomatoes

Change the **f** to **v** and add **es** to a singular noun ending in **f**.

   Example: leaf = leaves

Directions: Circle the correct plural form of each noun.

1. potato — (potatoes) — potatos — potatose
2. half — halfs — (halves) — halvs
3. mosquito — (mosquitoes) — mosquitoz — mosquitos
4. hero — heros — (heroes) — herose
5. loaf — (loaves) — loafs — loafes
6. zero — (zeroes) — zeros — zeroz
7. calf — calfs — (calves) — calfz
8. leaf — (leaves) — leafs — leafes
9. shelf — shelfs — shelvs — (shelves)
10. hoof — (hooves) — hoofs — hoofes

Page 19

Plural Nouns

Some words have special plural forms.

   Example: leaf = leaves

Directions: Some of the words in the Word Bank are special plurals. Finish each sentence with a plural noun from the Word Box. Then, write the letters from the boxes in the blanks at the bottom to solve the puzzle.

Word Bank			
tooth	teeth	mouse	mice
child	children	woman	women
foot	feet	man	men

1. I lost my two front t e e t h
2. My sister has two pet m i c e
3. Her favorite book is *Little* w o m e n
4. The circus clown had big f e e t
5. The teacher played a game with the c h i l d r e n

Take good care of this pearly plural!

t e e t h
1 2 3 4 5

Page 20

Collective Nouns

Collective nouns are used to represent a group. They are used with a singular verb.

   Example: **The mob of children was** excited for the parade to start.

Directions: First, underline the collective noun in each sentence. Then, circle the singular verb that goes with each collective noun.

1. The crowd of people (was) were) scared by Aunt Betty's monster truck.
2. The army (wear, (wears) blue uniforms in the parade.
3. The scout troop (throw, (throws) candy to the children.
4. The football team (marches) march) behind the scout troop.
5. The largest group in the parade ((is) are) the high school marching band.
6. The parade committee (ride, (rides) on a float covered with yellow daisies.
7. The public (follows) follow) the last float to the community park.
8. The school ((has) have) a picnic for everyone in the parade.
9. The school choir (sing, (sings) several songs for the people.

Page 21

Singular Possessive Nouns

A **singular possessive noun** shows ownership. To form a singular possessive noun, add an **apostrophe** and the letter **s** (**'s**) to the end of a singular noun.

   Example: Susan **Moore's** lunchbox
              Tony's baseball

Directions: Read Mrs. Goldfinger's will. Write the correct possessive noun above each sentence that uses a phrase like **belongs to**.

   Example: Mrs. Goldfinger's Last Will and Testament
   ~~Last Will and Testament of Mrs. Goldfinger~~

Being of sound mind,

              Aunt Minnie's Antique chair
I leave ~~the antique chair in my living room, which belonged to my Aunt Minnie,~~ to the Toon Town Oldies-but-Goodies Museum. I give to Digger J.
              my mother's herbs
Goldfinger my collection of ~~herbs that belonged to my mother.~~ ~~The flag~~
   My father's flag   Aunt Theodora Tutor's school
~~that belonged to my father~~ will go to ~~the school that is run by my Aunt~~
              My Aunt's book collection
~~Theodora Tutor. The book collection that once belonged to my aunt~~ will
                        my friend Millie Molly's yo-yo
be donated to the college. I give ~~my gold-plated yo-yo, which~~
~~belonged to my friend, Millie Molly,~~ to my mailman, Lawrence

Letter. Finally, to my nephew, Harry Hoo, I give ~~the owl that~~
   Uncle Hugh's owl!
~~belonged to my Uncle Hugh.~~

Page 22

Singular Possessive Nouns

To make a singular noun show **possession** or ownership, add an **apostrophe** and the letter **s** (**'s**).

   Examples: **Deandre**   **Deandre's** hiking shoes are muddy.
               tree   The **tree's** limbs are heavy with snow.

Directions: Change each noun to its possessive form.

1. snake _____snake's_____
2. rock _____rock's_____
3. bird _____bird's_____
4. lizard _____lizard's_____
5. plant _____plant's_____
6. shrub _____shrub's_____
7. turtle _____turtle's_____

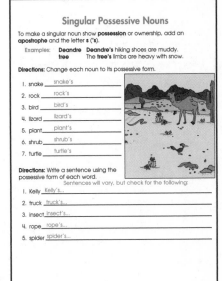

Directions: Write a sentence using the possessive form of each word.
Sentences will vary, but check for the following:

1. Kelly _____Kelly's..._____
2. truck _____truck's..._____
3. insect _____insect's..._____
4. rope _____rope's..._____
5. spider _____spider's..._____

Page 23

Plural Possessive Nouns

A **plural possessive noun** shows that something belongs to more than one person, place, or thing. To make a plural noun possessive, add only an **apostrophe** after the **s** or **es** ending. If the plural does not end in **s**, add an **apostrophe** and **s** ('s).

Examples: the toys of the brothers = the brothers' toys
the shoes of the women = the women's shoes

Directions: Change the words below to show the plural possessive nouns.

the truck belonging to the twins   the bows the girls are wearing

<u>the twins' truck</u>   <u>the girls' bows</u>

the toys of the children   the trays of the waiters

<u>the childrens' toys</u>   <u>the waiters' trays</u>

the ties belonging to the men   the lawns of our neighbors

<u>the men's ties</u>   <u>the neighbors' lawns</u>

the books belonging to the teachers   the book projects of all the classes

<u>the teachers' books</u>   <u>the classes' book projects</u>

the flowers belonging to the gardeners   the bones for the dogs

<u>the gardeners' flowers</u>   <u>the dogs' bones</u>

Page 24

Plural Possessive Nouns

To make a plural noun that ends with **s** show **possession** or ownership, add an **apostrophe** after the **s**.

Examples: boys   The **boys'** mother took them to the skate park.

If the plural noun does not end in **s**, add an **apostrophe** and the letter **s**.

Examples: men   The **men's** fitting room is on the left.

Directions: Change each plural noun to its possessive form.

1. cups <u>cups'</u>   6. children <u>children's</u>
2. hamburgers <u>hamburgers'</u>   7. parents <u>parents'</u>
3. french fries <u>french fries'</u>   8. milkshakes <u>milkshakes'</u>
4. workers <u>workers'</u>   9. sundaes <u>sundaes'</u>
5. straws <u>straws'</u>   10. fish <u>fishes'</u>

Directions: Write a sentence using the possessive form of each plural noun.

Sentences will vary, but check for the following:

1. girls <u>girls'...</u>
2. women <u>women's...</u>
3. hats <u>hats'...</u>
4. snacks <u>snacks'...</u>
5. yo-yos <u>yo-yos'...</u>

Page 25

Articles

An **article** is a word that comes before a noun. **A**, **an**, and **the** are articles. We use **a** before a word that begins with a consonant. We use **an** before a word that begins with a vowel.

Example: a peach   an apple 🍎

Directions: Write **a** or **an** in the sentences below.

Example: My bike had <u>a</u> flat tire.

1. They brought <u>a</u> goat to the farm.
2. My mom wears <u>an</u> old pair of shoes to mow the lawn.
3. We had <u>a</u> party for my grandfather.
4. Everybody had <u>an</u> ice-cream cone after the game.
5. We bought <u>a</u> picnic table for our backyard.
6. We saw <u>a</u> lion sleeping in the shade.
7. It was <u>an</u> evening to be remembered.
8. He brought <u>a</u> blanket to the game.
9. <u>An</u> exit sign was above the door.
10. They went to <u>an</u> orchard to pick apples.
11. He ate <u>an</u> orange for lunch.

Page 26

Articles

A, **an**, and **the** are special words called **articles**. **A** and **an** are used to introduce singular nouns. Use **a** when the next word begins with a consonant sound. Use **an** when the next word begins with a vowel sound.

Examples: a chair   an antelope

The is used to introduce both singular and plural nouns.

Examples: **the** beaver   **the** flowers

Directions: Underline the correct article for each word.

1. (<u>the</u>, an) field   16. (a, <u>an</u>) glove
2. (a, <u>an</u>) award   17. (<u>the</u>, an) net
3. (<u>an</u>, the) ball   18. (a, <u>the</u>) skates
4. (a, <u>the</u>) wheels   19. (a, <u>the</u>) tennis shoes
5. (a, <u>an</u>) inning   20. (<u>a</u>, an) touchdown
6. (<u>an</u>, the) sticks   21. (a, <u>the</u>) ice
7. (<u>the</u>, a) goalposts   22. (<u>a</u>, an) wave
8. (<u>a</u>, an) obstacle   23. (<u>the</u>, an) skateboard
9. (a, <u>an</u>) umpire   24. (a, <u>the</u>) water
10. (an, <u>the</u>) quarterback   25. (<u>the</u>, a) goggles
11. (a, <u>the</u>) outfield   26. (an, <u>the</u>) scoreboard
12. (<u>the</u>, an) surfboard   27. (a, <u>the</u>) spectators
13. (an, <u>the</u>) team   28. (<u>the</u>, an) uneven bars
14. (an, <u>the</u>) shin guards   29. (a, <u>the</u>) hurdles
15. (<u>a</u>, an) helmet   30. (<u>a</u>, an) time-out

Page 27

Articles

A, **an**, and **the** are words called **articles**. **A** and **an** refer to any one thing. Use **a** before a word that starts with a consonant sound. Use **an** before a word that starts with a vowel sound or a silent h. **The** refers to a specific thing.

Examples: Every duck in **the** pond wanted a bath.
It was **an** easy thing to do in **an** hour.

Directions: Complete the story below by filling in the articles **a**, **an**, or **the**.

<u>The</u> park on Saturday was full of animals. <u>An</u> ant was nibbling on my sandwich before I could get it in my mouth! <u>A</u> deer was behind <u>the</u> fence watching all <u>the</u> animals and people. <u>The</u> children were running and leaping through <u>the</u> grass, chasing <u>a</u> chipmunk. <u>A</u> park ranger made sure <u>the</u> picnic area was kept clean. When I looked down by my feet, I spotted <u>an</u> apple slice there. It wasn't there for long, though. Before I could pick it up, <u>a</u> squirrel snatched it and ran away! <u>The</u> sun was peeking through <u>the</u> thick-leaved trees and casting just enough warmth for <u>a</u> turtle that was wading in <u>a</u> pond. Even though I was only at <u>the</u> park for <u>an</u> hour, it was my most exciting visit ever.

Directions: Write the article **a** or **an** before each animal listed below.

<u>a</u> hippopotamus   <u>a</u> flamingo   <u>an</u> emperor penguin
<u>a</u> cockatoo   <u>a</u> California condor   <u>a</u> sloth
<u>a</u> chameleon   <u>a</u> robin   <u>a</u> sailfish
<u>a</u> falcon   <u>a</u> beetle   <u>a</u> blue macaw
<u>a</u> giraffe   <u>a</u> flying squirrel   <u>an</u> anteater
<u>a</u> starfish   <u>an</u> owl   <u>an</u> eel
<u>an</u> elephant   <u>an</u> albatross   <u>a</u> shark

Page 28

Articles

A, **an**, and **the** are called **articles**. **A** and **an** are articles that come before any person, place, or thing. **A** comes before a word that begins with a consonant. **An** comes before a word that begins with a vowel. **The** is the article that comes before a specific person, place, or thing.

Example: I saw **a** Tyrannosaurus Rex and **an** Allosaurus in **a** museum, and I saw **the** most complete dinosaur in Haddonfield, New Jersey.

Directions: Finish each sentence by filling in the correct article.

1. <u>A</u> bone was found about ten feet under the ground.
2. <u>The</u> crew member who found it dusted it carefully to remove dirt.
3. Once in the lab, Dr. Dexterous examined <u>the</u> find.
4. Three of <u>the</u> dino-diggers took <u>an</u> airplane to Phoenix where they had special equipment to date the bone.
5. At <u>the</u> university, the scientists used <u>a</u> special process to figure out how old <u>the</u> bone was.
6. They also found out that <u>the</u> bone was not from <u>a</u> dinosaur but from <u>a</u> human.

Page 29

Page 30

Action Words – Verbs

A **verb** is a word that tells what is happening in a sentence.

Word Bank

answers	play	studies	race
read	eats	yell	hugs
dances	swims	chats	

Directions: Write each verb from the Word Bank in the correct blank.

Sara has a busy day at school.
First, she _answers_ the teacher's
question, and then she _studies_
for her spelling test. At 11:30 a.m., she
eats her lunch and
chats with her friends.

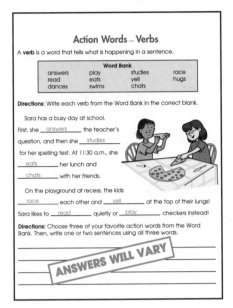

On the playground at recess, the kids
race each other and _yell_ at the top of their lungs!
Sara likes to _read_ quietly or _play_ checkers instead!

Directions: Choose three of your favorite action words from the Word Bank. Then, write one or two sentences using all three words.

ANSWERS WILL VARY

Page 31

Action Verbs

Action verbs show some kind of action. We use them to show what someone or something does, did, or will do.

Example: We **hike** down the trail.

Directions: Underline the action verbs in each rule.

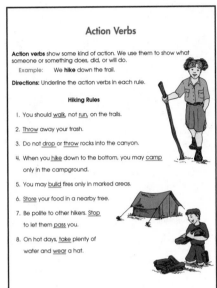

Hiking Rules

1. You should <u>walk</u>, not <u>run</u>, on the trails.
2. <u>Throw</u> away your trash.
3. Do not <u>drop</u> or <u>throw</u> rocks into the canyon.
4. When you <u>hike</u> down to the bottom, you may <u>camp</u> only in the campground.
5. You may <u>build</u> fires only in marked areas.
6. <u>Store</u> your food in a nearby tree.
7. Be polite to other hikers. <u>Stop</u> to let them <u>pass</u> you.
8. On hot days, <u>take</u> plenty of water and <u>wear</u> a hat.

Page 32

Action Verbs

Verbs are action words. They tell what is happening in a sentence. Some verbs are boring and used too often. You can make your writing clearer and more exciting by changing some verbs.

Examples: Barbara **put** peanut butter on her bread.
Barbara **slathered** peanut butter on her bread.

Directions: Change the underlined word in each sentence to a verb from the Word Bank to make the sentence more exciting.

Word Bank

thundered	streaked	explained	scurried	splashed
danced	grumbled	pitched	cried	hopped
steered	gathered	rescued	sailed	shrieked

1. _____ Dad <u>drove</u> the car toward the beach.
2. _____ The seagulls pla__ at the edge of the water.
3. _____ Waves ___ sand.
4. _____ ___ seashells at the seashore.
5. _____ "__at's that?" Petra <u>said</u>.
6. _____ "It's a sand crab," Bobby <u>said</u>.
7. _____ The sand crabs <u>went</u> away when he lifted the rock.
8. _____ Sam <u>ran</u> across the hot sand.
9. _____ Jessica <u>swam</u> in the surf.
10. _____ The beach ball <u>went</u> through the air.

ANSWERS WILL VARY

Page 33

Action Verbs

Action verbs tell what the subject of the sentence is doing.

Examples: run, jump, talk, throw, load, fight, read

Directions: Read the story below. Underline each action verb.

The Unexpected Fall

One Saturday, Mac and his father <u>hiked</u> in the desert near Superstition Mountain. Mac <u>ran</u> ahead, anxious to <u>see</u> if he could <u>find</u> the Lost Dutchman's gold mine. Mac and his father <u>looked</u> up at the rocky mountain. Saguaro cactuses <u>stood</u> guard. White clouds <u>scurried</u> across the noon sky. The puffy white balls looked so close that Mac <u>reached</u> up to <u>touch</u> them.

As he <u>jumped</u> up, his father <u>shouted</u>.
"<u>Watch</u> out!"

Mac <u>saw</u> the *Beware! Danger!* sign too late. Suddenly, his feet <u>went</u> out from under him, and he <u>slid</u> down a hole. When he <u>stopped</u> sliding, he was underground in the dark. He was in a cave.
He heard his father <u>yell</u>,
"Are you okay?"

Page 34

Action Verbs

Directions: Answer each question using a verb from the Word Bank. Write a sentence using that verb.

Word Bank

| stir | clap | drag | hug | plan | grab |

Which verb means to put your arms around someone?

hug

ANSWERS WILL VARY

Which verb means to mix something with a spoon?

stir

ANSWERS WILL VARY

Which verb means to pull something along the ground?

drag

ANSWERS WILL VARY

Which verb means to take something suddenly?

grab

ANSWERS WILL VARY

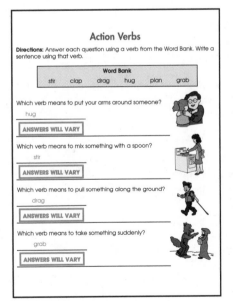

Page 35

Action Verbs

A word that tells what is happening in a sentence is called a **verb**. Verbs are **action words**.

Directions: Finish each sentence with the correct action word from the Word Bank.

Word Bank

| discovers | eats | shoots | dances | drives |

Duffy _drives_ his new, red car.
The lady _dances_ on the stage.
Coby _shoots_ the arrow at the target.
Judy _eats_ pumpkin pie.
The archaeologist _discovers_ the hidden doorway.

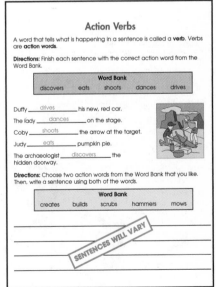

Directions: Choose two action words from the Word Bank that you like. Then, write a sentence using both of the words.

Word Bank

| creates | builds | scrubs | hammers | mows |

SENTENCES WILL VARY

Action Verbs

A **verb** is the action word in a sentence that tells what something or someone does.

Examples: run, jump, skip

Directions: Draw a box around the verb in each sentence below.

1. Spiders ⬚spin webs of silk.
2. A spider ⬚waits in the center of the web for its meals.
3. A spider ⬚sinks its sharp fangs into insects.
4. Spiders ⬚eat many insects.
5. Spiders ⬚make their nests with silk.
6. Female spiders ⬚wrap silk around their eggs to protect them.

Directions: Finish each sentence with the correct word from the Word Bank.

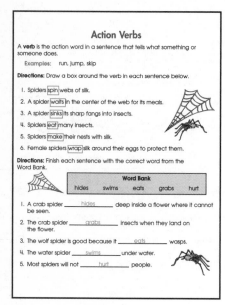

Word Bank				
hides	swims	eats	grabs	hurt

1. A crab spider ___hides___ deep inside a flower where it cannot be seen.
2. The crab spider ___grabs___ insects when they land on the flower.
3. The wolf spider is good because it ___eats___ wasps.
4. The water spider ___swims___ under water.
5. Most spiders will not ___hurt___ people.

Page 36

The Verb "Be"

Most verbs name an action. The verb **be** is different. It tells about someone or something. **Am, is,** and **are** are forms of the the verb **be**.

Use **is** with one person, place, or thing.

Example: Mr. Wu **is** my teacher.

Use **are** with more than one person, place, or thing or with the word **you.**

Examples: We **are** studying mummies.
You **are** happy.

Use **am** with the word **I.**

Example: I **am** happy today.

Directions: Fill in each blank with the correct form of the verb **be (is, am,** or **are).**

1. My house ___is___ brown.
2. My favorite color ___is___ blue.
3. We ___are___ baking cookies today.
4. I ___am___ going to the movies on Saturday.
5. My friends ___are___ going with me.
6. What ___is___ your phone number?
7. You ___are___ standing on my foot.
8. I ___am___ four feet tall.
9. The firefighter ___is___ driving the engine.
10. Charles and I ___are___ playing football.
11. The band ___is___ playing "The Star-Spangled Banner."
12. Denver ___is___ east of Los Angeles.
13. You ___are___ a nice person.
14. ___Am___ I your best friend?

Page 37

Linking Verbs

A **linking verb** does not show action. It links the subject of the sentence with a noun or adjective. Forms of **to be** are linking verbs.

Example: Thomas Jefferson **was** a president of the United States.

Directions: Write a linking verb in each blank.

1. The class's writing assignment ___is___ a report on U.S. Presidents.
2. The due date for our report ___is___ tomorrow.
3. I ___am___ glad I chose to write about Thomas Jefferson.
4. He ___was___ the youngest delegate to the First Continental Congress.
5. The colonies ___were___ angry at England.
6. Thomas Jefferson ___was___ a great writer, so he was asked to help write the Declaration of Independence.
7. The signing of that document ___is___ an important historical event.
8. As President, Jefferson ___was___ responsible for organizing the Louisiana Purchase.
9. He ___was___ the second president to live in the White House.
10. Americans ___are___ fortunate for the part Thomas Jefferson played in our country's history.

Page 38

Linking Verbs

A **linking verb** connects the subject in a sentence to the words in the **predicate.** The predicate is the part of the sentence that contains the verb. Forms of the verb **to be (is, are,** and **am)** are the most commonly used linking verbs.

Example: I **am** sick.
Mrs. Potter **is** our neighbor.

Directions: Finish each sentence with the correct linking verb from the Word Bank. You can use the same word twice.

Word Bank				
is	am	was	are	were

ANSWERS MAY VARY SLIGHTLY

1. The oldest saguaro cactus ___was___ over 250 years old.
2. The cactus wrens ___are___ in the hole.
3. The coyotes ___were___ wild.
4. I ___am___ cold as I paddle down the river.
5. The saguaro cactus ___is___ a flowering plant.
6. The flower of the saguaro cactus ___is___ the state flower of Arizona.

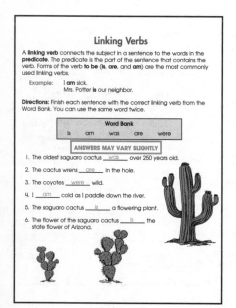

Page 39

Linking Verbs

Linking verbs connect the noun to a descriptive word. Linking verbs are often forms of the verb **be.**

Directions: The linking verb is underlined in each sentence. Circle the two words that are being connected.

Example: The (cat) is (fat)

1. My favorite (food) is (pizza).
2. The (car) was (red).
3. (I) am (tired).
4. (Books) are (fun).
5. The (garden) is (beautiful).
6. (Pears) taste (juicy).
7. The (airplane) looks (large).
8. (Rabbits) are (furry).

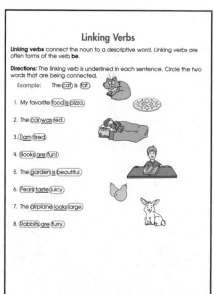

Page 40

Helping Verbs

A **helping verb** is a word used with an action verb.

Examples: might, shall, are

Directions: Finish each sentence with an appropriate helping verb from the Word Bank.

Word Bank			
can	could	must	might
may	would	should	will
shall	did	does	do
had	have	has	am
are	were	is	
be	being	been	

Example: Tomorrow, I ___might___ play soccer.

1. Mom ___may___ buy my new soccer shoes tonight.
2. Yesterday, my old soccer shoes ___were___ ripped by the cat.
3. I ___am___ going to ask my brother to go to the game.
4. He usually ___does___ not like soccer.
5. But, he ___will___ go with me because I am his sister.
6. He ___has___ promised to watch the entire soccer game.
7. He has ___been___ helping me with my homework.
8. I ___can___ spell a lot better because of his help.
9. Maybe I ___could___ finish the semester at the top of my class.

Page 41

Helping Verbs

Sometimes an **action verb** needs help from another verb called a **helping verb**.

Common Helping Verbs					
am	can	does	is	shall	will
are	could	had	may	should	would
be	did	has	might	was	
been	do	have	must	were	

Directions: Underline the action verb in each sentence. Then, finish each sentence with the best helping verb.

1. Jasmine's family ___is___ planning a recycling project.
   (is, had, are)

2. They ___are___ talking to their neighbors.
   (is, may, are)

3. Mr. Chavez ___will___ look for old newspapers and magazines.
   (will, do, were)

4. The Ong children ___are___ gathering bags to collect plastic bottles.
   (should, are, did)

5. Jasmine ___might___ open a lemonade stand to keep us cool.
   (have, was, might)

6. Mrs. Zanuto said she ___would___ drive us to the recycling center. (would, be, are)

7. We ___must___ respect our planet.
   (have, must, are)

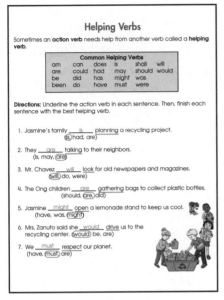

Page 42

Helping Verb

A **helping verb** "helps" another verb to show action.

Examples: I **was** turning.
He **should have** turned.
They **must have been** turning.

Directions: Finish each sentence below. Fill in the verb phrase by using the verb shown and adding a helping verb from the Word Bank. Try to use a different helping verb in each sentence.

Example: The flowers ___are growing___ tall.
(to grow)

ANSWERS WILL VARY

1. Freddie ___might listen___ in class.
   (to listen)

2. Lori ___did eat___ her vegetables.
   (to eat)

3. I ___will do___ my homework later.
   (to do)

4. They ___are going___ to the movie.
   (to go)

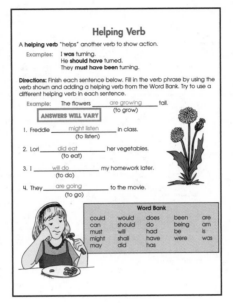

Word Bank				
could	would	does	been	are
can	should	do	being	am
must	will	had	be	is
might	shall	have	were	was
may	did	has		

Page 43

Verbs "Went" and "Gone"

The word **went** is used without a helping verb.

Examples:
Correct: Susan **went** to the store.
Incorrect: Susan **has went** to the store.

The word **gone** is used with a helping verb.

Examples:
Correct: Susan **has gone** to the store.
Incorrect: Susan **gone** to the store.

Directions: Write **C** in the blank if the verb is used correctly. Draw an **X** in the blank if the verb is not used correctly.

Example: ___C___ She has gone to my school since last year.

1. ___C___ Has not he been gone a long time?
2. ___X___ He has went to the same class all year.
3. ___X___ I have went to that doctor since I was born.
4. ___C___ She is long gone!
5. ___X___ Who among us has not gone to get a drink yet?
6. ___C___ The class has gone on three field trips this year.
7. ___C___ The class went on three field trips this year.
8. ___X___ Who has not went to the board with the right answer?
9. ___C___ We have not gone on our vacation yet.
10. ___X___ Who is went for the pizza?
11. ___C___ The train has been gone for two hours.
12. ___C___ The family had gone to the movies.
13. ___X___ Have you went to visit the new bookstore?
14. ___C___ He has gone on and on about how smart you are!

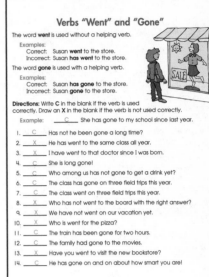

Page 44

The Verb "Be"

Some forms of the verb **to be** can be used as **main verbs** or **helping verbs**.

Examples: **main:** They **are** quiet.
helping: They **are being** quiet.

Directions: Circle the form of **to be** in each sentence below. Then, write **main** or **helping** in the blank to show how the verb is being used.

1. _helping_ Ruth has (been) playing soccer every day this week.
2. _helping_ He (was) teaching us to read.
3. _main_ The lunches (were) good.
4. _helping_ Janie (was) planning on leaving school.
5. _main_ My baby sister (is) unhappy.

Directions: Circle the correct form of **to be** in each sentence. Then, rewrite the sentence.

1. Julie (been, (has been)) the best student in our class.
   Julie has been the best student in our class.

2. Emily (be, (will be)) a very good scientist.
   Emily will be a very good scientist.

3. Soon, he (been, (will be)) a student hall monitor.
   Soon, he will be a student hall monitor.

4. Our school year (been, (has been)) good so far.
   Our school year has been good so far.

5. Brendan and Janie (be, (are)) both shy.
   Brendan and Janie are both shy.

Page 45

Verbs

Verbs are the action words in a sentence. There are three kinds of verbs: **action verbs**, **linking verbs**, and **helping verbs**.

An **action verb** tells the action of a sentence.

Examples: run, hop, skip, sleep, jump, talk, snore
Michael **ran** to the store.

A **linking verb** joins the subject and predicate of a sentence.

Examples: am, is, are, was, were
Michael **was** at the store.

A **helping verb** is used with an action verb to "help" the action of the sentence.

Examples: am, is, are, was, were
Matthew **was** helping Michael.

Directions: Underline the verbs in each sentence. Above the verb, write **A** if it is an action verb, **L** if it is a linking verb, or **H** if it is a helping verb.

Example: Amy <u>jumps</u> rope.
(A above jumps)

1. Paul <u>was</u> <u>jumping</u> rope, too. (H A)
2. They <u>were</u> <u>working</u> on their homework. (H A)
3. The math problem <u>requires</u> a lot of thinking. (A)
4. Addition problems <u>are</u> fun to do. (L)
5. The baby <u>sleeps</u> in the afternoon. (A)
6. Grandma <u>is</u> also <u>napping</u>. (H A)
7. Sam <u>is</u> <u>going</u> to bed. (H A)
8. John <u>paints</u> a lovely picture of the sea. (A)
9. The colors in the picture <u>are</u> soft and pale. (L)

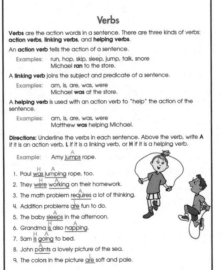

Page 46

Present-Tense Verbs

When something is happening right now, it is in the **present tense**. There are two ways to write verbs in the present tense: in the **simple present tense** and in **present tense with a helping verb**.

Examples: simple present tense: The dog **walks**.
present tense with a helping verb: The dog **is walking**.

Directions: Rewrite each sentence using a different form of the verb.

Example: He lists the numbers.
He is listing the numbers.

1. She is pounding the nail.
   She pounds the nail.

2. My brother toasts the bread.
   My brother is toasting the bread.

3. They search for the robber.
   They are searching for the robber.

4. The teacher lists the pages.
   The teacher is listing the pages.

5. They are spilling the water.
   They spill the water.

6. Ken and Amy load the packages.
   Ken and Amy are loading the packages.

Page 47

Present-Tense Verbs

When a **present-tense verb** tells what one person or thing is doing now, it often ends in **s**.

Example: She **sings**.

When a verb is used with **you, I,** or **we,** we do not add an **s**.

Example: I **sing**.

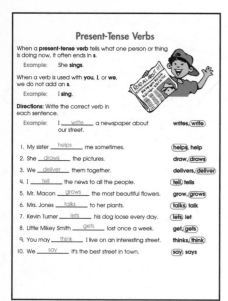

Directions: Write the correct verb in each sentence.

Example: I __write__ a newspaper about
our street. · **writes,** write

1. My sister __helps__ me sometimes. · **helps,** help
2. She __draws__ the pictures. · draw, **draws**
3. We __deliver__ them together. · delivers, **deliver**
4. I __tell__ the news to all the people. · **tell,** tells
5. Mr. Macon __grows__ the most beautiful flowers. · grow, **grows**
6. Mrs. Jones __talks__ to her plants. · **talks,** talk
7. Kevin Turner __lets__ his dog loose every day. · **lets,** let
8. Little Mikey Smith __gets__ lost once a week. · get, **gets**
9. You may __think__ I live on an interesting street. · thinks, **think**
10. We __say__ it's the best street in town. · **say,** says

Page 48

Present-Tense Verbs

Directions: Use each verb below in two sentences that tell about something that is happening now. Write the verb as both simple present tense and present tense with a helping verb.

Example: run

Mia runs to the store.   Mia is running to the store.
(simple present tense)   (present tense + helping verb)

1. hatch _____
2. check _____
3. spell _____
4. blend _____   *SENTENCES WILL VARY*
5. lick _____
6. cry_____
7. write _____
8. dream_____

Page 49

Present-Tense Verbs

The **present tense** of a verb tells about something that is happening now, happens often, or is about to happen. These verbs can be written in **simple present tense** (The bird sings.) or in **present tense with a helping verb** (The bird is singing.).

Directions: Write each sentence again, using the verb **is** and writing the **ing** form of the verb.

Example: He cooks the cheeseburgers.
He Is cooking the cheeseburgers.

1. Sharon dances to that song.
Sharon is dancing to that song.
2. Frank washed the car.
Frank is washing the car.
3. Mr. Benson smiles at me.
Mr. Benson is smiling at me.

Directions: Finish each sentence below. Tell something that is happening now. Be sure to use the helping verb **is** and the **ing** form of the action verb.

Example: The big, brown dog is barking.

1. The little baby _____
2. Most nine-year-olds _____   *ANSWERS WILL VARY*
3. The monster on television _____

Page 50

Past-Tense Verbs

The **past tense** of a verb tells about something that has already happened. We add a **d** or an **ed** to most verbs to show that something has already happened.

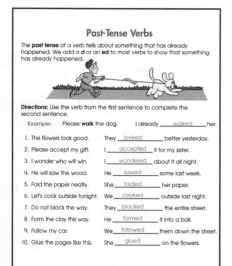

Directions: Use the verb from the first sentence to complete the second sentence.

Example: Please **walk** the dog.   I already __walked__ her.

1. The flowers look good.   They __looked__ better yesterday.
2. Please accept my gift.   I __accepted__ it for my sister.
3. I wonder who will win.   I __wondered__ about it all night.
4. He will saw the wood.   He __sawed__ some last week.
5. Fold the paper neatly.   She __folded__ her paper.
6. Let's cook outside tonight.   We __cooked__ outside last night.
7. Do not block the way.   They __blocked__ the entire street.
8. Form the clay this way.   He __formed__ it into a ball.
9. Follow my car.   We __followed__ them down the street.
10. Glue the pages like this.   She __glued__ on the flowers.

Page 51

Past-Tense Verbs

When you write about something that has already happened, you add **ed** to most verbs. There is another way to write about something in the past tense.

Examples: The dog walked. = The dog was walking.
The cats played. = The cats were playing.

Directions: Write each sentence again, using the verb in a different way.

Example: The baby pounded the pans.
The baby was pounding the pans.

1. Gary loaded the car by himself.
Gary was loading the car by himself.
2. They searched for a long time.
They were searching for a long time.
3. The water spilled over the edge.
The water was spilling over the edge.
4. Dad toasted the rolls.
Dad was toasting the rolls.

Page 52

Past-Tense Verbs

To write about something that already happened, you can add **ed** to the verb.

Example: Yesterday, we **talked**.

You can also use the helping verbs **was** and **were** and add **ing** to the action verb.

Example: Yesterday, we **were talking**.

When a verb ends with **e**, you usually drop the **e** before adding **ing**.

Examples: grade = was grading   weave = were weaving
tape = was taping   sneeze = were sneezing

Directions: Write two sentences for each verb below. Tell about something that has already happened. Write the verb both ways.

Example: stream
The rain **streamed** down the window.
The rain **was streaming** down the window.

1. grade
_____
2. tape
_____
3. weave   *SENTENCES WILL VARY*
_____
4. sneeze
_____
_____

Page 53

Past-Tense Verbs

To make many verbs past tense, add **ed**.

Examples: cook = cooked   wish = wished   play = played

When a verb ends in a **silent e**, drop the **e** and add **ed**.

Examples: hope = hoped   hate = hated

When a verb ends in **y** after a consonant, change the **y** to **i** and add **ed**.

Examples: hurry = hurried   marry = married

When a verb ends in a single consonant after a single short vowel, double the final consonant before adding **ed**.

Examples: stop = stopped   hop = hopped

Directions: Make the present-tense verb past-tense.

Example: call ___called___

1. copy	copied	10. reply	replied
2. frown	frowned	11. top	topped
3. smile	smiled	12. clean	cleaned
4. live	lived	13. scream	screamed
5. talk	talked	14. clap	clapped
6. name	named	15. mop	mopped
7. list	listed	16. soap	soaped
8. spy	spied	17. choke	choked
9. phone	phoned	18. scurry	scurried

Page 54

Past-Tense Verbs

Present-tense verbs tell what is happening now. **Past-tense verbs** tell what happened in the past.

To change most action verbs to past tense, add **ed**.
Example: jump = jumped

To change verbs that end in **e** to past tense, add **d**.
Example: race = raced

To change verbs that end in a consonant followed by a **y** to past tense, change the **y** to **i** and add **ed**.
Example: try = tried

To change verbs that end with a vowel followed by a consonant to past tense, double the consonant and add **ed**.
Example: stop = stopped

Directions: Fill in each blank with the past tense of the verb.

I was ___invited___ (invite) to a birthday party. So, my mom, my sister, and I ___hurried___ (hurry) to the mall to buy a gift. We ___hopped___ (hop) off the elevator. "Don't touch anything!" Mom said. So, I ___touched___ (touch) everything. I ___pulled___ (pull) the sweaters off the tables. I ___tried___ (try) on all the hats. I ___played___ (play) hide-and-seek with my sister. She ___cried___ (cry) when I ___tripped___ (trip) her. I ___hugged___ (hug) her to make her feel better. We ___stopped___ (stop) at a candy shop. I ___licked___ (lick) my lips when I saw the chewy bears. I ___begged___ (beg) my mom to buy some. She ___refused___ (refuse). I ___decided___ (decide) to get my friend chewy bears. I ___smiled___ (smile) as the salesperson ___wrapped___ (wrap) the gift. I ___carried___ (carry) the candy out to the car. What do you think ___happened___ (happen) to the gift?

Page 55

Irregular Verbs

Irregular verbs are verbs that you do not change from the present tense to the past tense by adding **d** or **ed**.

Example: sing = sang

Directions: Read the sentence and underline the verbs. Choose the past-tense form of the verb from the Word Bank and write it next to the sentence.

Word Bank			
blew	came	flew	gave
grew	made	sang	took
wore			

Example: Dad will make a cake tonight. ___made___

1. I will probably grow another inch this year. ___grew___
2. I will blow out the candles. ___blew___
3. Everyone will give me presents. ___gave___
4. I will wear my favorite red shirt. ___wore___
5. My cousins will come from out of town. ___came___
6. It will take them four hours. ___took___
7. My Aunt Betty will fly in from Cleveland. ___flew___
8. She will sing me a song. ___sang___

Page 56

Irregular Verbs

There are some verbs that you do not change to past tense by simply adding **ed**. These verbs are spelled differently. They are called **irregular verbs**.

Examples: **present:** fly, sing, run, swim, begin, eat, buy, bring, take
past: flew, sang, ran, swam, began, ate, bought, brought, took

Directions: Read each sentence. Underline all the irregular verbs.

1. Jeremy climbed to the top of the mountain and sang.
2. Moisha ran into town.
3. After breakfast, Tony and Cara went into town and bought books.
4. Jennifer found a stable, rented a horse, and rode on a trail by the river.
5. I put on my bathing suit and swam in the river.
6. Dr. Dexterous flew a helicopter over the forest.
7. Yolanda went exploring and found an arrowhead.
8. Carl found the best Mexican restaurant where he ate tacos and burritos.

Page 57

Irregular Verbs

Past tense tells about what happened in the past. To make a regular verb past tense, add **d** or **ed** to the verb. Irregular verbs do not form the past tense by adding **d** or **ed**.

Examples: **regular verbs:** paint = painted   try = tried
irregular verbs: fly = flew   eat = ate

Directions: Rewrite each sentence below in the past tense.

1. First, Aunt Betty picks out the paint for the shutters.
First, Aunt Betty picked out the paint for the shutters.

2. Then, Aunt Betty and Jenny make food for the picnic.
Then, Aunt Betty and Jenny made food for the picnic.

3. Next, they stop to get gas for the car.
Next, they stopped to get gas for the car.

4. After they shop, Aunt Betty begins to wash the car.
After they shopped, Aunt Betty began to wash the car.

5. Finally, Aunt Betty's sisters arrive to have dinner.
Finally, Aunt Betty's sisters arrived to have dinner.

Page 58

Irregular Verbs

Directions: Circle the verb that completes each sentence.

1. Scientists will try to (find, found) the cure.
2. Eric (brings, brought) his lunch to school yesterday.
3. Every day, Betsy (sings, sang) all the way home.
4. Jason (breaks, broke) the vase last night.
5. The ice had (freezes, frozen) in the tray.
6. Mitzi has (swims, swum) in that pool before.
7. Now I (choose, chose) to exercise daily.
8. The teacher has (rings, rung) the bell.
9. The boss (speaks, spoke) to us yesterday.
10. She (says, said) it twice already.

Page 59

Page 60

Irregular Verbs

Verbs that do not become past tense when you add **ed** are called **irregular verbs**. The spellings of these verbs change.

Example:	**present**	**past**
	begin, begins	began
	eat, eats	ate

Directions: Finish each sentence with the past tense of the irregular verb.

1. Sam almost ___fell___ (fall) when he tripped over the curb.
2. Diana made sure she ___took___ (take) bug spray on her hike.
3. Dave ___ran___ (run) over to his friend's house.
4. Tim ___broke___ (break) off a long piece of grass to put in his mouth.
5. Eve ___knew___ (know) the path along the river well.
6. The clouds ___began___ (begin) to turn gray.
7. Kathy ___threw___ (throw) a small piece of bread to the ducks.
8. Everyone ___ate___ (eat) a very nutritious meal after the long adventure.
9. We all ___slept___ (sleep) very well that night.

Page 61

The Irregular Verb "to Do"

It is important to use the correct form of **to do** whenever you speak or write.

Examples: Tara and Nan **do** stretching exercises.
Sara **did** the most sit-ups.

Directions: Circle the correct form of **to do** in each sentence.

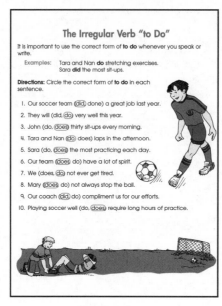

1. Our soccer team (did, done) a great job last year.
2. They will (did, do) very well this year.
3. John (do, does) thirty sit-ups every morning.
4. Tara and Nan (do, does) laps in the afternoon.
5. Sara (do, does) the most practicing each day.
6. Our team (does, do) have a lot of spirit.
7. We (does, do) not ever get tired.
8. Mary (does, do) not always stop the ball.
9. Our coach (did, do) compliment us for our efforts.
10. Playing soccer well (do, does) require long hours of practice.

Page 62

The Irregular Verb "Be"

The verb **be** is different from all other verbs. The present-tense forms of **be** are **am**, **is**, and **are**. The past-tense forms of **be** are **was** and **were**. The verb **to be** is written in the following ways:

singular: I am, you are, he is, she is, it is
plural: we are, you are, they are

Directions: Finish each sentence with the correct form of **be** from the Word Bank.

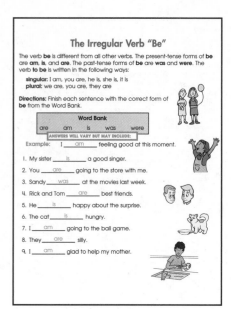

Word Bank				
are	am	is	was	were

ANSWERS WILL VARY BUT MAY INCLUDE:

Example: I ___am___ feeling good at this moment.

1. My sister ___is___ a good singer.
2. You ___are___ going to the store with me.
3. Sandy ___was___ at the movies last week.
4. Rick and Tom ___are___ best friends.
5. He ___is___ happy about the surprise.
6. The cat ___is___ hungry.
7. I ___am___ going to the ball game.
8. They ___are___ silly.
9. I ___am___ glad to help my mother.

Page 63

The Irregular Verb "Be"

Be is an irregular verb. The present-tense forms of be are **be**, **am**, **is**, and **are**. The past-tense forms of be are **was** and **were**.

Directions: Write the correct form of **be** in the blanks.

Example: I ___am___ so happy for you!

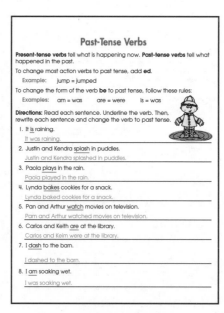

1. Jared ___was___ unfriendly yesterday.
2. English can ___be___ a lot of fun to learn.
3. They ___are___ among the nicest people I know.
4. They ___were___ late yesterday.
5. She promises she ___is___ going to arrive on time.
6. I ___am___ nervous right now about the test.
7. If you ___are___ happy now, then so am I.
8. He ___was___ as nice to me last week as I had hoped.
9. He can ___be___ very nice.
10. Would you ___be___ mad if I moved your desk?
11. He ___was___ waiting at the door for me yesterday.

Page 64

Past-Tense Verbs

Present-tense verbs tell what is happening now. **Past-tense verbs** tell what happened in the past.

To change most action verbs to past tense, add **ed**.

Example: jump = jumped

To change the form of the verb **be** to past tense, follow these rules:

Examples: am = was   are = were   is = was

Directions: Read each sentence. Underline the verb. Then, rewrite each sentence and change the verb to past tense.

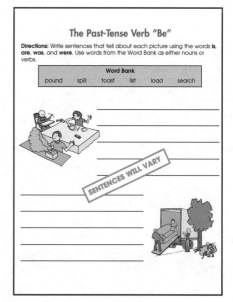

1. It <u>is</u> raining.
   It was raining.
2. Justin and Kendra <u>splash</u> in puddles.
   Justin and Kendra splashed in puddles.
3. Paola <u>plays</u> in the rain.
   Paola played in the rain.
4. Lynda <u>bakes</u> cookies for a snack.
   Lynda baked cookies for a snack.
5. Pan and Arthur <u>watch</u> movies on television.
   Pam and Arthur watched movies on television.
6. Carlos and Keith <u>are</u> at the library.
   Carlos and Keim were at the library.
7. I <u>dash</u> to the barn.
   I dashed to the barn.
8. I <u>am</u> soaking wet.
   I was soaking wet.

Page 65

The Past-Tense Verb "Be"

Directions: Write sentences that tell about each picture using the words **is**, **are**, **was**, and **were**. Use words from the Word Bank as either nouns or verbs.

Word Bank					
pound	spill	toast	list	load	search

SENTENCES WILL VARY

Irregular Verbs: Past-Tense

Irregular verbs change completely in the past tense. Unlike regular verbs, past-tense forms of irregular verbs are not formed by adding **ed**.

Example: The past tense of **go** is **went**.
The past tense of **break** is **broke**.

A **helping verb** helps to tell about the past. **Has**, **have**, and **had** are helping verbs that you can use with action verbs to show that the action happened in the past. The past-tense form of the irregular verb sometimes changes when a helping verb is added.

Present Tense Irregular Verb	Past Tense Irregular Verb	Past Tense Irregular Verb With Helper
go	went	have/has/had gone
see	saw	have/has/had seen
do	did	have/has/had done
bring	brought	have/has/had brought
sing	sang	have/has/had sung
drive	drove	have/has/had driven
swim	swam	have/has/had swum
sleep	slept	have/has/had slept

Directions: Choose four verbs from the chart. For each verb, write one sentence using the past-tense form without a helping verb. Then, write one sentence using the past-tense form with a helping verb.

1. _____
2. _____
3. _____
4. _____

SENTENCES WILL VARY

Page 66

Irregular Verbs With Helpers

Past-tense verbs that do not have an **ed** or **d** ending are called **irregular verbs**.

present	past	past participle
ring	rang	has rung, have rung
see	saw	has seen, have seen

Directions: Fill in the missing verbs in the chart.

Present	Past	Past-Tense Irregular Verb With Helper
do, does		has or have done
go, goes	went	has or have
know, knows		has or have known
fall, falls		has or have fallen
speak, speaks	spoke	has or have
stand, stands		has or have stood
write, writes		has or have written
draw, draws	drew	has or have

Directions: Circle the correct verb form in the parentheses.

1. Dad and I (went, gone) on a walk in the park one morning.
2. More than six inches of snow had (fall, fallen).
3. Yesterday, the tall trees (stand, stood) silently in their white overcoats.
4. A rabbit (ran, run) away as we approached it.
5. We (heard, hears) a cardinal's call from the oak tree.
6. A squirrel's nest (sat, sitted) in a tree overhead.
7. It (took, taken) us nearly an hour to make it back home.

Page 67

Regular and Irregular Verbs

Verbs that show action happening now are in the **present** tense. Verbs that show action happening in the past are in the **past** tense.

Examples: **present:** The fire department **puts** out fires.
past: The fire department **put** out fires yesterday.

Directions: Circle the verb (present or past) that finishes each sentence.

1. The police department (chases, chased) criminals every day.
2. Two days ago, our team (won, wins) the town trophy.
3. My teacher always (wears, wore) glasses.
4. The mailman (delivers, delivered) the wrong mail yesterday.
5. At last night's game, the mayor's daughter (sing, sang) the "Star-Spangled Banner."
6. A fire truck (races, raced) down the street this morning.
7. The bank (opens, opened) at 8 a.m. on Mondays.
8. When the score was (tie, tied), the pitcher threw a curve ball.
9. I (worked, work) at the library last week.

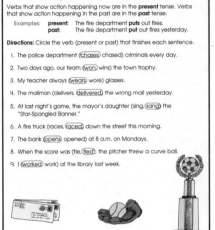

Page 68

Verb Tense

ANSWERS MAY VARY

Directions: Use verbs to complete the story below.

Last week, Amy and I ____entered____ a contest. We were supposed to make a card to give to a child in a hospital. First, we ____folded____ a big sheet of white paper in half to make the card. Then, we ____decided____ to draw a rainbow on the front.

Amy started coloring the rainbow all by herself. "Wait!" I said. "We both ____entered____ the contest. Let me help!"

"Okay," Amy said. "We can ____share____. You ____add____ a color, and then I'll ____add____ a color." It was more fun when we ____shared____. When we finished making the rainbow, we ____decided____ to ____add____ a sun to the picture. I cut the sun out of yellow paper. Then, Amy ____glued____ it just above the rainbow. Well, our card didn't win the contest, but it did make a little boy with a broken leg smile. Amy and I felt so happy! We ____decided____ to go right home and make some more cards!

Page 69

Verb Forms

Directions: Finish each sentence with the correct verb form.

1. Before the wheel, people ____dragged____ heavy loads. **drag, dragged**
2. No one knows who ____invented____ the wheel. **invented, invent**
3. The Sumerians ____were____ some of the first people to use the wheel. **were, are**
4. They ____made____ the first wheels out of wood and stone. **make, made**
5. The wheels ____were____ very heavy. **be, were**
6. Then, people ____thought____ of spokes. **think, thought**
7. Spokes helped the wheels ____turn____ more easily. **turn, turned**
8. Soon, people were ____building____ roads. **built, building**
9. I ____am____ glad that the wheel was invented. **is, am**
10. There ____are____ many things that move on wheels. **is, are**
11. Cars and trucks ____have____ wheels. **has, have**
12. A potter ____make____ pots on a wheel. **make, made**
13. A wool maker ____spin____ wool on a spinning wheel. **spin, spun**
14. Amusement park rides ____have____ wheels. **have, has**
15. My favorite set of wheels ____is____ on my bike. **is, am**

Page 70

Future-Tense Verbs

The **future tense** of a verb tells about something that will happen in the future. **Will** or **shall** are the helping verbs that are usually used with future tense.

Directions: Change the verb tense in each sentence to future tense.

Example: She cooks dinner.
She will cook dinner.

1. He plays baseball.
   He will play baseball.
2. She walks to school.
   She will walk to school.
3. Bobby talks to the teacher.
   Bobby will talk to the teacher.
4. I remember to vote.
   I will remember to vote.
5. Jack mows the lawn every week.
   Jack will mow the lawn every week.
6. We go on vacation soon.
   We will go on vacation soon.

Page 71

Future-Tense Verbs

To change a verb to the future tense, you usually add the helping verb **will**.

Example: He **will** work.

Directions: Circle each verb that is in the future tense.

In the Jungle

We (will walk) through the hot, dark jungle. Monkeys (will swing) from the trees and parrots (will squawk) as they fly around us. Tigers (will growl) and roar. We (will eat) our lunches under a giant fern. I hope a hungry gorilla (will join) us for lunch. We (will share) our bananas. After lunch, we (will pick) more papayas, bananas, and mangos.

When the sun begins to set, we (will store) our fruit in a tree and pitch our tent. We (will build) a fire. Around the fire, we (will tell) scary stories and then try to fall asleep.

Page 72

Future-Tense Verbs

Verbs in the **future tense** tell what will happen in the future. The helping verb **will** is usually used with the action verb to make the future tense.

Example: We **will take** a trip to see the pyramids.

Directions: First, underline the verb in each sentence. Then, write the verb in future tense on the line after each sentence.

1. We <u>ask</u> questions about the pyramids. __will ask__

2. The explorer <u>answers</u> our questions. __will answer__

3. Explorers <u>find</u> pyramids in Central and South America and Egypt. __will find__

4. The explorers <u>visit</u> the pyramid of Cheops in Egypt. __will visit__

5. The explorers <u>study</u> the history and architecture of the pyramids. __will study__

6. The explorers <u>compare</u> the pyramids in Egypt with the pyramids in Central and South America. __will compare__

7. The explorers <u>write</u> about what they saw. __will write__

8. The photographer <u>donates</u> his pictures to the project. __will donate__

Page 73

Future-Tense Verbs

Verb tense tells time in a sentence. The **future tense** tells about what will happen in the future. The helping verb **will** is usually used with the action verb to show future time.

Example: Tomorrow we **will go** to our aunt's house.

Directions: Write each sentence below in the future tense.

1. I pick up groceries at the store.
   I will pick up groceries at the store.

2. I call the painter to paint the shutters.
   I will call the painter to paint the shutters.

3. The neighborhood builds a float for the parade.
   The neighborhood will build a float for the parade.

4. There is a picnic at City Hall.
   There will be a picnic lunch at City Hall.

5. Jenny comes to visit.
   Jenny will come to visit.

Page 74

Using "ing" Verbs

Use the helping verbs **is** and **are** when describing something happening right now. Use the helping verb **was** and **were** when describing something that already happened.

Directions: Finish each sentence by adding **ing** to the verb and using the helping verb **is**, **are**, **was**, or **were**.

Examples:
When it started to rain, we ___were raking___ the leaves.
                              rake

When the soldiers marched up that hill, Captain Stevens
___was commanding___ them.
command

| ANSWERS MAY VARY BUT CHECK FOR: |

1. Now, the police ___...accusing___ them of stealing the money.
                        accuse

2. Look! The eggs ___...hatching___ .
                       hatch

3. A minute ago, the sky ___...glowing___ .
                            glow

4. My dad says he ___...treating___ us to ice cream!
                       treat

5. She ___...sneezing___ the whole time we were at the mall.
          sneeze

6. While we were at recess, he ___...grading___ our tests.
                                   grade

7. I hear something. Who ___...talking___ ?
                            talk

8. As I watched, the workers ___...grinding___ the wood into little chips.
                                grind

Page 75

Using "ing" Verbs

Using **ing** verbs can make your writing more interesting to read. Compare these lists of verbs:

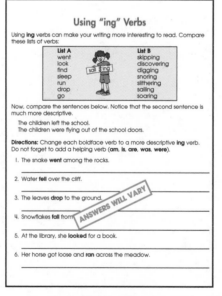

List A	List B
went	skipping
look	discovering
find	digging
sleep	snoring
run	slithering
drop	sailing
go	soaring

Now, compare the sentences below. Notice that the second sentence is much more descriptive.

The children left the school.
The children were flying out of the school doors.

Directions: Change each boldface verb to a more descriptive **ing** verb. Do not forget to add a helping verb (**am, is, are, was, were**).

1. The snake **went** among the rocks.

2. Water **fell** over the cliff.

3. The leaves **drop** to the ground.

4. Snowflakes **fall** from

5. At the library, she **looked** for a book.

6. Her horse got loose and **ran** across the meadow.

ANSWERS WILL VARY

Page 76

Using "ing" Verbs

Directions: Using descriptive **ing** verbs, write five sentences about activities you do every day.

Example: Peter is scarfing down his breakfast so he will not miss the bus.

1. _____

2. _____

3. _____

4. _____

5. _____

SENTENCES WILL VARY

Page 77

Page 78

Verb Tense

Not only do verbs tell the action of a sentence, but they also tell when the action takes place. This is called the **verb tense**. There are three verb tenses: past, present, and future tense.

Present-tense verbs tell what is happening now.

Examples: Jane **spells** words with long vowel sounds.
Stan **is standing** out in the rain.

Past-tense verbs tell about action that has already happened.

Examples: stay = stayed   John **stayed** home yesterday.
talk = was talking   Sally **was talking** to her mom.

Future-tense verbs tell what will happen in the future. Future-tense verbs are made by putting the word **will** before the verb.

Example: paint = will paint   Susie and Sherry **will paint** the house.

Directions: Look at each verb below. Write whether the verb tense is past, present, or future.

Example: watches ___present___

Verb	Tense		Verb	Tense
1. wanted	past		7. writes	present
2. will eat	future		8. vaulted	past
3. was squawking	past		9. were sleeping	past
4. yawns	present		10. will sing	future
5. crawled	past		11. is speaking	present
6. will hunt	future		12. will cook	future

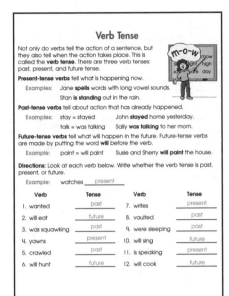

Page 79

Verb Tense

Verbs can be in the **past**, **present**, or **future**.

Directions: Match each sentence with the correct verb tense. **(Think:** When did each thing happen?)

It will rain tomorrow. — past
He played golf. — present
Molly is sleeping. — future
Jack is singing a song. — past
I will buy a kite. — present
Dad worked hard today. — future

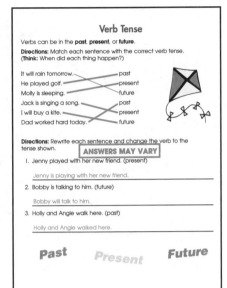

Directions: Rewrite each sentence and change the verb to the tense shown.

ANSWERS MAY VARY

1. Jenny played with her new friend. (present)

Jenny is playing with her new friend.

2. Bobby is talking to him. (future)

Bobby will talk to him.

3. Holly and Angie walk here. (past)

Holly and Angie walked here.

Past   *Present*   **Future**

Page 80

Verb Tense

Directions: Write **PRES** for present tense, **PAST** for past tense, or **FUT** for future tense.

1. __FUT__ She will help him study.
2. __PAST__ She helped him study.
3. __PRES__ She helps him study.
4. __PAST__ She promised she would help him study.

Directions: Write the past-tense form of each verb.

1. cry   cried
2. sigh   sighed
3. hurry   hurried
4. pop   popped

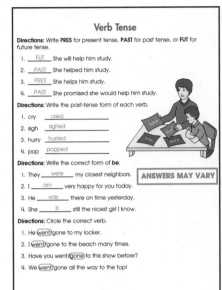

Directions: Write the correct form of **be**.

1. They __were__ my closest neighbors.
2. I __am__ very happy for you today.
3. He __was__ there on time yesterday.
4. She __is__ still the nicest girl I know.

ANSWERS MAY VARY

Directions: Circle the correct verb.

1. He (went)/gone to my locker.
2. I (went)/gone to the beach many times.
3. Have you went/(gone) to this show before?
4. We (went)/gone all the way to the top!

Page 81

Verb Tense

Directions: Read each sentence below. Underline the verbs. Above each verb, write whether it is past, present, or future tense.

Example: The crowd was booing the referee. *(past)*

1. Sally will compete on the balance beam. *(future)*
2. Matt marches with the band. *(present)*
3. Nick is marching, too. *(present)*
4. The geese swooped down to the pond. *(past)*
5. Dad will fly home tomorrow. *(future)*
6. They were looking for a new book. *(past)*
7. Presently, they are going to the garden. *(present)*
8. The children will pick the ripe vegetables. *(future)*
9. Grandmother canned the green beans. *(past)*

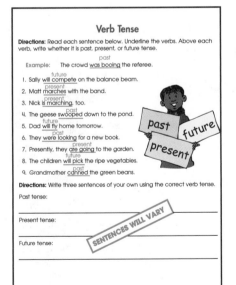

Directions: Write three sentences of your own using the correct verb tense.

Past tense:
_____

Present tense:
_____

Future tense:
_____

SENTENCES WILL VARY

Page 82

Verbs: Present, Past, and Future Tense

The **present tense** of a verb tells what is happening now.

Examples: I **am** happy.   I **run** fast.

The **past tense** of a verb tells what has already happened.

Examples: I **was** happy.   I **ran** fast.

The **future tense** of a verb refers to what is going to happen. The word **will** usually comes before the future tense of a verb.

Examples: I **will be** happy.   I **will run** fast.

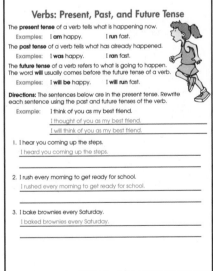

Directions: The sentences below are in the present tense. Rewrite each sentence using the past and future tenses of the verb.

Example: I think of you as my best friend.
I thought of you as my best friend.
I will think of you as my best friend.

1. I hear you coming up the steps.
I heard you coming up the steps.
_____

2. I rush every morning to get ready for school.
I rushed every morning to get ready for school.
_____

3. I bake brownies every Saturday.
I baked brownies every Saturday.
_____

Page 83

Verbs: Present, Past, and Future Tense

Directions: Read each sentence below. Write **PRES** if the sentence is in the present tense. Write **PAST** if the sentence is in the past tense. Write **FUT** if the sentence is in the future tense.

Example: __FUT__ I will be thrilled to accept the award.

1. __FUT__ Will you go with me to the dentist?
2. __PAST__ I thought he looked familiar!
3. __PAST__ They ate every single slice of pizza.
4. __PRES__ I run myself ragged sometimes.
5. __PRES__ Do you think this project is worthwhile?
6. __PAST__ No one has been able to repair the broken plate.
7. __PRES__ Thoughtful gifts are always nice.
8. __PAST__ I like the way he sang!
9. __FUT__ With a voice like that, he will go a long way.
10. __PRES__ I hope that they visit soon.
11. __PAST__ I wanted that coat very much.
12. __FUT__ She will be happy to take your place.
13. __PRES__ Everyone thinks the test will be easy.
14. __PRES__ Collecting stamps is her favorite hobby.

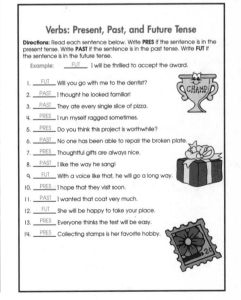

Adjectives

Adjectives are words that tell more about nouns, such as a **happy** child, a **cold** day, or a **hard** problem. Adjectives can tell **how many** (**one** airplane) or **which one** (**those** shoes).

Directions: The nouns are in bold letters. Circle the adjectives that describe the nouns.

Example: Some people have (unusual) **pets**.

1. Some people keep (wild) **animals**, like lions and bears.
2. (These) **pets** need special care.
3. (These) **animals** want to be free.
4. Even (small) **animals** can be difficult to care for if they are wild.
5. Raccoons and squirrels are not (tame) **pets**.
6. Never touch a (wild) **animal** that may be sick.

Directions: Finish the story below by writing your own adjectives. Use your imagination.

My Cat

My cat is a very _____ animal. She has _____ and _____ fur. Her favorite _____ ball.

She has _____ has a _____ tail. She has a _____ and _____ whiskers. I think she is the _____ cat in the world!

ANSWERS WILL VARY

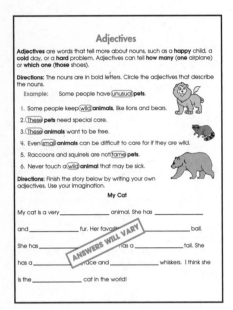

Page 84

Describing Words: Adjectives

A word that **describes** a noun is called an **adjective**. Adjectives tell what something is like. Fill in each blank below using an adjective from the Word Bank.

Word Bank
tiny   lumpy   pink   spotted   scary

Although the diamond was __tiny__, it sparkled like a huge spotlight.

"This bed is really uncomfortable. It is too __lumpy__!" said Max.

The __scary__ monster in my living room was only a dream.

The __spotted__ black and white dog is called a Dalmatian.

"__Pink__ is my favorite color!" said the princess.

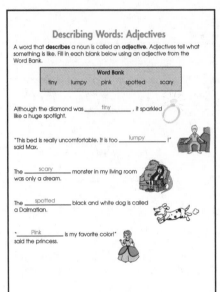

Page 85

Describing Words: Adjectives

A word that **describes** a noun is called an **adjective**.

Directions: Finish each sentence below using the adjectives from the Word Bank.

Word Bank
black   ugly   thousands   soft   expensive   hairy

The __soft__ mattress was very __expensive__ to buy because it was made of __thousands__ of downy feathers.

The __black__, __hairy__ spider was so __ugly__ that everybody was afraid to look at it. All it really needed was a haircut!

Directions: Finish each sentence below using the adjectives from the Word Bank.

Word Bank
hungry   delicate   loud   beautiful   tall   scary

Brown bears can be very __scary__ when they are __hungry__. They stand up __tall__ and let out __loud__ growls.

Roses are __delicate__ flowers and quite __beautiful__. Their petals feel like smooth velvet.

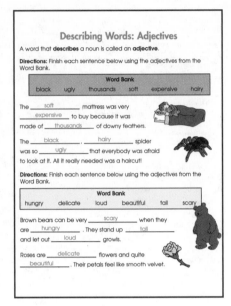

Page 86

Adjectives

Adjectives can tell the color, size, and number of the nouns they describe.

Directions: Look at the pictures. Then, complete the charts.

Noun	What Color?	What Size?	What Number?
flowers	red	small	two

Noun	What Color?	What Size?	What Number?
elephants	gray	large	two

Noun	What Color?	What Size?	What Number?
turtles	green	small	four

Noun	What Color?	What Size?	What Number?
tree	green	large	one

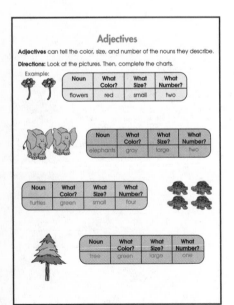

Page 87

Adjectives

Adjectives are describing words. They tell **how many**, **what kind**, or **which one**. When you use adjectives in your writing, you are making the sentences clearer and more interesting.

Example: The car speeds away.
The **sleek**, **red** car speeds away.

Directions: Use words from the Word Bank to make the story below more interesting.

Word Bank
beautiful   magical   pointy   fat   cruel   huge   wonderful   silly   fantastic   fun   blue   cold   funny   exciting   shy   rusty   strong   tiny   sweet

Once upon a time, there was a _____ princess who wore a _____ hat. She lived in _____ castle with her _____ ess was bored. "There is nothing to do," _____ princess complained. She wandered of _____ garden in search of adventure. "What _____ is I see?" she cried. There was a _____ box next to a _____ tree. The princess opened the lid to find a _____ cloak. "This is a _____ cloak!" she exclaimed. But when she slipped it on, the _____ princess vanished!

ANSWERS WILL VARY

Page 88

Adjectives

Adjectives are words that describe nouns by telling **what kind**, **how many**, or **which one**.

Examples: **ten-thousand tiny**, **black** tarantulas
talented chefs
tall, **shiny** skyscrapers

Directions: Underline the adjectives that describe each noun listed below.

1. a <u>bright</u>, <u>red</u> fire engine
2. <u>four</u> <u>awesome</u> firemen
3. a <u>tall</u>, <u>wooden</u> ladder
4. <u>two</u> <u>black-and-white</u> dalmations
5. a <u>soft</u> bed
6. a <u>skinny</u> fire pole
7. a <u>white</u> gazebo
8. the <u>ten</u> members of the band
9. a <u>red-and-white</u> banner
10. <u>magnificent</u> fireworks

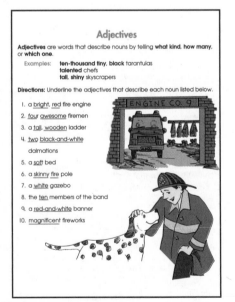

Page 89

Page 90

Adjectives

Adjectives tell which one, how many, or what kind.

Example: **These three red** apples.

Directions: Underline the nouns in each sentence below. Circle the adjectives that describe the nouns. Then, write each adjective that you circled in the correct category.

1. The lovely, pink flower has five blossoms.
2. These white roses have a sweet fragrance.
3. Each flower has several dainty petals.
4. The refreshing aroma of the sweet-scented lavender filled the air.
5. These five yellow sunflowers are tall plants.

Which one?	What kind?	How many?
1. the	lovely	five
	pink	
2. these	white	
a	sweet	
3. each	dainty	several
4. the	refreshing	
the	sweet-scented	
5. these	yellow	five
	tall	

Page 91

Adjectives

Adjectives are words that describe nouns by telling **what kind, how many,** or **which one.**

Directions: Write three adjectives for each noun below. Do not use an adjective more than once. The first one is done for you.

book	foot	house
long		
good		
short		
car	chips	cloud
butterflies	shoes	flute
clown	flowers	pizza

ANSWERS WILL VARY

Page 92

Adjectives

Directions: Underline the adjectives in the story.

The Best Soup I Ever Had

I woke up one cold winter morning and decided to make a delicious pot of hot vegetable soup. First, I put sweet white onions in the big gray pot. Then, I added orange carrots and dark green broccoli. The broccoli looked just like tiny trees. I added fresh, juicy tomatoes and crisp potatoes next. I cooked the soup for a long, long time. This soup turned out to be the best soup I ever had.

Directions: Rewrite two of the sentences from the story. Substitute your own adjectives for the words that you underlined.

1. _____

2. _____

ANSWERS WILL VARY

Page 93

Adjectives

Adjectives tell more about nouns. Adjectives are describing words.

Examples: **scary** animals   **bright** glow   **wet** frog

Directions: Add at least two adjectives to each sentence below. Use your own words or words from the Word Bank.

Word Bank						
pale	soft	sticky	burning	furry	glistening	peaceful
faint	shivering	slippery	gleaming	gentle	foggy	tangled

Example: The stripe was blue.
The wide stripe was light blue.

1. The frog had eyes.

2. The house was a sight.

3. A boy heard a noise.

4. The girl tripped over a toad.

5. A tiger ran through the room.

6. They saw a glow in the window.

7. A pan was sitting on the stove.

8. The boys were eating french fries.

ANSWERS WILL VARY

Page 94

Adjectives

Adjectives tell a noun's size, color, shape, texture, taste, brightness, darkness, personality, sound, and so on.

Examples: **color** — red, yellow, green, black
size — small, large, huge, tiny
shape — round, square, rectangular, oval
texture — rough, smooth, soft, scaly
brightness — glistening, shimmering, dull, pale
personality — gentle, grumpy, happy, sad

Directions: Follow the instructions below.

1. Look at an apple, orange, or other piece of fruit. Write adjectives that describe its size, color, shape, and texture.

2. Take a bite of fruit. Write adjectives that describe its taste, texture, and smell.

3. Use the adjectives from above to write a cinquain about your fruit. A **cinquain** is a five-line poem. See the form and sample poem below.

Form:	Line 1 — noun	**Example:**	Apple
	Line 2 — two adjectives		red, smooth
	Line 3 — three sounds		cracking, smacking, slurping
	Line 4 — four-word phrase		tastes sour and delicious
	Line 5 — noun		Apple

ANSWERS WILL VARY

Page 95

Adjectives

Directions: Finish each sentence below with the correct adjective from the Word Bank.

Word Bank					
polite	careless	neat	shy	selfish	thoughtful

1. Someone who is quiet and needs some time to make new friends is _____shy_____.

2. A person who says "please" and "thank you" is _____polite_____.

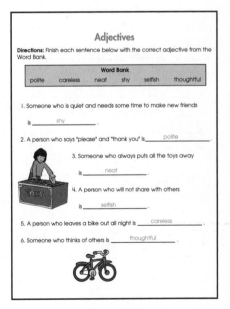

3. Someone who always puts all the toys away is _____neat_____.

4. A person who will not share with others is _____selfish_____.

5. A person who leaves a bike out all night is _____careless_____.

6. Someone who thinks of others is _____thoughtful_____.

Complete Book of Grammar and Punctuation
Grades 3–4

Adjectives: Explaining Sentences

Directions: Use a word from the Word Bank to tell about a person in each picture below. Then, write a sentence that explains why you chose that word.

Word Bank					
polite	neat	careless	shy	selfish	thoughtful

The word I picked: _____

I chose this word because . . .

_____

_____

The word I picked: _____

I chose this word because . . .

ANSWERS WILL VARY

The word I picked: _____

I chose this word because . . .

Page 96

Adjectives

Directions: Look at each picture. Then, add adjectives to each sentence. Use colors, numbers, words from the Word Bank, and any other words you need to describe each picture.

Word Bank		
polite	neat	careless
shy	selfish	thoughtful

Example: The boy shared his pencil.

The polite boy shared his red pencil.

The girl dropped her coat.

The boy played with cars.

ANSWERS WILL VARY

The boy put books away.

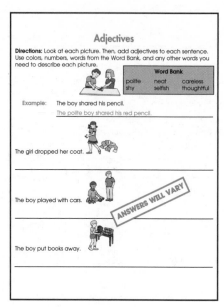

Page 97

Adjectives: Create a Word Puzzle

Directions: Make your own word puzzle! Write the words from the Word Bank in the puzzle below. Write some words across and others from top to bottom. Make some words cross each other. Fill the extra squares with other letters. See if someone else can find the words from the Word Bank in your puzzle!

Word Bank					
polite	neat	careless	shy	selfish	thoughtful

Example: Your puzzle will look like the one below. It has two of the words from the Word Bank in it. Can you find them?

l	a	e	n	x	f	y	h
c	a	r	e	l	e	s	s
y	u	a	a	r	n	m	z
g	w	i	t	b	l	v	s

Now, make your own puzzle!

PUZZLES WILL VARY

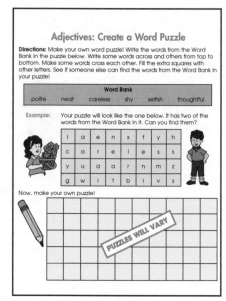

Page 98

Adjectives

Adjectives describe nouns. They tell **how many**, **what kind**, or **which one**.

Examples: **seven** children, **purple** flowers, **that** toy

Directions: Write three adjectives to describe each noun.

puppy	desert
storm	city
ANSWERS WILL VARY	
beetle	tulip
computer	snow

Page 99

Adjectives: Using the Five Senses

When you are writing, you can use your five senses to help you describe something. Think about what you might see, hear, smell, taste, and feel.

Example: **See:**   shiny, round

Taste: spicy, sweet

Hear: squeaky, roaring

Feel: sharp, prickly

Smell: rotten, smoky

Directions: Write two describing words for each noun. Use your five senses to help you.

1. strawberry   _____
2. pony   _____
3. sand   _____
4. leather coat   _____
5. golf ball   _____
6. bicycle chain   _____
7. paper   _____

ANSWERS WILL VARY

Directions: Now, use two of the nouns and describing words from above to write a descriptive sentence.

ANSWERS WILL VARY

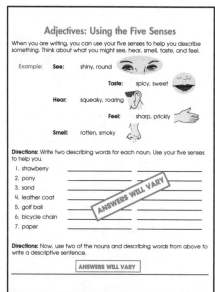

Page 100

Adjectives Plus "er"

The suffix **er** is often added to adjectives to compare two things.

Examples: My feet are **large**.
Your feet are **larger** than my feet.

When an adjective ends with one consonant, double the final consonant before adding **er**. When a word ends in two or more consonants, add **er**.

Examples: big = bigger (single consonant)
bold = bolder (two consonants)

When an adjective ends in **y**, change the **y** to **i** before adding **er**.

Examples: easy = easier
greasy = greasier
breezy = breezier

Directions: Use the correct rule to add **er** to the words below.

Example: fast   _underline faster_

1. thin	_thinner_	10. fat	_fatter_
2. long	_longer_	11. poor	_poorer_
3. few	_fewer_	12. juicy	_juicier_
4. ugly	_uglier_	13. early	_earlier_
5. silly	_sillier_	14. clean	_cleaner_
6. busy	_busier_	15. thick	_thicker_
7. grand	_grander_	16. creamy	_creamier_
8. lean	_leaner_	17. deep	_deeper_
9. young	_younger_	18. lazy	_lazier_

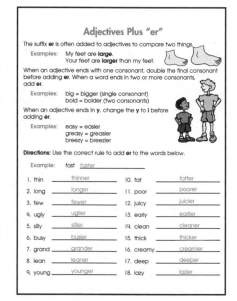

Page 101

Adjectives: Making Comparisons

Adjectives that compare two things usually end in **er**.

Example: Ants are **smaller** than ladybugs.

Adjectives that compare three or more things usually end in **est**.

Example: February is the **shortest** month of the year.

Directions: Underline the adjective that best completes each sentence.

1. Margery is the (stronger, <u>strongest</u>) girl in third grade.
2. The blue sailboat is (<u>faster</u>, fastest) than the red sailboat.
3. July is usually (<u>hotter</u>, hottest) than January.
4. Which instrument is the (louder, <u>loudest</u>) one in the orchestra?
5. Turtles are (<u>slower</u>, slowest) than rabbits.
6. Travis is the (funnier, <u>funniest</u>) student in our class.
7. Your slice of cake is (<u>thicker</u>, thickest) than mine.
8. Frogs jump (<u>higher</u>, highest) than mice.
9. Mount Everest is the (taller, <u>tallest</u>) mountain in the world.
10. The summer solstice is the (longer, <u>longest</u>) day of the year.

Directions: Write a sentence for each adjective listed below. Use the adjective to compare two or more things.

1. short _____
2. bright _____ ANSWERS WILL VARY
3. smart _____
4. cold _____

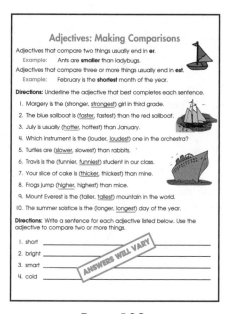

Page 102

Adding "er" and "est" to Adjectives

Directions: Circle the correct adjective for each sentence.

Example: Of all the students in the gym, her voice was the (louder, (loudest)).

1. "I can tell you are ((busier) busiest) than I am," he said to the librarian.
2. If you and Carl stand back to back, I can see which one is ((taller) tallest).
3. She is the (kinder, (kindest)) teacher in the whole building.
4. Wow! That is the (bigger, (biggest)) pumpkin I have ever seen!
5. I believe your flashlight is ((brighter), brightest) than mine.
6. "This is the (cleaner, (cleanest)) your room has been in a long time," Mother said.
7. The leaves on that plant are ((prettier), prettiest) than the ones on the window sill.

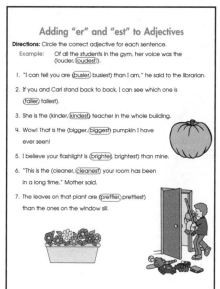

Page 103

Adjectives That Compare

Add **er** to most **adjectives** when comparing two nouns. Add **est** to most adjectives when comparing three or more nouns.

Example: The forecaster said this winter is **colder** than last winter. It is the **coldest** winter on record.

Directions: Finish each sentence with the correct form of the adjective.

1. The weather map showed that the ___coldest___ place of all was Marquette, Michigan. (cold)
2. The ___warmest___ city of all was Phoenix, Arizona. (warm)
3. Does San Diego get ___hotter___ than San Francisco? (hot)
4. The ___deepest___ snow of all fell in the Twin Cities. (deep)
5. The snowfall was two inches ___deeper___ than in Buffalo. (deep)
6. The ___windiest___ place of all was Chicago, Illinois. (windy)
7. The ___strongest___ winds of all blew there. (strong)
8. The ___foggiest___ city in the U.S. was Bangor, Maine. (foggy)
9. Seattle was the ___rainiest___ of all the cities. (rainy)
10. It is usually ___rainier___ in Seattle than in Portland. (rainy)

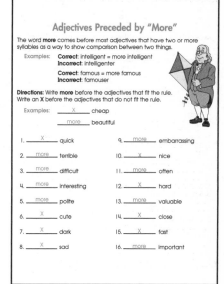

Page 104

Adjectives Plus "est"

The ending **est** is often added to adjectives to compare more than two things.

Example: My glass is **full**.
Your glass is **fuller**.
His glass is **fullest**.

When an adjective ends with one consonant, you usually double the final consonant before adding **est**.

Examples: big = biggest (short vowel)
steep = steepest (long vowel)

When an adjective ends in **y**, change the **y** to **i** before adding **est**.

Example: easy = easiest

Directions: Use the correct rule to add **est** to the words below.

Example: thin ___thinnest___

1. skinny ___skinniest___
2. cheap ___cheapest___
3. busy ___busiest___
4. loud ___loudest___
5. kind ___kindest___
6. dreamy ___dreamiest___
7. ugly ___ugliest___
8. pretty ___prettiest___
9. early ___earliest___
10. big ___biggest___
13. silly ___silliest___
14. tall ___tallest___
15. quick ___quickest___
16. red ___reddest___
17. happy ___happiest___
18. high ___highest___
19. wet ___wettest___
20. clean ___cleanest___

Page 105

Adjectives Plus "er" or "More"

Directions: Add the word or words needed in each sentence.

1. I thought the book was ___more interesting___ than the movie. (interesting)
2. Do you want to carry this box? It is ___lighter___ than the one you have now. (light)
3. I noticed you are moving ___slower___ this morning. Does your ankle still bother you? (slow)
4. She stuck out her lower lip and said, "Your ice-cream cone is ___bigger___ than mine!" (big)
5. Mom said my room was ___cleaner___ than it has been in a long time. (clean)

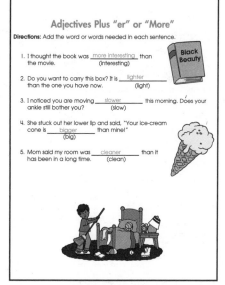

Page 106

Adjectives Preceded by "More"

The word **more** comes before most adjectives that have two or more syllables as a way to show comparison between two things.

Examples: **Correct:** intelligent = more intelligent
Incorrect: intelligenter

Correct: famous = more famous
Incorrect: famouser

Directions: Write **more** before the adjectives that fit the rule. Write an **X** before the adjectives that do not fit the rule.

Examples: ___X___ cheap
___more___ beautiful

1. ___X___ quick
2. ___more___ terrible
3. ___more___ difficult
4. ___more___ interesting
5. ___more___ polite
6. ___X___ cute
7. ___X___ dark
8. ___X___ sad
9. ___more___ embarrassing
10. ___X___ nice
11. ___more___ often
12. ___X___ hard
13. ___more___ valuable
14. ___X___ close
15. ___X___ fast
16. ___more___ important

Page 107

Adjectives Plus "est" or "Most"

Directions: Add the word or words needed to complete each sentence.

Example: The star over there is the ___brightest___ of all!
(bright)

1. "I believe this is the ___most delightful___ time I have ever had," said Mackenzie.
(delightful)

2. That game was the ___most exciting___ one of the whole year!
(exciting)

3. I think this tree has the ___greenest___ leaves.
(green)

4. We will need the ___sharpest___ knife you have.
(sharp)

5. Everyone agreed that your chocolate chip cookies were the ___most delicious___ of all.
(delicious)

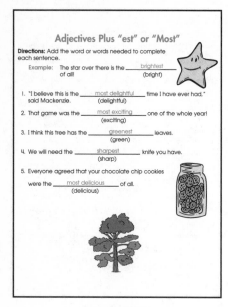

Page 108

Adjectives Plus "Most"

The word **most** comes before most adjectives that have two or more syllables as a way to show comparison between more than two things.

Examples:
Correct: intelligent = most intelligent
Incorrect: intelligentest

Correct: famous = most famous
Incorrect: famousest

Directions: Read the groups of sentences below. In the last sentence of each group, write the adjective with the word **most**.

Example: My uncle is intelligent.
My aunt is more intelligent.
My cousin is the _____ most intelligent

1. I am thankful.
My brother is more thankful.
My parents are the _____ most thankful

2. Your sister is polite.
Your brother is more polite.
You are the _____ most polite

3. The blouse was expensive.
The sweater was more expensive.
The coat was the _____ most expensive

4. The class was fortunate.
The teacher was more fortunate.
The principal was the _____ most fortunate

5. The cookies were delicious.
The cake was even more delicious.
The brownies were the _____ most delicious

6. That painting is beautiful.
The sculpture is more beautiful.
The finger painting is the _____ most beautiful

Page 109

Adjectives That Break the Rules

The adjectives **good** and **bad** do not follow the rules. Instead of using **er** and **est** or the words **more** and **most**, they use different spellings to compare two or more things.

good   better   best

Examples:
good — This is a **good** book.
better — My book is **better** than your book.
best — This is the **best** book I've ever read.

bad — The weather is **bad** today.
worse — The weather is **worse** today than yesterday.
worst — Today's weather is the **worst** of the winter.

Directions: Circle the form of the adjective that finishes each sentence.

1. This is the (bad, worse, (worst)) pizza I have ever eaten.
2. My shoes are in (bad, (worse) worst) condition than yours.
3. My grades are the (good, better, (best)) in the class.
4. Plastic cups make ((good), better, best) paint containers.
5. This tool is the (good, better, (best)) one I have.
6. The bumpy drive was a ((bad), worse, worst) one.
7. My brownies are (good, (better) best) than yours.
8. This is a ((bad), worse, worst) snowstorm.
9. This one looks even (good, (better) best) than that one.
10. My brother's room looks (bad, (worse) worst) than mine.

Page 110

Pronouns

Pronouns are words that are used in place of nouns.
Examples: he, she, it, they, him, them, her, him

Directions: Read each sentence. Write the pronoun that takes the place of each noun.

Example: The **monkey** dropped the banana. ___It___

1. **Dad** washed the car last night. — He
2. **Mary** and **David** took a walk in the park. — They
3. **Peggy** spent the night at her grandmother's house. — She
4. The **players** lost their game. — They
5. **Mike Van Meter** is a great soccer player. — He
6. The **parrot** can say five different words. — It
7. **Megan** wrote a story in class today. — She
8. They gave a party for **Teresa**. — Her
9. Everyone in the class was happy for **Ted**. — Him
10. The children petted the **giraffe**. — It
11. Linda put the **kittens** near the warm stove. — Them
12. **Gina** made a chocolate cake for my birthday. — She
13. **Pete** and **Matt** played baseball on the same team. — They
14. Give the books to **Herbie**. — Him

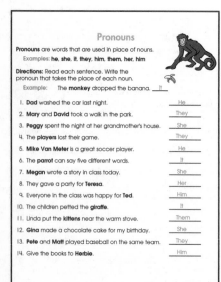

Page 111

Pronouns

Singular Pronouns				Plural Pronouns			
I	me	my	mine	we	us		our
you	your	yours		ours	you		your
he	she	him	her	yours	they		them
his	hers	it	its	their	theirs		

Directions: Underline the pronouns in each sentence.

1. Mom told <u>us</u> to wash <u>our</u> hands.
2. Did <u>you</u> go to the store?
3. <u>We</u> should buy <u>him</u> a present.
4. <u>I</u> called <u>you</u> about <u>their</u> party.
5. <u>Our</u> house had damage on <u>its</u> roof.
6. <u>They</u> want to give <u>you</u> a prize at <u>our</u> party.
7. <u>My</u> cat ate <u>my</u> sandwich.
8. <u>Your</u> coat looks like <u>his</u> coat.

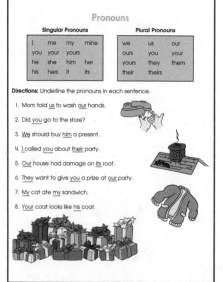

Page 112

Pronouns

A **pronoun** is a word that takes the place of a noun.
Example: Meg gave the ball to Dave.
He was glad to get **it**.

Directions: Read the sentences below. After each pronoun, write the word or words that the pronoun stands for.

Most penguins live near the South Pole. They (_penguins_) spend most of their time underwater searching for food. Penguins surface for air and get enough of it (___air___) to fill the air sacs throughout their bodies. These (_air sacs_) make it possible for them (_penguins_) to stay underwater for long periods of time.

Although penguins have wings, they (___wings___) are not used for flying. Their wings are like flippers. They (___wings___) are used for swimming.

Penguins feel best in very cold water but leave it (___water___) to nest and raise their young. A penguin's nest is very odd. It (___nest___) is simply a pile of stones on a rocky shore. The female lays one to three eggs. They (___eggs___) are chalky white. After a time, the female passes her eggs to the male. He (___male___) tucks them (___eggs___) into a skin flap under his body to keep them (___eggs___) warm. It (_skin flap_) is lined with thick, soft down. The parents take turns feeding the babies when they (___eggs___) hatch.

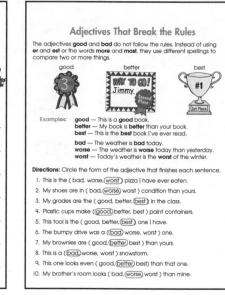

Page 113

Page 114

Nouns and Pronouns

Pronouns can be substituted for nouns that are repeated.

Example: Mother made the beds.
Then, ~~Mother~~ started the laundry.

The noun **Mother** is used in both sentences.
The pronoun **she** could be used in place
of **Mother** the second time.

Directions: Cross out nouns when they appear a second and/or third time.
Write a pronoun that could be used instead.

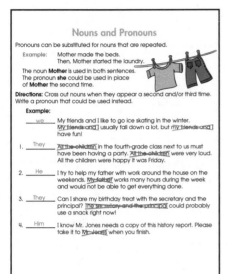

Example:

_we_ My friends and I like to go ice skating in the winter. ~~My friends and I~~ usually fall down a lot, but ~~my friends and I~~ have fun!

1. _They_ ~~All the children~~ in the fourth-grade class next to us must have been having a party. ~~All the children~~ were very loud. All the children were happy it was Friday.

2. _He_ I try to help my father with work around the house on the weekends. ~~My father~~ works many hours during the week and would not be able to get everything done.

3. _They_ Can I share my birthday treat with the secretary and the principal? ~~The secretary and the principal~~ could probably use a snack right now!

4. _Him_ I know Mr. Jones needs a copy of this history report. Please take it to ~~Mr. Jones~~ when you finish.

Page 115

Pronouns

A **pronoun** is a word that takes the place of a noun in a sentence.

Examples: I, my, mine, me
we, our, ours, us
you, your, yours
he, his, him
she, her, hers
it, its
they, their, theirs, them

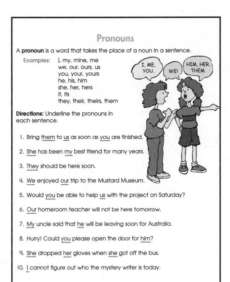

Directions: Underline the pronouns in each sentence.

1. Bring <u>them</u> to <u>us</u> as soon as <u>you</u> are finished.

2. <u>She</u> has been <u>my</u> best friend for many years.

3. <u>They</u> should be here soon.

4. <u>We</u> enjoyed <u>our</u> trip to the Mustard Museum.

5. Would <u>you</u> be able to help <u>us</u> with the project on Saturday?

6. <u>Our</u> homeroom teacher will not be here tomorrow.

7. <u>My</u> uncle said that <u>he</u> will be leaving soon for Australia.

8. Hurry! Could <u>you</u> please open the door for <u>him</u>?

9. <u>She</u> dropped <u>her</u> gloves when <u>she</u> got off the bus.

10. <u>I</u> cannot figure out who the mystery writer is today.

Page 116

Nouns and Pronouns

Directions: Cross out nouns when they appear a second or third time. Write a pronoun that could be used instead.

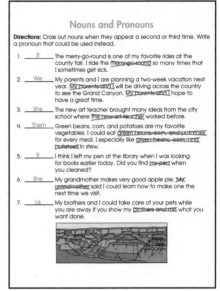

1. _It_ The merry-go-round is one of my favorite rides at the county fair. I ride the ~~merry-go-round~~ so many times that I sometimes get sick.

2. _We_ My parents and I are planning a two-week vacation next year. ~~My parents and I~~ will be driving across the country to see the Grand Canyon. ~~My parents and I~~ hope to have a great time.

3. _She_ The new art teacher brought many ideas from the city school where ~~the new art teacher~~ worked before.

4. _Them_ Green beans, corn, and potatoes are my favorite vegetables. I could eat ~~green beans, corn, and potatoes~~ for every meal. I especially like ~~green beans, corn, and potatoes~~ in stew.

5. _It_ I think I left my pen at the library when I was looking for books earlier today. Did you find ~~my pen~~ when you cleaned?

6. _She_ My grandmother makes very good apple pie. ~~My grandmother~~ said I could learn how to make one the next time we visit.

7. _Us_ My brothers and I could take care of your pets while you are away if you show my ~~brothers and me~~ what you want done.

Page 117

Pronoun Referents

A **pronoun referent** is the noun or nouns a pronoun refers to.

Example: **Green beans, corn,** and **potatoes** are my favorite vegetables. I could eat **them** for every meal.

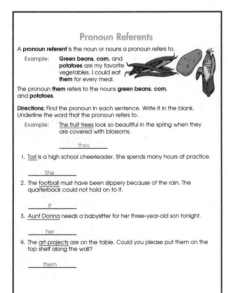

The pronoun **them** refers to the nouns **green beans, corn,** and **potatoes.**

Directions: Find the pronoun in each sentence. Write it in the blank. Underline the word that the pronoun refers to.

Example: The <u>fruit trees</u> look so beautiful in the spring when they are covered with blossoms.

they

1. <u>Tori</u> is a high school cheerleader. She spends many hours at practice.

She

2. The <u>football</u> must have been slippery because of the rain. The quarterback could not hold on to it.

_It_

3. <u>Aunt Donna</u> needs a babysitter for her three-year-old son tonight.

her

4. The <u>art projects</u> are on the table. Could you please put them on the top shelf along the wall?

them

Page 118

Pronoun Referents

Directions: Read each sentence carefully. Draw a line to connect each sentence to the correct pronoun.

1. All the teachers in our building said _____ could use a day off!

2. The whole cast spent a lot of time in rehearsals for the school play. _____ should go very well.

3. Uncle Mike is driving around in a very old car. I know _____ would like to buy a new one.

4. Mr. Barker is having some trouble programming that DVD player. Can you help _____?

5. There are too many books on the shelf. I know I cannot fit all of _____ into this small box.

6. Ms. Hart slipped on the bleachers at the football game. That is why_____ is using crutches.

him

It

they

she

them

he

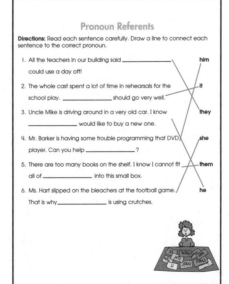

Page 119

Pronoun Referents

Directions: Find the pronoun in each sentence. Write it in the blank. Underline the word that the pronoun refers to.

1. Did <u>Aaron</u> see the movie _Titanic_? Jay thought it was a very good movie.

_It_

2. Maysie can help you with the spelling words now, <u>Tasha</u>.

you

3. The new <u>tennis coach</u> said to call him after 6:00 tonight.

him

4. <u>Jim, John, and Jason</u> called to say they would be later than planned.

they

5. <u>Mrs. Burns</u> enjoyed the cake her class made for the surprise party.

her

6. The <u>children</u> are waiting outside. Ask Josh to take the pinwheels out to them.

them

7. <u>Mrs. Taylor</u> said to go on ahead because she will be late.

she

8. The <u>whole team</u> must sit on the bus until the driver gives us permission to get off.

_us_

9. <u>Dad</u> said the umbrella did a poor job of keeping the rain off him.

him

10. The <u>umbrella</u> was blowing around too much. That is probably why it did not do a good job.

_It_

Page 120

Possessive Pronouns

Possessive pronouns show ownership.

Example: **his** hat, **her** shoes, **our** dog

We can use the pronouns **my, our, you, his, her, its,** and **their** before a noun.

Example: That is **my** bike.

We can use the pronouns **mine, yours, ours, his, hers, theirs,** and **its** without a noun.

Example: That is mine.

Directions: Rewrite each sentence using a pronoun instead of the word or words in bold letters.

Example: My **dog's** bowl is brown. **Its** bowl is brown.

1. That is **Lisa's** book.
   That is hers.
2. This is **my pencil**.
   This is mine.
3. This hat is **your hat**.
   This hat is yours.
4. Fifi is **Kevin's** cat.
   Fifi is his cat.
5. That beautiful house is **our home**.
   That beautiful house is ours.
6. The **gerbil's** cage is too small.
   Its cage is too small.

Page 121

Possessive Pronouns

A **possessive pronoun** takes the place of a possessive noun.

Examples: Belinda's bicycle is red. Shane and Bob's cat is gray.
Her bicycle is red. **Their** cat is gray.

Possessive Pronouns						
my	your	her	his	its	our	their

Directions: Draw a line from each possessive noun to the correct possessive pronoun.

1. Leticia's — their
2. the boat's — our
3. the children's — their
4. the class' — his
5. my friends' and my — its
6. Matthew's — her

Directions: Write a sentence using each possessive pronoun.

1. _____
2. _____
3. _____ ANSWERS WILL VARY
4. _____
5. _____
6. _____
7. _____

Page 122

Possessive Pronoun

A **possessive pronoun** shows ownership. It can replace a possessive noun. Some possessive pronouns can be used before a noun and some can be used alone.

Examples: Used before a noun: **my, your, its, her, his, our,** and **their.**
Used alone: **mine, yours, his, hers, yours,** and **theirs.**

Directions: Read each pair of sentences. If the correct possessive pronoun is used in the second sentence, circle **Right.** If it is not, circle **Wrong.**

1. An archaeologist studies people's remains.
   An archaeologist studies **their** remains. (Right) Wrong
2. The important discovery was the scientist's.
   The important discovery was **hers**. (Right) Wrong
3. She found part of a potter's wheel.
   She found part of **their** wheel. Right (Wrong)
4. Other treasures were found on the scientist's dig.
   Other treasures were found on **their** dig. Right (Wrong)
5. The pottery shards belonged to all of us on the crew.
   The pottery shards were **ours**. (Right) Wrong
6. Experts say the Pharoah's tomb took years to build.
   Experts say **their** tomb took years to build. Right (Wrong)
7. A Pharoah's tomb was said to be cursed.
   Its tomb was said to be cursed. Right (Wrong)
8. One theory about the mummy's curse is in the book.
   One theory about **its** curse is in the book. (Right) Wrong
9. The scientist's belief is that it is just superstition.
   Her belief is that it is just superstition. (Right) Wrong

Page 123

Possessive Pronouns

Possessive Pronouns show ownership. **My, mine, your, yours, his, her, hers, our, ours, their,** and **theirs** are possessive pronouns.

Example: **His** house was painted red and black.

Directions: Underline the possessive pronouns in each sentence of the story.

When I first saw this island, I knew it was as close to home as I could get. When the ten monks decided to join me, it became <u>our</u> home. Although we built all of these Chinese-looking buildings together, most were <u>theirs</u>. One hut was <u>ours</u> to share as a place to meditate and eat <u>our</u> meals. <u>Their</u> other buildings were used for living. One monk's hut was unusual. He had painted zebra stripes all along <u>his</u> walls. The monks kept <u>their</u> gardens around <u>their</u> living areas. <u>My</u> house was also built like the houses in China. Some of <u>our</u> other living quarters were more like the huts of African villages. We all lived together, sharing <u>our</u> food and sharing what was <u>mine, theirs,</u> and <u>ours</u>.

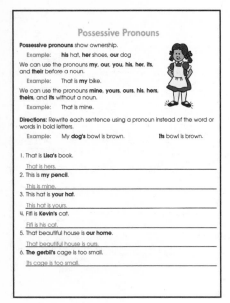

Page 124

Possessive Pronouns

A **possessive pronoun** is a pronoun that shows ownership. Possessive pronouns include **my, mine, your, yours, his, her, hers, our, ours, its, their,** and **theirs.**

Example: **My** car runs faster than **yours.**
Their friend went to the zoo.

Directions: Read the article. Underline each possessive pronoun.

There are many kinds of sharks, and <u>their</u> sizes vary greatly. They can be from six-inches to over forty-feet long. A shark does not have many bones in <u>its</u> body. <u>Its</u> body is quite different from <u>your</u> body. Much of <u>its</u> body is made of cartilage, which is similar to the material in <u>your</u> nose.

<u>Our</u> fear of sharks is well-founded. <u>Their</u> behavior is unpredictable. Many fishermen have had <u>their</u> catch eaten by sharks. For millions of years, the seas have been <u>their</u> domain. <u>Their</u> time on Earth began long before <u>our</u> species appeared here.

Directions: Substitute a possessive pronoun for the word or words in parentheses.

1. (A shark's) _Its_ hearing is very sharp.
2. Sharks can hear (divers') _their_ sounds underwater.
3. (Dan's) _His_ friend wrote a report about sharks.
4. (Janie's) _Her_ report gave us interesting facts.
5. the report used (Dan's and Tim's) _their_ pictures.
6. (Janie's) _Her_ report was more interesting than (Jack's) _his_ .

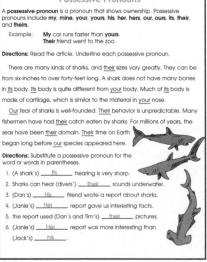

Page 125

Subject pronouns

The subject of a sentence can be a noun or a **pronoun.** A pronoun can take the place of a noun. **Subject pronouns** include **I, you, he, she, it, we,** and **they.**

Examples: **The mayor** closed the office door.
He closed the office door.

Directions: Write the correct pronoun above the subject noun in each sentence.

1. Andrew is Mayor Sneak's administrative _He_ assistant.
2. Mayor Sneak has a huge computer. _He_
3. The door to Mayor Sneak's office was closed. _It_
4. The custodians swept the floor. _They_
5. My class waited for a tour. _We_
6. Mayor Sneak sneaked out. _He_
7. Andrew met us instead. _He_
8. Andrew and our class had a good time on our tour. _We_

Subject Pronouns

Subject Pronouns can take the place of the subject in a sentence. The **subject pronouns** are: **I**, **you**, **he**, **she**, **it**, **we**, **you**, and **they**.

Examples: **My brother** washed the car.
He washed the car.

Directions: Fill in the blanks with subject pronouns.

Dear Mayor Sneak,

___I___ would like to announce that a woman in your office is taking office supplies home. ___She___ has taken paper clips and staples. Last Tuesday, ___I___ saw this person put a large item in a box. ___It___ looked very heavy.

Later, when everything was dark and quiet, ___I___ heard a growl. A female cat was growling as if ___she___ wanted to warn someone of an intruder. The security guard was asleep in his chair by the door. ___He___ did not see the thief escape with the large item in the box.

___You___ may want to look into this matter.

Sincerely,
A Silent Observer

Page 126

Object Pronouns

Object pronouns take the place of the person, place, or thing that is the object of the sentence. Object pronouns include: **me, you, her, him, it, us,** and **them**.

Example: He wanted to find **a dinosaur**.
He wanted to find **it**.

Directions: The objects in each sentence is underlined. Write the pronoun that can replace the object on the line following each sentence.

1. Henry turned the duty of standing guard over to <u>Maya</u>.
   ___her___

2. Everyone wanted to thank <u>Chuck</u> for making the dinner.
   ___him___

3. After we cleaned the dishes, we gathered around the fire to listen to <u>Hillary</u> sing.
   ___her___

4. We were just about ready for bed when we heard <u>a strange noise</u>.
   ___it___

5. Several of the crew raced to the river and saw <u>a large, furry shape</u>.
   ___it___

6. But the mysterious visitor was too quick for most of <u>the crew</u>.
   ___them___

7. Jason ran after <u>the mysterious creature</u>.
   ___it___

Page 127

Subject and Object Pronouns

A **pronoun** is a word that takes the place of a noun.
A **subject pronoun** takes the place of a noun in the subject of a sentence.
An **object pronoun** takes the place of a noun that follows a verb or a word like **to, from, of, at, with,** or **by**.

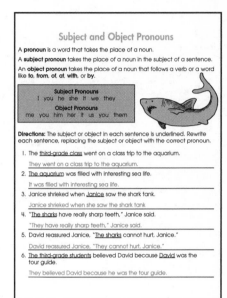

Subject Pronouns
I   you   he   she   it   we   they
Object Pronouns
me   you   him   her   it   us   you   them

Directions: The subject or object in each sentence is underlined. Rewrite each sentence, replacing the subject or object with the correct pronoun.

1. The <u>third-grade class</u> went on a class trip to the aquarium.
   They went on a class trip to the aquarium.

2. <u>The aquarium</u> was filled with interesting sea life.
   It was filled with interesting sea life.

3. Janice shrieked when <u>Janice</u> saw the shark tank.
   Janice shrieked when she saw the shark tank.

4. "<u>The sharks</u> have really sharp teeth," Janice said.
   "They have really sharp teeth," Janice said.

5. David reassured Janice, "<u>The sharks</u> cannot hurt, Janice."
   David reassured Janice, "They cannot hurt, Janice."

6. <u>The third-grade students</u> believed David because <u>David</u> was the tour guide.
   They believed David because he was the tour guide.

Page 128

Subject and Object Pronouns

I and **we** are **subject pronouns. Me** and **us** are **object pronouns.**

Examples: **subject pronoun:** Mark and **I** are on our way to the park.
We just love to launch rockets!

object pronoun: Will Sara come with **me**?
Please feel welcome to join **us**.

Directions: Choose the correct pronoun to complete each sentence. Write it in the blank.

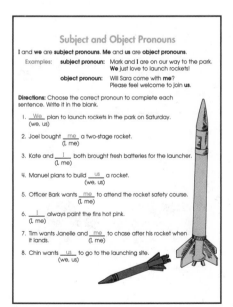

1. ___We___ plan to launch rockets in the park on Saturday.
   (we, us)

2. Joel bought ___me___ a two-stage rocket.
   (I, me)

3. Kate and ___I___ both brought fresh batteries for the launcher.
   (I, me)

4. Manuel plans to build ___us___ a rocket.
   (we, us)

5. Officer Bark wants ___me___ to attend the rocket safety course.
   (I, me)

6. ___I___ always paint the fins hot pink.
   (I, me)

7. Tim wants Janelle and ___me___ to chase after his rocket when it lands.
   (I, me)

8. Chin wants ___us___ to go to the launching site.
   (we, us)

Page 129

Subject and Object Pronouns

Pronouns are words that take the place of nouns in a sentence. Some pronouns take the place of subjects. Some take the place of objects.

Examples: **subject pronouns:** I, you, he, she, it, we, you, they
object pronouns: me, you, him, her, it, us, you, them

Directions: Write the correct subject or object pronoun above each underlined noun.

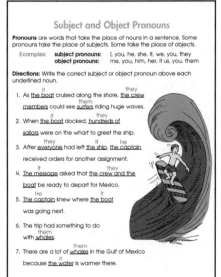

1. As <u>the boat</u> cruised along the shore, <u>the crew</u> ^{it} ^{they}
   <u>members</u> could see <u>surfers</u> riding huge waves. ^{them}

2. When <u>the boat</u> docked, <u>hundreds of</u> ^{it} ^{they}
   <u>sailors</u> were on the wharf to greet the ship.

3. After <u>everyone</u> had left <u>the ship</u>, <u>the captain</u> ^{they} ^{it} ^{he}
   received orders for another assignment.

4. <u>The message</u> asked that <u>the crew and the</u> ^{It} ^{they}
   <u>boat</u> be ready to depart for Mexico.

5. <u>The captain</u> knew where <u>the boat</u> ^{He} ^{it}
   was going next.

6. The trip had something to do ^{them}
   with <u>whales</u>.

7. There are a lot of <u>whales</u> in the Gulf of Mexico ^{them}
   because <u>the water</u> is warmer there. ^{it}

Page 130

Adverbs

Adverbs are words that tell **when, where,** or **how.**

Adverbs of time tell when.

Example:
The train left **yesterday**.
Yesterday is an adverb of time. It tells when the train left.

Adverbs of place tell where.

Example:
The girl walked **away**.
Away is an adverb of place. It tells where the girl walked.

Adverbs of manner tell how.

Example:
The boy walked **quickly**.
Quickly is an adverb of manner. It tells how the boy walked.

Directions: Write the adverb from each sentence in the first column. In the second column, write whether it is an adverb of time, place, or manner.

Example:
The family ate downstairs. ___downstairs___ ___place___

1. The relatives laughed loudly. ___loudly___ ___manner___
2. We will finish tomorrow. ___tomorrow___ ___time___
3. The snowstorm will stop soon. ___soon___ ___time___
4. She sings beautifully! ___beautifully___ ___manner___
5. The baby slept soundly. ___soundly___ ___manner___
6. The elevator stopped suddenly. ___suddenly___ ___manner___
7. Does the plane leave today? ___today___ ___time___
8. The phone call came yesterday. ___yesterday___ ___time___

Page 131

Adverbs of Time

Directions: Choose a word or group of words from the Word Bank that finishes each sentence.

Word Bank	
in 2 weeks	last winter
next week	at the end of the day
soon	right now
2 days ago	tonight

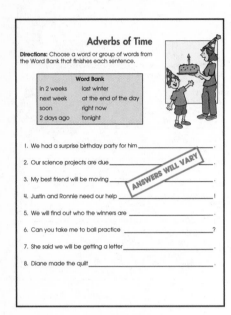

1. We had a surprise birthday party for him _____

2. Our science projects are due _____

3. My best friend will be moving _____

4. Justin and Ronnie need our help _____!

5. We will find out who the winners are _____

6. Can you take me to ball practice _____?

7. She said we will be getting a letter _____

8. Diane made the quilt _____

ANSWERS WILL VARY

Page 132

Adverbs of Place

Directions: Choose one word from the Word Bank to finish each sentence. Make sure the adverb you choose makes sense with the rest of the sentence.

Word Bank			
inside	upstairs	below	everywhere
home	somewhere	outside	there

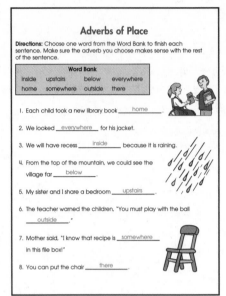

1. Each child took a new library book _____home_____

2. We looked _____everywhere_____ for his jacket.

3. We will have recess _____inside_____ because it is raining.

4. From the top of the mountain, we could see the village far _____below_____.

5. My sister and I share a bedroom _____upstairs_____.

6. The teacher warned the children, "You must play with the ball _____outside_____."

7. Mother said, "I know that recipe is _____somewhere_____ in this file box!"

8. You can put the chair _____there_____.

Page 133

Adverbs of Manner

Directions: Choose a word from the Word Bank to finish each sentence. Make sure the adverb you choose makes sense with the rest of the sentence. You will use one word twice.

Word Bank					
quickly	carefully	loudly	easily	carelessly	slowly

ANSWERS MAY VARY BUT MAY INCLUDE...

1. The scouts crossed the old bridge _____carefully_____.

2. We watched the turtle move _____slowly_____ across the yard.

3. Everyone completed the math test _____easily_____.

4. The quarterback scampered _____quickly_____ down the sideline.

5. The mother _____carefully_____ cleaned the child's sore knee.

6. The fire was caused by someone _____carelessly_____ tossing a match.

7. The alarm rang _____loudly_____ while we were eating.

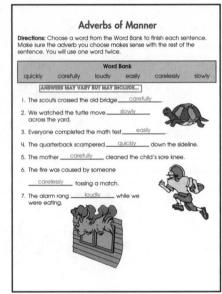

Page 134

Adverbs

Like adjectives, **adverbs** are describing words. They describe verbs. Adverbs tell **how, when,** or **where** action takes place.

Examples:	**How**	**When**	**Where**
	slowly	yesterday	here
	gracefully	today	there
	swiftly	tomorrow	everywhere
	quickly	soon	

Hint: To identify an adverb, first locate the verb. Then, ask yourself if there are any words that tell how, when, or where the action takes place.

How? When? Where?

Directions: Read each sentence below. Underline the adverb. Then, write whether it tells how, when, or where.

Example:	At the end of the day, the children ran <u>quickly</u> home from school.	how
1. They will have a spelling test <u>tomorrow</u>.		time
2. <u>Slowly</u>, the children filed to their seats.		manner
3. The teacher sat <u>here</u> at her desk.		place
4. She will pass the tests back <u>later</u>.		time
5. The students received their grades <u>happily</u>.		manner

Directions: Write four sentences of your own using any of the adverbs above.

_____

ANSWERS WILL VARY

Page 135

Adverbs

Adverbs are words that describe verbs. They tell **where, how,** or **when.**

Directions: Circle the adverb in each of the following sentences.

Example: The doctor worked (carefully.)

1. The skater moved (gracefully) across the ice.

2. They returned their call (quickly).

3. We (easily) learned the new words.

4. He did the work (perfectly).

5. She lost her purse (somewhere).

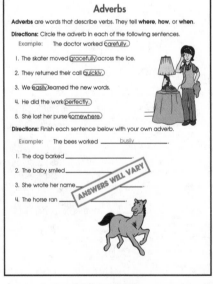

Directions: Finish each sentence below with your own adverb.

Example: The bees worked _____busily_____

1. The dog barked _____

2. The baby smiled _____

3. She wrote her name _____

4. The horse ran _____

ANSWERS WILL VARY

Page 136

Adverbs

An **adverb** tells more about a verb. Adverbs can tell **how, when,** or **where** an action takes place.

Examples:	**how:**	Kallie drove the car **slowly**.
	when:	Kallie drove the car **then**.
	where:	Kallie drove the car **far**.

Directions: Circle the adverbs that tell how, when, or where something happened.

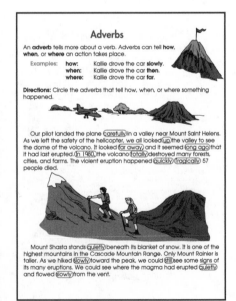

Our pilot landed the plane (carefully) in a valley near Mount Saint Helens. As we left the safety of the helicopter, we all looked (up) the valley to see the dome of the volcano. It looked (far away) and it seemed (long ago) that it had last erupted. (In 1980,) the volcano (totally) destroyed many forests, cities, and farms. The violent eruption happened (quickly) (tragically) 57 people died.

Mount Shasta stands (quietly) beneath its blanket of snow. It is one of the highest mountains in the Cascade Mountain Range. Only Mount Rainier is taller. As we hiked (slowly) toward the peak, we could (still) see some signs of its many eruptions. We could see where the magma had erupted (quietly) and flowed (slowly) from the vent.

Page 137

Page 138

Adverbs

Adverbs describe verbs. They usually tell **how, when,** or **where** an action happened.

Examples: The horse walked **slowly**.
We went riding **yesterday**.

Directions: Finish each sentence with an adverb from the Word Bank.

Word Bank

| slowly | carefully | yesterday | recklessly | nearby |
| there | softly | later | happily | beautifully |

ANSWERS MAY VARY BUT MAY INCLUDE...

1. Sandy _____happily_____ at her ice-cream cone.
2. Put your backpack _____there_____ .
3. Milo skated _____recklessly_____ and broke his wrist.
4. Tyler visited the museum _____yesterday_____ .
5. When the baby is asleep, we must speak _____softly_____ .
6. I have soccer practice _____later_____ .
7. The bear watched her cubs play _____nearby_____ .
8. Charlotte sings _____beautifully_____ .
9. Mother decorated the cake _____carefully_____ .
10. The jellyfish swims _____slowly_____ .

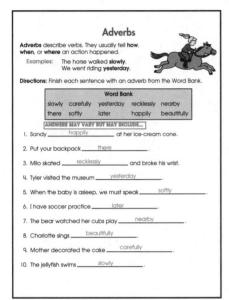

Page 139

Adverbs

An **adverb** tells more about a verb. Adverbs can tell **when, where,** or **how** an action takes place.

Example: I sleep **often**.

Directions: Finish each sentence with an adverb from the Word Bank.

ANSWERS MAY VARY BUT MAY INCLUDE...

1. When hiking in the desert, _____always_____ stay on the marked trails.
2. Do not go too _____near_____ a rattlesnake, or it will attack.
3. Stay _____far_____ away from floods during storms. The water can be dangerous.
4. Apply sunscreen _____generously_____ .
5. Take breaks _____frequently_____ . Do not wear yourself out.
6. When walking in the desert, walk _____slowly_____ and _____carefully_____ .
7. Approach any strange object _____cautiously_____ .
8. Make sure you look _____up_____ and _____down_____ the trail so you do not trip.
9. On hot days, drink water _____often_____ to keep you from getting sick.
10. Break in boots _____before_____ you wear them hiking.

Word Bank

| near | before | down | slowly | always | frequently |
| carefully | far | up | cautiously | often | generously |

Page 140

Adverbs

An **adverb** tells more about a verb. Adverbs can tell **when, where,** or **how**.

Directions: Write three adverbs to describe each verb. Do not use an adverb more than once.

run	dance	tripped
fly	play	jump
read	sing	growl
laugh	write	eat

ANSWERS WILL VARY

Page 141

Adverbs

Directions: Read each sentence. Then, answer the questions.

Example: Charles ate hungrily.
who? Charles (subject)
what? ate (verb)
how? hungrily (adverb)

1. She dances slowly.
who? She
what? dances
how? slowly

2. The girl spoke carefully.
who? The girl
what? spoke
how? carefully

3. My brother ran quickly.
who? My brother
what? ran
how? quickly

4. Jean often walks home.
who? Jean
what? walks
how? often

5. The children played loudly.
who? children
what? played
how? loudly

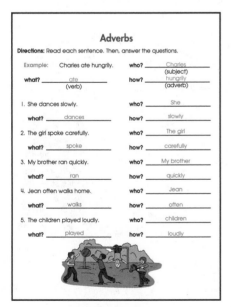

Page 142

Adverbs

Adverbs tell **when, where,** or **how** about the verb in a sentence. Many adverbs end in **ly** when answering the question, "How?"

Examples: I celebrated my birthday **today**. (When?)
Children sat **near** me. (Where?)
I **excitedly** opened my gifts. (How?)

Directions: Underline the adverb in each sentence. Then, write **when, where,** or **how** on the line to tell which question it answers.

1. The children played quietly at home. how
2. We went to the movie yesterday. when
3. My friends came inside to play. where
4. The child cut his meat carefully. how
5. The girls ran upstairs to get their coats. where
6. The play-off games start tomorrow. when
7. The boys walked slowly. how
8. The teacher said, "Write your name neatly." how

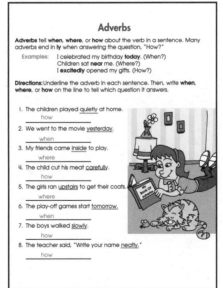

Page 143

Adverbs

Adverbs tell **when, where,** or **how** an action takes place.

Directions: Circle the adverbs that can tell about the verb.

study	painted	laugh
(later)	(colorfully)	(happily)
(well)	(joyfully)	fun
(often)	beautiful	(today)
math	oranges	(loudly)

listen	drive	plant
(quietly)	(everywhere)	seeds
(attentively)	road	(deep)
important	(cautiously)	(sometimes)
(carefully)	(there)	(slowly)

cried	run
(yesterday)	(swiftly)
tears	(fast)
(sadly)	(again)
(silently)	races

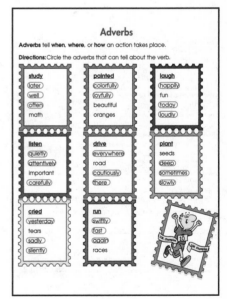

Adverbs

Directions: Circle the 12 adverbs in the story. Then, write them in the correct spaces to show if they tell when, where, or how about the verb.

Robert and Tom *went* (inside) to dress for the movies. They planned to watch *Sonic Man* (today).

"Hurry, or we will be late!" called Tom (loudly).

They ran (quickly) to the bus stop and waited (impatiently) for the bus to arrive.

At the theater, the line wound (outside). The boys worried they would have to return (tomorrow).

The line moved (slowly) as the boys waited (nervously). "I hope they have tickets left," moaned Robert (quietly).

"Yes, we have seats left," said a ticket seller who stood (nearby).

The movie began (immediately) as the boys settled in their seats.

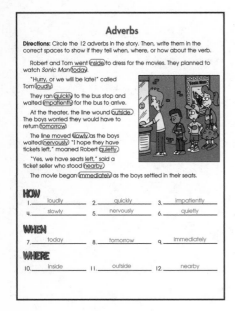

HOW
1. loudly   2. quickly   3. impatiently
4. slowly   5. nervously   6. quietly

WHEN
7. today   8. tomorrow   9. immediately

WHERE
10. inside   11. outside   12. nearby

Page 144

Adverbs

Directions: Finish each sentence with an adverb that tells how, when, or where about the verb.

1. Our team played _____ . (when)
2. Brian writes _____ . (how)
3. The cows move _____ . (how)
4. Melissa will dance _____ . (when)
5. My dog went _____ . (where)
6. We ra_____ . (how)
7. The ch___ sang _____ . (how)
8. The cat purred _____ . (where)
9. Hillary spoke _____ . (how)
10. We will go on our vacation _____ . (when)
11. The sign goes _____ . (where)
12. Mother brought the groceries _____ . (where)
13. David read the directions _____ . (how)
14. We will be leaving _____ . (when)
15. We have three bedrooms _____ . (where)
16. We will arrive _____ . (when)
17. The mother bird leaves the nest _____ . (when)
18. Do not let the cat _____ . (where)

ANSWERS MAY VARY

Where?
The monkeys are inside.

Page 145

Adverbs

Adverbs are words that describe verbs. Adverbs tell **where**, **when**, or **how**. Most adverbs end in **ly**.

Directions: Finish each sentence with the correct part of speech.

Example:
Hank	wrote	here.
who? (noun)	what? (verb)	where? (adverb)

1. _____ was lost _____
   who? (noun)   what? (verb)   where? (adverb)

2. _____ _____ quickly
   who? (noun)   (verb)   how? (adverb)

3. _____ felt _____
   who? (noun)   what? (verb)   how? (adverb)

4. My brother _____ _____
   who? (noun)   what? (verb)   when? (adverb)

5. _____ woke up _____
   who? (noun)   what? (verb)   when? (adverb)

6. _____ _____ gladly
   who? (noun)   what? (verb)   how? (adverb)

ANSWERS WILL VARY

Page 146

Adverbs

Adverbs show comparison by adding **er** or **est** to the end of the word. Add **er** when the adverb compares two actions. Add **est** when the adverb compares three or more actions.

Example: The clarinets played **louder** than the flutes.
             The trumpets played the **loudest** of all the instruments.

Directions: Finish the following sentences by using a comparative form of the underlined adverb.

1. The airplane flew <u>high</u>.
   The airplane flew ___higher___ than the bird.
   The jet flew ___highest___ of all.

2. Jack's car raced <u>fast</u>.
   Jim's car raced ___faster___ than Jack's car.
   Ted's car raced ___fastest___ of all.

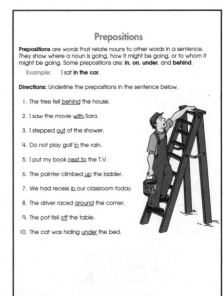

You can also show comparison by adding the word **more**, **most**, **less**, or **least** in front of the adverb. These words are usually added to adverbs ending in **ly**.

Directions: Add **more**, **most**, **less**, or **least** to each adverb to show comparison.   *ANSWERS MAY VARY BUT MAY INCLUDE...*

1. Andrew travels overseas ___more___ frequently than Eric.
2. Vanessa travels overseas ___most___ often of all her friends.
3. Raquel drives her car ___less___ skillfully than Sara.
4. Dave drives ___least___ expertly of all.
5. Aaron uses his boat ___more___ often than Tim.
6. Tim sails ___less___ often than Aaron.

Page 147

Prepositions

Prepositions show relationships between the noun or pronoun and another noun in the sentence. The preposition comes before that noun.
Example: The book is (on) the table.

Common Prepositions				
above	behind	by	near	over
across	below	in	off	through
around	beside	inside	on	under

Directions: Circle the prepositions in each sentence.

1. The dog ran fast (around) the house.
2. The plates (in) the cupboard were clean.
3. Put the card (inside) the envelope.
4. The towel (on) the sink was wet.
5. I planted flowers (in) my garden.
6. My kite flew high (above) the trees.
7. The chair (near) the counter was sticky.
8. (Under) the ground, worms lived (in) their homes.
9. I put the bow (around) the box.
10. (Beside) the pond, there was a playground.

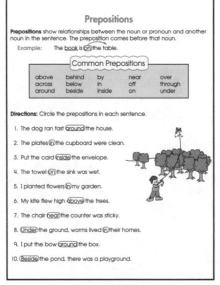

Page 148

Prepositions

Prepositions are words that relate nouns to other words in a sentence. They show where a noun is going, how it might be going, or to whom it might be going. Some prepositions are: **in**, **on**, **under**, and **behind**.
Example: I sat **in the car**.

Directions: Underline the prepositions in the sentence below.

1. The tree fell <u>behind</u> the house.
2. I saw the movie <u>with</u> Sara.
3. I stepped <u>out</u> of the shower.
4. Do not play golf <u>in</u> the rain.
5. I put my book <u>next to</u> the T.V.
6. The painter climbed <u>up</u> the ladder.
7. We had recess <u>in</u> our classroom today.
8. The driver raced <u>around</u> the corner.
9. The pot fell <u>off</u> the table.
10. The cat was hiding <u>under</u> the bed.

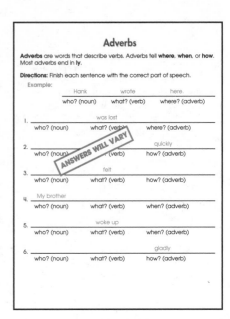

Page 149

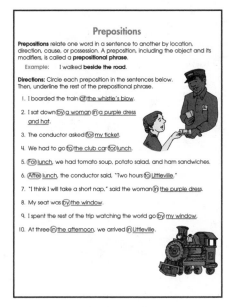

Prepositions

Prepositions relate one word in a sentence to another by location, direction, cause, or possession. A preposition, including the object and its modifiers, is called a **prepositional phrase**.

Example: I walked **beside the road**.

Directions: Circle each preposition in the sentences below. Then, underline the rest of the prepositional phrase.

1. I boarded the train (at) the whistle's blow.
2. I sat down (by) a woman (in) a purple dress and hat.
3. The conductor asked (for) my ticket.
4. We had to go (to) the club car (for) lunch.
5. (For) lunch, we had tomato soup, potato salad, and ham sandwiches.
6. (After) lunch, the conductor said, "Two hours (to) Littleville."
7. "I think I will take a short nap," said the woman (in) the purple dress.
8. My seat was (by) the window.
9. I spent the rest of the trip watching the world go (by) my window.
10. At three (in) the afternoon, we arrived (in) Littleville.

Page 150

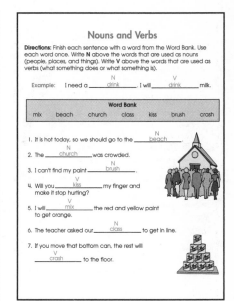

Nouns and Verbs

A **noun** names a **person, place,** or **thing.** A **verb** tells what something does or what something is. Some words can be nouns and verbs, depending on how they are used.

Directions: Finish the sentences in each pair with a word from the Word Bank. The word will be a noun in the first sentence and a verb in the second sentence.

Word Bank			
mix	kiss	brush	crash

1. Did your dog ever give you a _____kiss_____ ?
   (noun)
   I have a cold, so I cannot _____kiss_____ you today.
   (verb)
2. I brought my comb and my _____brush_____ .
   (noun)
   I will _____brush_____ the leaves off your coat.
   (verb)
3. Was anyone hurt in the _____crash_____ ?
   (noun)
   If you are not careful, you will _____crash_____ into me.
   (verb)
4. We bought a cake _____mix_____ at the store.
   (noun)
   I will _____mix_____ the eggs together.
   (verb)

Page 151

Nouns and Verbs

Directions: Finish each sentence with a word from the Word Bank. Use each word once. Write **N** above the words that are used as nouns (people, places, and things). Write **V** above the words that are used as verbs (what something does or what something is).

Example: I need a ___drink___ (N). I will ___drink___ (V) milk.

Word Bank						
mix	beach	church	class	kiss	brush	crash

1. It is hot today, so we should go to the ___beach___ (N).
2. The ___church___ (N) was crowded.
3. I can't find my paint ___brush___ (N).
4. Will you ___kiss___ (V) my finger and make it stop hurting?
5. I will ___mix___ (V) the red and yellow paint to get orange.
6. The teacher asked our ___class___ (N) to get in line.
7. If you move that bottom can, the rest will ___crash___ (V) to the floor.

Page 152

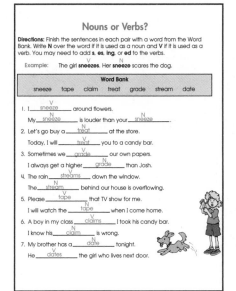

Nouns or Verbs?

Directions: Finish the sentences in each pair with a word from the Word Bank. Write **N** over the word if it is used as a noun and **V** if it is used as a verb. You may need to add **s, es, ing,** or **ed** to the verbs.

Example: The girl **sneezes.** Her **sneeze** scares the dog.

Word Bank						
sneeze	tape	claim	treat	grade	stream	date

1. I ___sneeze___ (V) around flowers.
   My ___sneeze___ (N) is louder than your ___sneeze___ (N).
2. Let's go buy a ___treat___ (N) at the store.
   Today, I will ___treat___ (V) you to a candy bar.
3. Sometimes we ___grade___ (V) our own papers.
   I always get a higher ___grade___ (N) than Josh.
4. The rain ___streams___ (V) down the window.
   The ___stream___ (N) behind our house is overflowing.
5. Please ___tape___ (V) that TV show for me.
   I will watch the ___tape___ (N) when I come home.
6. A boy in my class ___claims___ (V) I took his candy bar.
   I know his ___claim___ (N) is wrong.
7. My brother has a ___date___ (N) tonight.
   He ___dates___ (V) the girl who lives next door.

Page 153

Nouns or Verbs?

Some words can be either **nouns** or **verbs**, depending on how they are used in a sentence.

Example: **noun:** The **paint** on Aunt Betty's shutters is wet.
         verb: They will **paint** the shutters again later today.

Directions: In each sentence below, the noun or the verb is in bold. Write **N** if the word is a noun or **V** if the word is a verb.

1. _N_ Aunt Betty said we need to look for a **ship**.
2. _V_ We will **ship** the picnic basket to the island.
3. _N_ There will be hardly any **light** in the forest.
4. _V_ Aunt Betty will **light** the way with her trusty flashlight.
5. _N_ We parked our car near the **water**.
6. _V_ On the way, Aunt Betty stopped to **water** some flowers.
7. _N_ Then, she picked some of the pink ones and put them in a **box**.
8. _V_ "I will **box** these for my friend in Hawaii," Aunt Betty said.
9. _N_ "It will be a **present** for my friend."
10. _V_ "I hope to **present** it to her tomorrow."
11. _V_ We will **play** all day on the island.
12. _N_ At night, we will see a **play**.

Page 154

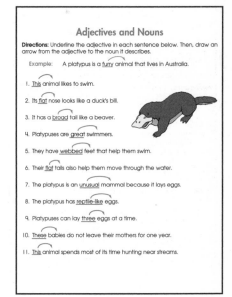

Adjectives and Nouns

Directions: Underline the adjective in each sentence below. Then, draw an arrow from the adjective to the noun it describes.

Example: A platypus is a <u>furry</u> animal that lives in Australia.

1. <u>This</u> animal likes to swim.
2. Its <u>flat</u> nose looks like a duck's bill.
3. It has a <u>broad</u> tail like a beaver.
4. Platypuses are <u>great</u> swimmers.
5. They have <u>webbed</u> feet that help them swim.
6. Their <u>flat</u> tails also help them move through the water.
7. The platypus is an <u>unusual</u> mammal because it lays eggs.
8. The platypus has <u>reptile-like</u> eggs.
9. Platypuses can lay <u>three</u> eggs at a time.
10. <u>These</u> babies do not leave their mothers for one year.
11. <u>This</u> animal spends most of its time hunting near streams.

Page 155

ANSWER KEY

Nouns, Pronouns, and Adjectives

Directions: Circle the nouns that show ownership. Draw a box around the pronouns. Underline the adjectives.

Example: Tropical birds live in warm, wet lands.
They live in dark forests and busy zoos.
The birds' feathers are bright.

1. A canary is a small finch.
2. It is named for the Canary Islands.
3. Ben's birds are lovebirds.
4. He says they are small parrots that like to cuddle.
5. His parents gave him the lovebirds for his birthday.
6. Lisa's bird is a talking myna bird.
7. Her neighbors gave it to her when they moved.
8. She thanked them for the wonderful gift.
9. She says its feathers are dark with an orange mark on each wing.
10. Some children's myna birds can be very noisy.
11. Parakeets are this country's most popular tropical birds.
12. Parakeets' cages have ladders and swings.
13. A parakeet's diet is made up of seeds.

Page 156

Adjectives and Adverbs

Directions: Write ADJ on the line if the bold word is an adjective. Write ADV if the bold word is an adverb.

Example: **ADV** That road leads **nowhere**.

1. **ADV** The squirrel was **nearby**.
2. **ADJ** Her **delicious** cookies were all eaten.
3. **ADV** Everyone rushed **indoors**.
4. **ADV** He **quickly** zipped his jacket.
5. **ADJ** She hummed a **popular** tune.
6. **ADJ** Her **sunny** smile warmed my heart.
7. **ADV** I hung your coat **there**.
8. **ADV** Bring that **here** this minute!
9. **ADV** We all walked **back** to school.
10. **ADJ** The **skinniest** boy ate the most food!
11. **ADJ** She acts like a **famous** person.
12. **ADJ** The **silliest** jokes always make me laugh.
13. **ADV** She must have parked her car **somewhere**!
14. **ADV** Did you take the test **today**?

Page 157

Adjectives and Adverbs

Directions: Finish each sentence by adding words that tell who, what, where, or when.

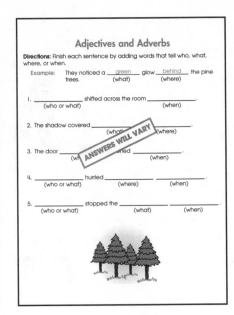

Example: They noticed a ___green___ glow ___behind___ the pine trees. (what) (where)

1. _____ shifted across the room _____.
(who or what) (when)

2. The shadow covered _____ _____.
(what) (where)

3. The door (wh... [ANSWERS WILL VARY] ...ned _____.
(when)

4. _____ hurried _____ _____.
(who or what) (where) (when)

5. _____ stopped the _____ _____.
(who or what) (what) (when)

Page 158

Adjectives and Adverbs

Directions: Read the story. Underline the adjectives. Circle the adverbs. Write the words in the correct column at the end of the story.

Surprise!

Emily and Elizabeth tiptoed quietly through the dark hallway. Even though none of the lights were lit, they knew the presents were there. Every year, the two sisters had gone to Mom and Dad's bedroom to wake them on Christmas morning. This year would be different, they decided.

Last night after supper, they had secretly plotted to look early in the morning before Mom and Dad were awake. The girls knew that Emily's red-and-green stocking and Elizabeth's striped stocking hung by the brick fireplace. They knew the beautiful tree was in the corner by the rocking chair.

"Won't Mom and Dad be surprised to awaken on their own?" asked Elizabeth quietly.

Emily whispered, "Click the overhead lights so we can see better."

"You don't have to whisper," said a voice.

There sat Mom and Dad as the Christmas-tree lights suddenly shone.

Dad said, "I guess the surprise is on you two!"

Adverbs		Adjectives	
quietly		dark	striped
there		none	brick
secretly		every	beautiful
early		two	rocking
better		this	Christmas-tree
suddenly		last	overhead
		different	
		red-and-green	

Page 159

Parts of Speech

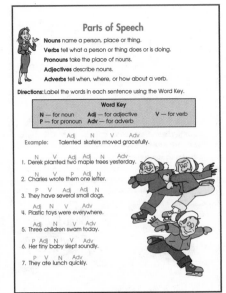

Nouns name a person, place or thing.
Verbs tell what a person or thing does or is doing.
Pronouns take the place of nouns.
Adjectives describe nouns.
Adverbs tell when, where, or how about a verb.

Directions: Label the words in each sentence using the Word Key.

Word Key		
N — for noun	Adj — for adjective	V — for verb
P — for pronoun	Adv — for adverb	

Example: Adj N V Adv
Talented skaters moved gracefully.

1. N Adj Adj N Adv
Derek planted two maple trees yesterday.

2. N V P Adj N
Charles wrote them one letter.

3. P V Adj Adj N
They have several small dogs.

4. Adj N V Adv
Plastic toys were everywhere.

5. Adj N V Adv
Three children swam today.

6. P Adj N V Adv
Her tiny baby slept soundly.

7. P V N Adv
They ate lunch quickly.

Page 160

Parts of Speech

Nouns, pronouns, verbs, adjectives, adverbs, and prepositions are all **parts of speech**.

Directions: Label each word in the sentence with the correct part of speech.

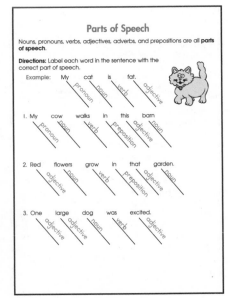

Example: My cat is fat.
pronoun noun verb adjective

1. My cow walks in this barn
pronoun noun verb preposition adjective noun

2. Red flowers grow in that garden.
adjective noun verb preposition adjective noun

3. One large dog was excited.
adjective adjective noun verb adjective

Page 161

Page 162

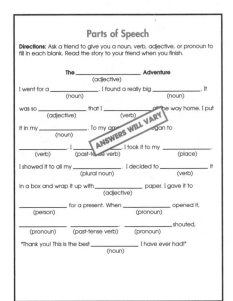

Parts of Speech

Directions: Ask a friend to give you a noun, verb, adjective, or pronoun to fill in each blank. Read the story to your friend when you finish.

The _____ Adventure
(adjective)

I went for a _____. I found a really big _____. It
(noun)   (noun)

was so _____ that I _____ all the way home. I put
(adjective)   (verb)

it in my _____. To my amazement, it began to
(noun)

_____. I _____. I took it to my _____.
(verb)   (past-tense verb)   (place)

I showed it to all my _____. I decided to _____ it
(plural noun)   (verb)

in a box and wrap it up with _____ paper. I gave it to
(adjective)

_____ for a present. When _____ opened it,
(person)   (pronoun)

_____ _____. _____ shouted,
(pronoun) (past-tense verb) (pronoun)

"Thank you! This is the best _____ I have ever had!"
(noun)

ANSWERS WILL VARY

Page 163

Parts of Speech

Directions: Write the part of speech for each underlined word on the correct numbered line below.

NOUN PRONOUN VERB ADJECTIVE ADVERB PREPOSITION

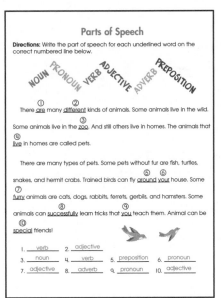

There ①are many ②different kinds of animals. Some animals live in the wild.
③
Some animals live in the zoo. And still others live in homes. The animals that
④
live in homes are called pets.

There are many types of pets. Some pets without fur are fish, turtles,
⑤   ⑥
snakes, and hermit crabs. Trained birds can fly around your house. Some
⑦
furry animals are cats, dogs, rabbits, ferrets, gerbils, and hamsters. Some
⑧   ⑨
animals can successfully learn tricks that you teach them. Animal can be
⑩
special friends!

1. _verb_   2. _adjective_
3. _noun_   4. _verb_   5. _preposition_   6. _pronoun_
7. _adjective_   8. _adverb_   9. _pronoun_   10. _adjective_

Page 164

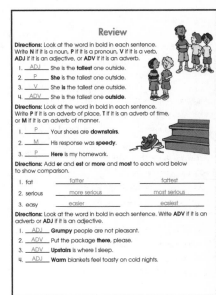

Review

Directions: Look at the word in bold in each sentence. Write **N** if it is a noun, **P** if it is a pronoun, **V** if it is a verb, **ADJ** if it is an adjective, or **ADV** if it is an adverb.

1. _ADJ_ She is the **tallest** one outside.
2. _P_ **She** is the tallest one outside.
3. _V_ She **is** the tallest one outside.
4. _ADV_ She is the tallest one **outside**.

Directions: Look at the word in bold in each sentence. Write **P** if it is an adverb of place, **T** if it is an adverb of time, or **M** if it is an adverb of manner.

1. _P_ Your shoes are **downstairs**.
2. _M_ His response was **speedy**.

Directions: Add **er** and **est** or **more** and **most** to each word below to show comparison.

1. fat   _fatter_   _fattest_
2. serious   _more serious_ _most serious_
3. easy   _easier_   _easiest_

Directions: Look at the word in bold in each sentence. Write **ADV** if it is an adverb or **ADJ** if it is an adjective.

1. _ADJ_ **Grumpy** people are not pleasant.
2. _ADV_ Put the package **there**, please.
3. _ADV_ **Upstairs** is where I sleep.
4. _ADJ_ **Warm** blankets feel toasty on cold nights.

Page 165

Sentences

A **sentence** has a **beginning** and an **ending**. A sentence tells a **complete thought**. When you write a sentence, make sure that all of it is there! Just a beginning or just an ending is not a complete sentence!

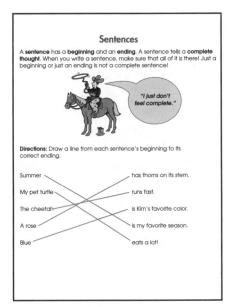

"I just don't feel complete."

Directions: Draw a line from each sentence's beginning to its correct ending.

Summer ————— has thorns on its stem.
My pet turtle ————— runs fast.
The cheetah ————— is Kim's favorite color.
A rose ————— is my favorite season.
Blue ————— eats a lot!

Page 166

Sentences

Every sentence must have two things: a **noun** or **pronoun** that tells who or what is doing something and a **verb** that tells what the noun is doing.

Directions: Add a **noun**, a **pronoun**, or a **verb** to complete each sentence. Be sure to begin your sentences with capital letters and end them with periods.

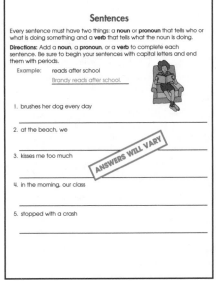

Example: reads after school
            Brandy reads after school.

1. brushes her dog every day

2. at the beach, we

3. kisses me too much

4. in the morning, our class

5. stopped with a crash

ANSWERS WILL VARY

Page 167

Sentences

Directions: Write one sentence about each picture. Write **N** above the noun in each sentence. Write **V** above the verb in each sentence.

ANSWERS WILL VARY

Subjects

A **subject** is a **noun** or a **pronoun**. It tells who or what the sentence is about.

Directions: Underline the subject in each sentence below.

Example: The <u>zebra</u> is a striped animal.

1. <u>Zebras</u> live in Africa.
2. <u>Zebras</u> are related to horses.
3. <u>Horses</u> have longer hair than zebras.
4. <u>Zebras</u> are good runners.
5. <u>Their</u> feet are protected by their hooves.
6. Some <u>animals</u> live in groups.
7. <u>These groups</u> are called herds.
8. <u>Zebras</u> live in herds with other grazing animals.
9. <u>Grazing animals</u> eat mostly grass.
10. <u>They</u> usually eat three times a day.
11. <u>They</u> often travel to water holes.

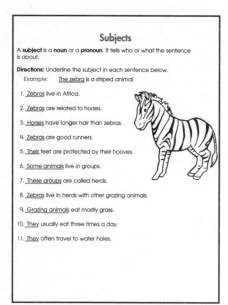

Page 168

Subjects

Directions: Finish each sentence below with a subject.

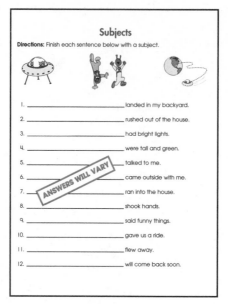

1. _____ landed in my backyard.
2. _____ rushed out of the house.
3. _____ had bright lights.
4. _____ were tall and green.
5. _____ talked to me.
6. _____ came outside with me.
7. _____ ran into the house.
8. _____ shook hands.
9. _____ said funny things.
10. _____ gave us a ride.
11. _____ flew away.
12. _____ will come back soon.

ANSWERS WILL VARY

Page 169

Subjects

Directions: Circle the subject in each sentence. Change the subject to make a new sentence. The word or words you add must make sense with the rest of the sentence.

Example: (Twelve students) signed up for the student council elections.

Only one person in my class signed up for the student council elections.

1. (Our whole family) went to the science museum last week.
   | ANSWERS WILL VARY |

2. (The funny story) made us laugh.
   | ANSWERS WILL VARY |

3. (The brightly colored kites) drifted lazily across the sky.
   | ANSWERS WILL VARY |

4. (My little brother and sister) spent the whole day at the amusement park.
   | ANSWERS WILL VARY |

5. (The tiny sparrow) made a tapping sound at my window.
   | ANSWERS WILL VARY |

Page 170

Predicates

A **predicate** always has a **verb**. It tells what the subject is doing, has done, or will do.

Directions: Underline the predicate in each sentence below.

Example: Woodpeckers <u>live in trees</u>.

1. They <u>hunt for insects in the trees</u>.
2. Woodpeckers <u>have strong beaks</u>.
3. They can <u>peck through the bark</u>.
4. You can <u>hear the pecking sound from far away</u>.

Directions: Circle each group of words that can be a predicate.

(have long tongues)   (pick up insects)

hole in bark   sticky substance

(help it to climb trees)   tree bark

Directions: Choose the correct predicate from above to finish each sentence below.

1. Woodpeckers _____ have long tongues _____.
2. They use their tongues to _____ pick up insects _____.
3. Its strong feet _____ help it to climb trees _____.

Page 171

Predicates

Directions: Write a predicate for each sentence below.

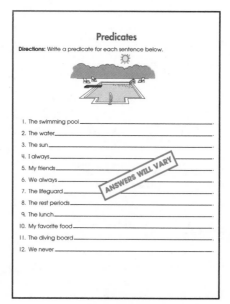

1. The swimming pool _____
2. The water _____
3. The sun _____
4. I always _____
5. My friends _____
6. We always _____
7. The lifeguard _____
8. The rest periods _____
9. The lunch _____
10. My favorite food _____
11. The diving board _____
12. We never _____

ANSWERS WILL VARY

Page 172

Predicates

Directions: Circle the predicate in each sentence. Change the predicate to make a new sentence. The words you add must make sense with the rest of the sentence.

Example: Twelve students (signed up for the student council elections.)

Twelve students were absent from my class today!

1. Our whole family (went to the science museum last week.)
   | ANSWERS WILL VARY |

2. The funny story (made us laugh.)
   | ANSWERS WILL VARY |

3. The brightly colored kites (drifted lazily across the sky.)
   | ANSWERS WILL VARY |

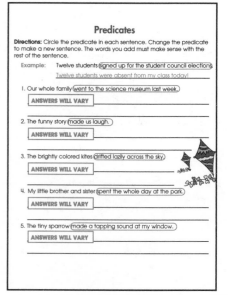

4. My little brother and sister (spent the whole day at the park.)
   | ANSWERS WILL VARY |

5. The tiny sparrow (made a tapping sound at my window.)
   | ANSWERS WILL VARY |

Page 173

Subject-Verb Agreement

The verb and subject in a sentence must match in number. This is called **subject-verb agreement**.

Present tense tells what is happening right now. If the verb is present tense and the subject refers to only one thing, then add an **s** or **es** to the verb.

Examples: The branch **sways** softly in the breeze.
Hannah **munches** on carrot sticks.

If the verb is present tense and the subject refers to more than one thing, then do not add an **s** or **es** to the verb.

Examples: Gophers **live** underground.
They **crush** plants.

Directions: Read each sentence. Underline the form of the verb that agrees with the subject.

1. Mary (receive, (receives)) a new bicycle on her birthday.
2. She (put, (puts)) on her helmet.
3. Tony and Jennifer ((ride), rides) to Mary's house.
4. Mary (jump, (jumps)) on the shiny red bike.
5. She (spin, (spins)) around in the driveway.
6. The friends ((laugh), laughs) as they ride.
7. They ((race), races) down the sidewalk.
8. The streamers ((fly), flies) in the wind.
9. Jennifer (reach, (reaches)) the finish line first.
10. Tony (finish, (finishes)) last.
11. Mary (enjoy, (enjoys)) her new bike.
12. They will all ((meet), meets) tomorrow for another ride.

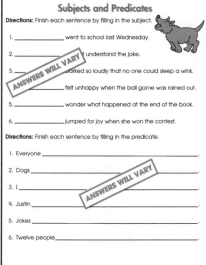

Page 174

Subject-Verb Agreement

In a sentence, the subjects and verbs must agree. When the subject is a single person, place, or thing, it is **singular**. You should match it to a **singular verb**. When the subject is more than one person, place, or thing, it is **plural**. You should match it to a **plural verb**.

Examples: **One** of my friends **is** going to see the Grand Canyon.
There **are** thirty-five **students** on the bus.

Directions: Finish each sentence, using the correct tense to make the subject and verb agree.

1. Thirty-five students ___are___ on their way to the Grand Canyon.
   (to be)

2. One of the students ___has___ a fear of heights and ___is___
   (to have)   (to be)
   scared of hiking down the narrow trails.

3. "There ___is___ one more stop before we get to the canyon," the
         (to be)
   bus driver said as he stopped the big bus.

4. When he stopped, there ___were___ thirty-five students who got off
                           (to be)
   the bus and ___went___ to see the sands of the Painted Desert.
               (to go)

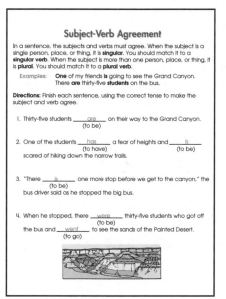

Page 175

Subject and Predicate

The **subject** of a sentence tells who or what the sentence is about. The subject can be a **noun** or a **pronoun**. The **predicate** of a sentence always has a **verb**. It tells what the subject is or does.

          subject   predicate
Example: The sailboat   took us to the island.

Directions: In each sentence, underline the subject and double underline the predicate.

1. We all climbed aboard the boat for the trip to the island.
2. Aunt Betty took the tiller.
3. We pushed off from the shore.
4. The lake was very quiet.
5. A few ducks followed our boat.
6. I fed them crusts of bread from our sandwiches.
7. I became more and more excited.
8. Aunt Betty gave me some binoculars.
9. I saw a man with a long beard wearing a strange outfit on the dock.

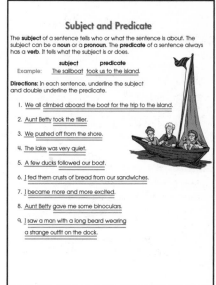

Page 176

Subject and Predicate

The **subject** of a sentence tells whom or what the sentence is about. It is always a noun or pronoun. The subject can be one word or more than one word.

The **predicate** is the part of the sentence that tells what the subject is or does. It always has a verb. The predicate can be one word or more than one word.

Directions: Match each subject to the correct predicate. Write the letter of the predicate in the space before the correct subject.

Subjects

1. _e_ Parker
2. _g_ The ballerina
3. _f_ My sister's parakeet
4. _d_ Our teacher
5. _a_ The amusement park ride
6. _h_ That ice-cream sundae
7. _b_ Emily
8. _c_ The goalie

Predicates

a. was closed for repairs.
b. dove into the freezing-cold pool.
c. made the save.
d. assigned the class lots of homework.
e. likes to ride his skateboard.
f. flew out of the window.
g. twirled on her toes.
h. is almost too sweet to eat!

Page 177

Subjects and Predicates

Directions: Finish each sentence by filling in the subject.

1. _____ went to school last Wednesday.
2. _____ understand the joke.
3. _____ barked so loudly that no one could sleep a wink.
4. _____ felt unhappy when the ball game was rained out.
5. _____ wonder what happened at the end of the book.
6. _____ jumped for joy when she won the contest.

~~ANSWERS WILL VARY~~

Directions: Finish each sentence by filling in the predicate.

1. Everyone _____.
2. Dogs _____.
3. I _____.
4. Justin _____.
5. Jokes _____.
6. Twelve people _____.

~~ANSWERS WILL VARY~~

Page 178

Subjects and Predicates

A **sentence** is a group of words that expresses a complete thought. It must have a subject and a predicate.

Examples: **Sentence:** John felt tired and went to bed early.
Not a sentence: Went to bed early.

Directions: Write S if the group of words is a complete sentence. Write NS if the group of words is not a sentence.

1. _NS_ Which one of you?
2. _S_ We're happy for the family.
3. _S_ We enjoyed the program very much.
4. _NS_ Felt left out and lonely afterwards.
5. _S_ Everyone said it was the best party ever!
6. _S_ No one knows better than I what the problem is.
7. _NS_ Seventeen of us!
8. _NS_ Quickly before they.
9. _S_ Squirrels are lively animals.
10. _S_ Not many people believe it really happened.
11. _S_ Certainly, we enjoyed ourselves.
12. _NS_ Tuned her out.

SUBJECTS & PREDICATES

Page 179

Subjects and Predicates

Directions: On page 179, some of the groups of words are not sentences. Rewrite them to make complete sentences.

1. _____

2. _____

3. _____

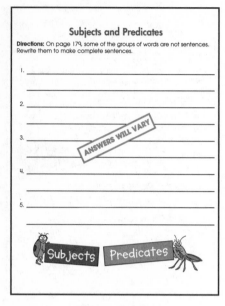

ANSWERS WILL VARY

4. _____

5. _____

Page 180

Compound Subjects

Compound subjects are two or more nouns that have the same predicate.

Directions: Combine the subjects to create one sentence with a compound subject.

Example: Jill can swing.
Whitney can swing.
Luke can swing.
Jill, Whitney, and Luke can swing.

1. Roses grow in the garden. Tulips grow in the garden.

   Roses and tulips grow in the garden.

2. Apples are fruit. Oranges are fruit. Bananas are fruit.

   Apples, oranges, and bananas are fruit.

3. Bears live in the zoo. Monkeys live in the zoo.

   Bears and monkeys live in the zoo.

4. Jackets keep us warm. Sweaters keep us warm.

   Jackets and sweaters keep us warm.

Page 181

Compound Subjects

The **subject** of a sentence tells who or what the sentence is about. A **compound subject** is two or more simple subjects joined by the word **and**.

Examples: **Toads** are amphibians. **Frogs** are amphibians.
Toads and frogs are amphibians.

Directions: If the sentence has a compound subject, write **CS** on the line. If the sentence does not have a compound subject, write **NO**.

1. NO An amphibian lives in the water and on land.
2. CS Frogs and salamanders are amphibians.
3. NO A salamander has a long body and a tail.
4. CS Adult frogs and toads do not have tails.
5. NO It is easy for them to move on land.
6. NO Frogs use their strong legs for leaping.
7. NO Toads have shorter legs and cannot jump as far.
8. CS The eyes and nose of a frog are on the top of its head.
9. NO Tree frogs are expert jumpers and can cling to things

Directions: Combine each set of sentences to make one sentence with a compound subject. Write the new sentence on the line.

1. Toads lay their eggs in water. Frogs lay their eggs in water.

   Toads and frogs lay their eggs in water.

2. Newts have tails. Salamanders have tails.

   Newts and salamanders have tails.

3. Tree frogs are noisy. Bullfrogs are noisy.

   Tree frogs and bullfrogs are noisy.

Page 182

Compound Subjects

Directions: Underline the simple subjects in each compound subject.

Example: <u>Dogs</u> and <u>cats</u> are good pets.

1. <u>Blueberries</u> and <u>strawberries</u> are fruit.
2. <u>Jesse</u>, <u>Jake</u>, and <u>Hannah</u> like school.
3. <u>Cows</u>, <u>pigs</u>, and <u>sheep</u> live on a farm.
4. <u>Boys</u> and <u>girls</u> ride the bus.
5. My <u>family</u> and <u>I</u> took a trip to Duluth.
6. <u>Fruits</u> and <u>vegetables</u> are good for you.
7. <u>Katarina</u>, <u>Lexi</u>, and <u>Mandi</u> like to go swimming.
8. <u>Petunias</u>, <u>impatiens</u>, <u>snapdragons</u>, and <u>geraniums</u> are all flowers.
9. <u>Coffee</u>, <u>tea</u>, and <u>milk</u> are beverages.
10. <u>Dave</u>, <u>Karla</u>, and <u>Tami</u> worked on the project together.

Page 183

Compound Predicates

Compound predicates have two or more verbs that have the same subject.

Directions: Combine the predicates to create one sentence with a compound predicate.

Example: We went to the zoo. We watched the monkeys.
We went to the zoo and watched the monkeys.

1. Students read their books. Students do their work.

   Students read their books and do their work.

2. Dogs can bark loudly. Dogs can do tricks.

   Dogs can bark loudly and do tricks.

3. The football player caught the ball. The football player ran.

   The football player caught the ball and ran.

4. My dad sawed wood. My dad stacked wood.

   My dad sawed and stacked wood.

5. My teddy bear is soft. My teddy bear has big brown eyes.

   My teddy bear is soft and has big brown eyes

Page 184

Compound Predicate

The **predicate** of a sentence tells who the subject is or what the subject is doing. A **compound predicate** is two or more simple predicates joined by the word **and**.

Example: Dad **picks up** Troy. Dad **drives** to the dentist.
Dad **picks up** Troy **and drives** to the dentist.

Directions: If the sentence has a compound predicate, write **CP** on the line. If the sentence does not have a compound predicate, write **NO**.

1. CP Dad and Troy park the car and go inside.
2. CP Troy reads and watches T.V. while waiting for the dentist.
3. NO Dad talks to another patient.
4. CP The hygienist comes into the waiting room and gets Troy.
5. CP The hygienist cleans, polishes, and X-rays Troy's teeth.
6. CP The dentist examines Troy's teeth and checks the X-rays.
7. NO The dentist gives Troy a toothbrush to take home.
8. NO Troy thanks the dentist.
9. NO Dad pays the dentist.

Directions: Combine each set of sentences to make one sentence with a compound predicate. Write the new sentence on the line.

1. Troy wiggles his tooth. Troy pulls it loose.

   Troy wiggles and pulls his tooth loose.

2. Troy smiles. Troy shows Dad the empty space in his mouth.

   Troy smiles and shows Dad the empty space in his mouth.

3. Dad laughs. Dad hugs Troy.

   Dad laughs and hugs Troy.

Page 185

Compound Predicates

Directions: Underline the verbs in each compound predicate.

Example: The fans <u>clapped</u> and <u>cheered</u> at the game.

1. The coach <u>talks</u> and <u>encourages</u> the team.

2. The cheerleaders <u>jump</u> and <u>yell</u>.

3. The basketball players <u>dribble</u> and <u>shoot</u> the ball.

4. The basketball <u>bounces</u> and <u>hits</u> the backboard.

5. The ball <u>rolls</u> around the rim and <u>goes</u> into the basket.

6. Everyone <u>leaps</u> up and <u>cheers</u>.

7. The team <u>scores</u> and <u>wins</u>!

Page 186

Simple and Complete Subjects

The **simple subject** of a sentence tells who or what the sentence is about. It does not contain any adjectives or articles.

Example: The **surface** of the ocean sometimes looks angry in a storm.

The **complete subject** of a sentence is all the words in the part of the sentence that tells about the subject. It can contain adjectives and articles.

Example: **The top of the ocean** sometimes looks angry in a storm.

Directions: Underline the simple subject and circle the complete subject in each sentence below.

1. (The killer <u>whale</u>) is found in all oceans.

2. (Killer <u>whales</u>, or orcas,) travel in groups or pods.

3. (<u>Pods</u>) can have from two to dozens of whales.

4. (Each <u>pod</u>) "talks" with its own set of underwater sounds.

5. Most of the crew <u>members</u>) had seen orcas before.

6. (The killer <u>whale</u>) has teeth, unlike some other whales.

7. (These <u>whales</u>) feed on salmon and other fish.

8. (<u>They</u>) do not usually attack people.

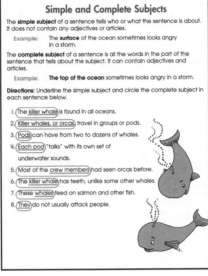

Page 187

Simple and Complete Subjects

The **simple subject** is who or what the sentence is about. It does not include any adjectives or articles.

Example: The flying cactus **critter** was huge.

The **complete subject** is the simple subject plus any adjectives or articles.

Examples: **The flying cactus critter** was huge.

Directions: Underline the simple subject and circle the complete subject in each sentence below.

1. (Many <u>deserts</u>) receive little rainfall.

2. (About one-fifth of the earth's <u>land</u>) consists of deserts.

3. (The largest <u>desert</u> in the world) is the Sahara.

4. (Most <u>towns</u> and <u>cities</u> in desert regions) must get water from wells or nearby rivers.

5. (<u>People</u> in desert regions) must protect themselves from the intense heat.

6. (<u>Deserts</u>) can consist of sand, gravel, and rocky hills and mountains.

7. (Many desert <u>soils</u>) are rich in minerals.

8. (An <u>oasis</u>) is an unusually wet area in a desert where many plants can grow.

9. (Most <u>deserts</u>) receive less than 10 inches of rainfall per year.

10. (Most desert <u>animals</u>) eat at night to avoid high daytime temperatures.

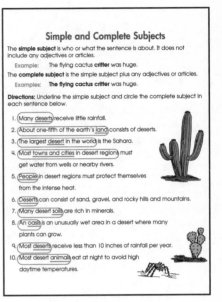

Page 188

Simple Predicates

A **simple predicate** is the main verb or verbs in the complete predicate.

Directions: Draw a line between the complete subject and the complete predicate. Circle the simple predicate.

Example: The ripe apples (fell) to the ground.

1. The farmer (scattered) feed for the chickens.

2. The horses (galloped) wildly around the corral.

3. The baby chicks (stayed) warm by the light.

4. The tractor (baled) hay.

5. The silo (was) full of grain.

6. The cows (waited) to be milked.

7. The milk truck (drove) up to the barn.

8. The rooster (woke) up everyone.

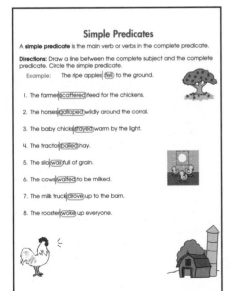

Page 189

Simple and Complete Predicates

The **simple predicate** tells what the subject is or does.

Example: I **created** a flying critter.

The **complete predicate** includes all of the words in the predicate (including adjectives, articles, and verbs).

Example: I **created a flying critter.**

Directions: Underline the simple predicate and circle the complete predicate in each sentence below.

1. All birds (<u>have</u> wings and feathers.)

2. There (<u>is</u> no other animal on earth that can travel faster than a bird.)

3. Some birds (<u>cannot</u> fly.)

4. Ostriches and penguins (<u>use</u> their wings for balance or to swim.)

5. Many birds (<u>have</u> vibrantly colored wings.)

6. People (<u>have</u> used birds as symbols on flags and in crests.)

7. The smallest bird (<u>is</u> the bee hummingbird.)

8. The largest bird, the ostrich, (<u>may grow</u> to be 8 feet tall.)

9. Birds (<u>live</u> all over the world.)

10. Some birds even (<u>live</u> in the Arctic and Antarctic.)

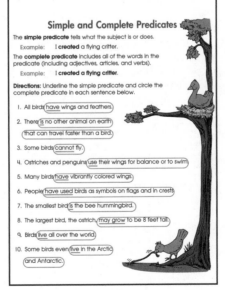

Page 190

Direct Objects

A **direct object** is the word or words that answer the question **whom** or **what** about the verb.

Examples: Aaron wrote a **letter.**
Letter is the direct object. It tells what Aaron wrote.

We heard **Tom.**
Tom is the direct object. It tells whom we heard.

Directions: Identify the direct object in each sentence. Write it in the blank.

1. __me__ My mother called me.

2. __it__ The baby dropped it.

3. __mayor__ I met the mayor.

4. __you__ I like you!

5. __them__ No one visited them.

6. __cat__ We all heard the cat.

7. __stars__ Jessica saw the stars.

8. __nap__ She needs a nap.

9. __bone__ The dog chewed the bone.

10. __doll__ He hugged the doll.

11. __radio__ I sold the radio.

12. __banana__ Douglas ate the banana.

13. __house__ We finally found the house.

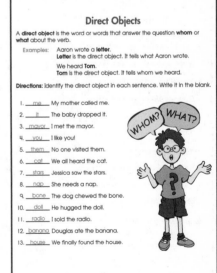

Page 191

Direct Objects

Directions: Finish each sentence by writing a direct object.

1. Eric sang _____
2. Our class rode _____
3. Jordan made _____
4. Keesha baked _____
5. All the children got _____
6. Our new principal read _____
7. My brother wrote _____
8. Sheree gave _____
9. The girls played _____
10. I bought _____
11. Mrs. Bernhard typed _____
12. Barb and Valerie traded _____
13. We all raked _____
14. Jennifer climbed _____

ANSWERS WILL VARY

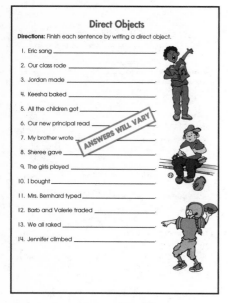

Page 192

Indirect Objects

An **indirect object** is the word or words that receive the action of the verb. An indirect objects tells **to whom** or **what** or **for whom** or **what** something is done.

Examples: He read **me** a funny story.

Me is the indirect object. It tells to whom something (reading a story) was done.

Directions: Identify the indirect object in each sentence. Write it in the blank.

1. The coach gave Bill a trophy. — a trophy
2. He cooked me a wonderful meal. — me
3. She told Maria her secret. — Maria
4. Someone gave my mother a gift. — my mother
5. The class gave the principal a new flag for the cafeteria. — the principal
6. The restaurant pays the waiter a good salary. — the waiter
7. You should tell your dad the truth. — your dad
8. She sent her son a plane ticket. — her son
9. The waiter served the patron a salad. — the patron
10. Grandma gave the baby a kiss. — the baby
11. I sold Steve some cookies. — Steve
12. He told us six jokes. — us
13. She brought the boy a sucker. — the boy

Page 193

Indirect Objects

Directions: Finish each sentence below with the correct indirect object from the Word Bank. Write the letter of the indirect object in the blank.

Word Bank			
a. the librarian	**b.** the coach	**c.** all the teachers	**d.** the class
e. Mom	**f.** the waiter	**g.** all of us	**h.** our parents

Example: __c__ The principal gave__ the notice about the meeting.

ANSWERS MAY VARY BUT MAY INCLUDE...

1. __e__ My sister told ___ the truth.
2. __d__ Our teacher told ___ the homework assignment.
3. __g__ Dad bought ___ a delicious treat.
4. __a__ She gave ___ her overdue books.
5. __h__ We helped ___ clean the house.
6. __f__ The customer gave ___ a good tip.
7. __b__ Michael told ___ about his sore leg.

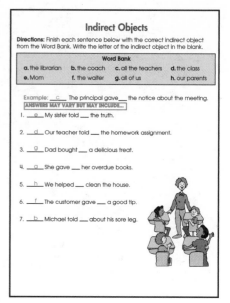

Page 194

Direct and Indirect Objects

Sentences can have direct and indirect objects. A **direct object** answers the question **what** or **whom** about the verb.

Example: Sharon told a story.

Told is the verb. If you ask, **what did Sharon tell**, you can figure out the direct object. Sharon told a story, so **story** is the direct object.

An **indirect object** receives the action of the verb. It answers the question **to what** or **to whom** is something done.

Example: Sharon told Jennifer a story.

If you ask, **to whom did sharon tell a story**, you can figure out the indirect object. Sharon told Jennifer a story, so **Jennifer** is the indirect object.

Directions: Circle the direct object and underline the indirect object in each sentence.

1. The teacher gave the class (a test.)
2. Josh brought Elizabeth (the book.)
3. Someone left (the cat) a present.
4. The poet read David (all his poems.)
5. My big brother handed me (the ticket.)
6. Luke told everyone (the secret.)
7. Jason handed his dad (the newspaper.)
8. Mother bought Jack (a suitcase.)
9. They cooked us (an excellent dinner.)
10. I loaned Jonathan (my bike.)
11. She threw him (a curve ball.)

Page 195

Direct and Indirect Objects

Directions: Finish each sentence by adding a direct object and an indirect object. Circle the direct object and underline the indirect object.

1. The happy clown gave _____
2. The smiling politician offered _____
3. My big brother handed _____
4. His uncle Seth works _____
5. The friendly waiter gave _____
6. Elizabeth told _____
7. My mother brought _____
8. He served _____
9. Jane should tell _____
10. Someone threw _____
11. The bookstore sent _____
12. The salesclerk gave _____
13. The magician brought _____
14. Her father cooked _____
15. Her boss pays. _____

ANSWERS WILL VARY

Page 196

Direct and Indirect Objects

Directions: Circle the direct object and underline the indirect object in each sentence. Then, write the direct and indirect objects in the correct columns.

Example: All the girls wrote (letters) to their friends.

1. Each child brought the teacher (an apple.)
2. My Dad gave my Mom (flowers) on their anniversary.
3. Christopher gave the class (a book report.)
4. The bus drivers gave the children (oranges.)
5. We showed Mom (the prizes.)
6. My brother gave Mom and Dad (his report card.)

Example:

	Direct Objects	Indirect Objects
	letters	friends
1.	an apple	the teacher
2.	flowers	my mom
3.	a book report	the class
4.	oranges	the children
5.	the prizes	Mom
6.	his report card	Mom and Dad

Page 197

Sentence Fragments

A **sentence** tells a complete thought. It has a **subject**—what or who the sentence is about. And it has a **predicate**—what happened to the subject or what the subject did.

A **sentence fragment** is **not a complete thought.**

Example: **Sentences:** The museum was open.
The movie starts at three o'clock.
Mr. Tillbury is coming for dinner.

Fragments: Because Mr. Tillbury.
The museum.
Starts at three o'clock.

Directions: Write **sentence** on the line before each complete sentence. Write **fragment** on the line before each fragment.

1. _fragment_ Because I like chocolate.
2. _sentence_ Paris is in France.
3. _sentence_ Nina likes fritters.
4. _fragment_ Washington, D.C., the capital of the USA.
5. _fragment_ The ancient ruins of the Incas.

Directions: Rewrite each fragment below so that it is a complete sentence.

1. _____ Likes to cook.
2. _____ Mr. Tillbury.
3. _____ Because fritters taste good.
4. _____ To bring to dinner.

ANSWERS WILL VARY

Page 198

Sentence Fragments

A **sentence** is a group of words that expresses a complete thought. It contains a subject and a predicate.

Example: Miranda eats pizza every day.

A **fragment** does not express a complete thought. It may be missing either the subject or the predicate.

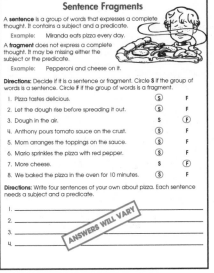

Example: Pepperoni and cheese on it.

Directions: Decide if it is a sentence or fragment. Circle **S** if the group of words is a sentence. Circle **F** if the group of words is a fragment.

	S	F
1. Pizza tastes delicious.	Ⓢ	F
2. Let the dough rise before spreading it out.	Ⓢ	F
3. Dough in the air.	S	Ⓕ
4. Anthony pours tomato sauce on the crust.	Ⓢ	F
5. Mom arranges the toppings on the sauce.	Ⓢ	F
6. Mario sprinkles the pizza with red pepper.	Ⓢ	F
7. More cheese.	S	Ⓕ
8. We baked the pizza in the oven for 10 minutes.	Ⓢ	F

Directions: Write four sentences of your own about pizza. Each sentence needs a subject and a predicate.

1. _____
2. _____
3. _____
4. _____

ANSWERS WILL VARY

Page 199

Sentence Fragments

A **sentence fragment** is only a part of a sentence. It does not express a complete thought.

Example: **fragment:** If I pass the test.
sentence: If I pass the test, I will graduate.

Directions: Write **S** if the group of words is a complete sentence. Write **F** if the group of words is a fragment.

1. _S_ The cactus looks just like Mom's pincushion for sewing.
2. _F_ Prickly pear cactus and hedgehog cactus.
3. _F_ Sucks up water when it rains.
4. _F_ Spines help.
5. _S_ The agave and ocotillo thrive in the desert.

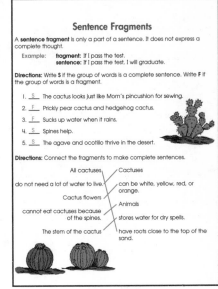

Directions: Connect the fragments to make complete sentences.

All cactuses → Cactuses
do not need a lot of water to live. → can be white, yellow, red, or orange.
Cactus flowers → Animals
cannot eat cactuses because of the spines. → stores water for dry spells.
The stem of the cactus → have roots close to the top of the sand.

Page 200

Word Order

Each sentence needs a **subject** and a **predicate** to be complete. Usually, the subject comes before the predicate. If the parts are not in order, the sentence may not make sense.

Example: **Incorrect:** Rode my bike to town I.
Correct: I rode my bike to town.

Directions: Draw a line to match the subject to the correct predicate. Then, write each complete sentence on the lines below to form a story.

goes along Waddle Lake. — It
Horses — will sing songs and have hayfights.
will be available after the ride. — will drink cider and eat pumpkin pie.
The townsfolk — will pull the wagons.
The hungry party-goers — Food
will be a wonderful night. — The hayride

The hayride goes along Waddle Lake.
Horses will pull the wagons.
Food will be available after the ride.
The townsfolk will sing songs and have hayfights.
The hungry party-goers will drink cider and eat pumpkin pie.
It will be a wonderful night.

Page 201

Word Order

The words in a sentence must be in a certain **order** for the sentence to make sense. If you change the order of the words in a sentence, you will change the meaning of the sentence as well.

Example: The ball hit the wall.
The wall hit the ball.

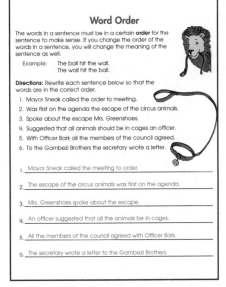

Directions: Rewrite each sentence below so that the words are in the correct order.

1. Mayor Sneak called the order to meeting.
2. Was first on the agenda the escape of the circus animals.
3. Spoke about the escape Mrs. Greenshoes.
4. Suggested that all animals should be in cages an officer.
5. With Officer Bark all the members of the council agreed.
6. To the Gambezi Brothers the secretary wrote a letter.

1. Mayor Sneak called the meeting to order.
2. The escape of the circus animals was first on the agenda.
3. Mrs. Greenshoes spoke about the escape.
4. An officer suggested that all the animals be in cages.
5. All the members of the council agreed with Officer Bark.
6. The secretary wrote a letter to the Gambezi Brothers.

Page 202

Word Order

Word order is the logical order of words in sentences.

Directions: Put the words in order so that each sentence tells a complete idea.

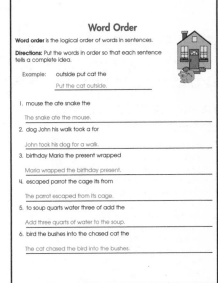

Example: outside put cat the
Put the cat outside.

1. mouse the ate snake the
The snake ate the mouse.
2. dog John his walk took a for
John took his dog for a walk.
3. birthday Maria the present wrapped
Maria wrapped the birthday present.
4. escaped parrot the cage its from
The parrot escaped from its cage.
5. to soup quarts water three of add the
Add three quarts of water to the soup.
6. bird the bushes into the chased cat the
The cat chased the bird into the bushes.

Page 203

Run-On Sentences

When you join together two or more sentences without punctuation, you have created a **run-on sentence**.

Examples:

Run-on sentence: I lost my way once did you?
Correct punctuation: I lost my way once. Did you?

Run-on sentence: I found the recipe it was not hard to follow.
Correct punctuation: I found the recipe. It was not hard to follow.

Directions: Rewrite each run-on sentence so that it becomes two or more sentences.

Example: Did you take my umbrella I cannot find it anywhere!

Did you take my umbrella? I cannot find it anywhere!

1. How can you stand that noise I cannot!

How can you stand that noise? I cannot!

2. The cookies are gone I see only crumbs.

The cookies are gone. I see only crumbs.

3. The dogs were barking they were hungry.

The dogs were barking. They were hungry.

4. She is quite ill please call a doctor immediately!

She is quite ill. Please call a doctor immediately!

5. The clouds piled up we knew the storm would hit soon.

The clouds piled up. We knew the storm would hit soon.

Page 204

Run-On Sentences

A **run-on sentence** is made up of two or more complete sentences that are joined together without the correct punctuation.

Example: **Run-On:**   I am a desert creature I love the heat
                 Correct: I am a desert creature. I love the heat.

Directions: Rewrite each run-on sentence so that it becomes two or more complete sentences.

I am a nocturnal animal I shed my skin and I eat rodents, lizards, and even birds. I can inject my poison through my fangs I have a rattle at the tip of my tail it tells when I may attack.

I am a nocturnal animal. I shed my skin and I eat rodents, lizards, and
even birds. I can inject my poison through my fangs. I have a rattle at
the tip of my tail. It tells when I may attack.

I am cold-blooded my body temperature is the same as the air around me I am a tiny animal that looks like the giant dinosaurs that lived a long time ago.

I am cold-blooded. My body temperature is the same as the air around
me. I am a tiny animal that looks like the giant dinosaurs that lived a long
time ago.

Page 205

Run-On Sentences

A **run-on sentence** is two or more sentences that run together. You can use punctuation and capitalization to make complete sentences.

Examples: **Run-On:**   Katelyn's garden is in the backyard
                 she works there each day.
              Correct: Katelyn's garden is in the backyard.
                 She works there each day.

Directions: Rewrite each run-on sentence correctly. Write two or more shorter sentences.

1. Katelyn cleared the garden she raked the leaves and collected rocks.

Katelyn cleared the garden. She raked the leaves and collected rocks.

2. Katelyn planted seeds she planted beans and pumpkins.

Katelyn planted seeds. She planted beans and pumpkins.

3. the seeds grow quickly they like warm sunshine.

The seeds grow quickly. They like warm sunshine.

4. Water helps the plants grow Katelyn waters them every day.

Water helps the plants grow. Katelyn waters them every day.

5. Insects visit Katelyn's garden some bugs are good.

Insects visit Katelyn's garden. Some bugs are good.

6. Pulling weeds is not very fun it is an important job.

Pulling weeds is not very fun. It is an important job.

7. Pumpkins grow very large beans grow very tall.

Pumpkins grow very large. Beans grow very tall.

8. Katelyn harvests the vegetables they taste good.

Katelyn harvests the vegetables. They taste good.

Page 206

Conjunctions

Words that join sentences or combine ideas, such as **and, but, or, because, when, after,** and **so,** are called conjunctions.

Examples:

I played the drums, **and** Sue played the clarinet.
She likes bananas, **but** I do not.
We could play music **or** just enjoy the silence.
I needed the book **because** I had to write a book report.
He gave me the book **when** I asked for it.
I asked her to eat lunch **after** she finished the test.
You wanted my bike **so** you could ride it.

Conjunctions can affect the meaning of a sentence.

Example: He gave me the book **when** I asked for it.
                 He gave me the book **after** I asked for it.

Directions: Choose the best conjunction to combine each pair of sentences.

Example: I like my hair curly. Mom likes my hair straight.

I like my hair curly, but Mom likes it straight.

1. I can remember what she looks like. I cannot remember her name.

I can remember what she looks like, but I cannot remember her name.

2. We will have to wash the dishes. We will not have clean plates for dinner.

We will have to wash dishes, or we will not have clean plates for dinner.

3. The yellow flowers are blooming. The red flowers are not.

The yellow flowers are blooming, but the red flowers are not.

4. I like banana cream pie. I like chocolate donuts.

I like banana cream pie, and I like chocolate donuts.

Page 207

Conjunctions

Directions: Use a conjunction from the Word Bank to combine the pairs of sentences.

Word Bank						
and	but	or	because	when	after	so

ANSWERS WILL VARY BUT MAY INCLUDE...

1. I like Leah. I like Ben.

I like Leah and I like Ben.

2. Should I eat the orange? Should I eat the apple?

Should I eat the orange or the apple?

3. You will get a reward. You turned in the lost item.

You will get a reward if you turned in the lost item.

4. I really mean what I say! You had better listen!

I really mean what I say, so you had better listen!

5. I like you. You are nice, friendly, helpful, and kind.

I like you because you are nice, friendly, helpful, and kind.

6. You can have dessert. You ate all your peas.

You can have dessert because you ate all your peas.

7. I like your shirt better. You should decide for yourself.

I like your shirt better, but you should decide for yourself.

8. We walked out of the building. We heard the fire alarm.

We walked out of the building when we heard the fire alarm.

9. I like to sing folk songs. I like to play the guitar.

I like to sing folk songs and play the guitar.

Page 208

"And," "But," "Or"

Directions: Write **and, but,** or **or** to finish each sentence.

ANSWERS WILL VARY BUT MAY INCLUDE...

1. I want to try that new hamburger place, _but_ Mom wants to eat at the Spaghetti Shop.

2. We could stay home, _or_ would you rather go to the game?

3. She went right home after school, _and_ he stopped at the store.

4. Mother held the piece of paneling, _and_ Father nailed it in place.

5. She babysat last weekend, _and_ her big sister went with her.

6. She likes raisins in her oatmeal, _but_ I prefer brown sugar.

7. She was planning on coming over tomorrow, _but_ I asked her if she could wait until the weekend.

8. Tomato soup with crackers sounds good to me, _or_ would you rather have vegetable beef soup?

Page 209

"And" or "But"

We can use **and** or **but** to make one longer sentence from two short ones.

Directions: Use **and** or **but** to make two short sentences into a longer, more interesting one.

Example: The skunk has black fur. The skunk has a white stripe.
           <u>The skunk has black fur and a white stripe.</u>

1. The skunk has a small head. The skunk has small ears.

   <u>The skunk has a small head and small ears.</u>

2. Skunks have short legs. Skunks can move quickly.

   <u>Skunks have short legs but can move quickly.</u>

3. Skunks sleep in hollow trees. Skunks sleep underground.

   <u>Skunks sleep in hollow trees and underground.</u>

4. Larger animals may try to chase a skunk. Skunks do not run away.

   <u>Larger animals may try to chase a skunk, but skunks do not run away.</u>

5. Skunks sleep during the day. Skunks hunt at night.

   <u>Skunks sleep during the day. Skunks hunt at night.</u>

Page 210

"When" or "After"

Directions: Write **when** or **after** to finish each sentence.

ANSWERS WILL VARY BUT MAY INCLUDE...

1. I knew we were in trouble <u>when</u> I heard the thunder in the distance.

2. We carried the baskets of cherries to the car <u>after</u> we were finished picking them.

3. Mother took off her apron <u>after</u> I reminded her that our dinner guests would be here any minute.

4. I wondered if we would have school tomorrow <u>after</u> I noticed the snow begin to fall.

5. The boys and girls all clapped <u>when</u> the magician pulled the colored scarves out of his sleeve.

6. I was startled <u>when</u> the phone rang so late last night.

7. You will need to get the film developed <u>after</u> you have taken all the pictures.

8. The children began to run <u>when</u> the snake started to move!

Page 211

"Because" or "So"

Directions: Write **because** or **so** to finish each sentence.

1. She cleaned the paint brushes <u>so</u> they would be ready in the morning.

2. Father called home complaining of a sore throat <u>so</u> Mom stopped by the pharmacy.

3. His bus will be running late <u>because</u> it has a flat tire.

4. We all worked together <u>so</u> we could get the job done sooner.

5. We took a variety of sandwiches on the picnic <u>because</u> we knew not everyone liked cheese and olives with mayonnaise.

6. All the school children were sent home <u>because</u> the electricity went off at school.

7. My brother wants us to meet his girlfriend <u>so</u> she will be coming to dinner with us on Friday.

8. He forgot to take his umbrella along this morning <u>so</u> now his clothes are very wet.

Page 212

Joining Sentences

Directions: Use **because**, **after**, or **when** to join each set of sentences into one longer sentence.

1. I pack my own lunch. I do not like the school's food.

   <u>I pack my own lunch because I do not like the school's food.</u>

2. I decided to be a zoo keeper. We visited the zoo.

   <u>I decided to be a zoo keeper when we visited the zoo.</u>

3. I am surprised there is such a crowd. It costs so much to get in.

   <u>I am surprised there is such a crowd because it costs so much to get in.</u>

4. I beat the eggs for two minutes. The recipe called for egg yolk.

   <u>I beat the eggs for two minutes because the recipe called for egg yolk.</u>

Page 213

Combining Sentences

Some simple sentences can be easily combined into one sentence.

Examples:
   Simple sentences: The bird sang. The bird was tiny.
   The bird was in the tree.
   Combined sentence: The tiny bird sang in the tree.

Directions: Combine each set of simple sentences into one sentence.

Example:
   The older girls laughed. They were friendly. They helped the little girls.
   <u>The older, friendly girls laughed as they helped the little girls.</u>

1. The dog was hungry. The dog whimpered. The dog looked at its bowl.

   <u>The hungry dog whimpered and looked at its bowl.</u>

2. Be quiet now. I want you to listen. You listen to my joke!

   <u>Be quiet now so you can listen to my joke!</u>

3. I lost my pencil. My pencil was stubby. I lost it on the bus.

   <u>I lost my stubby pencil on the bus.</u>

4. I see my mother. My mother is walking. My mother is walking down the street.

   <u>I see my mother walking down the street.</u>

5. Do you like ice cream? Do you like hot dogs? Do you like mustard?

   <u>Do you like ice cream, hot dogs, and mustard?</u>

6. Tell me you will do it! Tell me you will! Tell me right now.

   <u>Tell me right now that you will do it!</u>

Page 214

Using Fewer Words

Writing can be more interesting when you use fewer words. Combining sentences is easy when the subjects are the same. Notice how the comma is used.

Example: Sally woke up. Sally ate breakfast. Sally brushed her teeth.
           <u>Sally woke up, ate breakfast, and brushed her teeth.</u>

Combining sentences with more than one subject is a little more complicated. Notice how commas are used to "set off" information.

Examples: Jane went to the store. Jane is Sally's sister.
            <u>Jane went to the store with Sally, her sister.</u>

  Eddy Eddie likes to play with cars. Eddie is my younger brother.
            <u>Eddie, my younger brother, likes to play with cars.</u>

Directions: Write each pair of sentences as one sentence.

1. Jerry played soccer after school. He played with his best friend, Tom.

   <u>Jerry played soccer after school with his best friend, Tom.</u>

2. Spot likes to chase cats. Spot is my dog.

   <u>Spot, my dog, likes to chase cats.</u>

3. Lori and Janice both love ice cream. Janice is Lori's cousin.

   <u>Lori and Janice, Lori's cousin, both love ice cream.</u>

4. Jayna is my cousin. Jayna helped me move into my new apartment.

   <u>Jayna, my cousin, helped me move into my new apartment.</u>

5. Romeo is a big tomcat. Romeo loves to hunt mice.

   <u>Romeo, a big tomcat, loves to hunt mice.</u>

Page 215

Putting Ideas Together

Directions: Make each pair of sentences into one sentence. (You may have to change the verbs for some sentences—from **is** to **are**, for example.)

Example: Our house was flooded. Our car was flooded.
Our house and car were flooded.

1. Kenny sees a glow. Carrie sees a glow.

Kenny and Carry see a glow.

2. Our new stove came today. Our new refrigerator came today.

Our new stove and refrigerator came today.

3. The pond is full of toads. The field is full of toads.

The pond and field are full of toads.

4. Stripes are on the flag. Stars are on the flag.

Stripes and stars are on the flag.

5. The ducks took flight. The geese took flight.

The ducks and geese took flight.

6. Joe reads stories. Dana reads stories.

Joe and Dana read stories.

7. French fries taste good. Milkshakes taste good.

French fries and milkshakes taste good.

8. Justine heard someone groan. Kevin heard someone groan.

Justine and Kevin heard someone groan.

Page 216

Putting Ideas Together

Directions: Write each pair of sentences as one sentence.

Example:
Jim will deal the cards one at a time.
Jim will give four cards to everyone.
Jim will deal the cards one at a time and give four cards to everyone.

1. Amy won the contest. Amy claimed the prize.

Amy won the contest and claimed the prize.

2. We need to find the scissors. We need to buy some tape.

We need to find the scissors and buy some tape.

3. The stream runs through the woods. The stream empties into the East River.

The stream runs through the woods and empties into the East River.

4. Katie tripped on the steps. Katie has a pain in her left foot.

Katie tripped on the steps and has a pain in her left foot.

5. Grandpa took me to the store. Grandpa bought me a treat.

Grandpa took me to the store and bought me a treat.

6. Charity ran two miles. She walked one mile to cool down afterward.

Charity ran two miles and walked one mile to cool down afterward.

Page 217

Statements

A **statement** is a sentence that tells something.

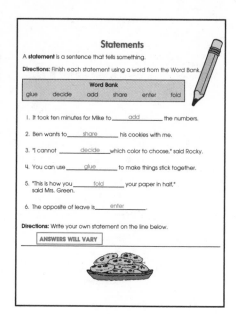

Directions: Finish each statement using a word from the Word Bank.

Word Bank					
glue	decide	add	share	enter	fold

1. It took ten minutes for Mike to ___add___ the numbers.

2. Ben wants to ___share___ his cookies with me.

3. "I cannot ___decide___ which color to choose," said Rocky.

4. You can use ___glue___ to make things stick together.

5. "This is how you ___fold___ your paper in half," said Mrs. Green.

6. The opposite of leave is ___enter___ .

Directions: Write your own statement on the line below.

ANSWERS WILL VARY

Page 218

Questions

Questions are asking sentences. They begin with a capital letter and end with a question mark. Many questions begin with the word **who, what, why, when, where,** or **how.**

Directions: Write six questions using the question words below. Make sure to end each sentence with a question mark.

1. Who _____

2. What _____

3. Why _____   ANSWERS WILL VARY

4. When _____

5. Where _____

6. How _____

Page 219

Writing Question Sentences

Directions: Rewrite each sentence to make it a question. In some cases, you will need to change the form of the verb.

Example: She slept soundly all day.
Did she sleep soundly all day?

1. The cookies are hot.

Are the cookies hot?

2. He put the cake in the oven.

Did he put the cake in the oven?

3. She lives in the blue house.

Does she live in the blue house?

4. He understood my directions.

Did he understand my directions?

5. Jessica ran faster than everyone.

Did Jessica run faster than everyone?

6. The bus was gone before he arrived.

Was the bus gone before he arrived?

7. His car is yellow.

Is his car yellow?

8. Elizabeth wants some more beans.

Does Elizabeth want some more beans?

Page 220

Statements and Questions

A **statement** tells some kind of information. It is followed by a period (.).

Examples: It is a rainy day.
We are going to the beach next summer.

A **question** asks for a specific piece of information. It is followed by a question mark (?).

Examples: What is the weather like today?
When are you going to the beach?

Directions: Write whether each sentence is a statement or question.

Example: Jamie went for a walk at the zoo.   statement

1. The leaves turn bright colors in the fall.   statement

2. When does the Easter Bunny arrive?   question

3. Madeleine went to the new art school.   statement

4. Is school over at 3:30?   question

5. Grandma and Grandpa are moving.   statement

6. Anthony went home.   statement

7. Did Mary go to Amy's house?   question

8. Who went to work late?   question

Directions: Write two statements and two questions below.

Statements:

_____

_____

Questions: ANSWERS WILL VARY

Page 221

Commands

A **command** is a sentence that tells someone or something to do something.

Directions: Finish each command with a word from the Word Bank.

Word Bank					
glue	decide	add	share	enter	fold

1. _Add_ a cup of flour to the cake batter.

2. _Decide_ how much paper you will need to write your story.

3. Please _glue_ the picture of the apple onto the paper.

4. _Enter_ through this door and leave through the other door.

5. Please _fold_ the letter and put it into an envelope.

6. _Share_ your toys with your sister.

Directions: Write four commands on the lines below.

ANSWERS WILL VARY

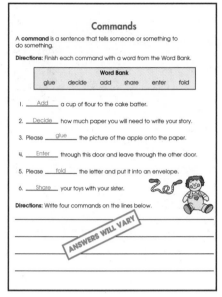

Page 222

Directions

A **direction** is a sentence written as a command.

Directions: Write the missing directions for these pictures. Begin each direction with one of the verbs from the Word Bank.

Word Bank					
glue	decide	add	share	enter	fold

How To Make a Peanut Butter and Jelly Sandwich:
ANSWERS WILL VARY BUT MAY INCLUDE:

1. Spread peanut butter on the bread.

2. Spread jelly on the bread.

3. Cut the sandwich in half.

4. Place the sandwich on a plate.

How To Make a Valentine:

1. Fold the paper in half.

2. Draw half of a heart.

3. Cut along the line you drew.

4. Glue the heart to a piece of paper.

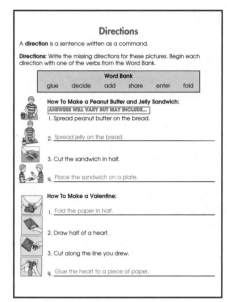

Page 223

Exclamations

Exclamation points end sentences or phrases that express strong feelings.

Example: **Wait!**
Don't forget to call!

Directions: Add an exclamation point at the end of each sentence that expresses strong feelings. Add a period at the end of each statement.

1. My parents and I watched television_._

2. The snow began falling around noon_._

3. Wow_!_

4. The snow was really coming down_!_

5. We turned the television off and looked out the window_._

6. The snow looked like a white blanket_._

7. How beautiful_!_

8. We decided to put on our coats and go outside_._

9. Hurry_!_

10. Get your sled_._

11. All the people on the street came out to see the snow_._

12. How wonderful_!_

13. The children began making a snowman_._

14. What a great day_!_

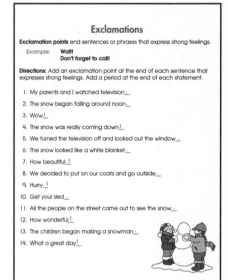

Page 224

Commands and Exclamations

A command tells someone to do something. It is followed by a period (.).

Examples: Get your math book. Do your homework.

An exclamation shows strong feeling or excitement. It is followed by an exclamation mark (!).

Examples: Watch out for that car! There's a snake!

Directions: Write whether each sentence is a command or an exclamation.

Examples:
Please clean your room. ___command___
Wow! Those fireworks are beautiful! ___exclamation___

1. Come to dinner now. ___command___

2. Color the sky and water blue. ___command___

3. Trim the paper carefully. ___command___

4. Here comes the bus! ___exclamation___

5. That is a lovely picture! ___exclamation___

6. Stop playing and clean up. ___command___

7. Brush your teeth before bedtime. ___command___

Directions: Write two commands and two exclamations below.
Commands:

Exclamations:

ANSWERS WILL VARY

Page 225

Four Kinds of Sentences

Directions: Write **S** if the sentence is a statement, **Q** if the sentence is a question, **C** if the sentence is a command, or **E** if the sentence is an exclamation. End each sentence with a period, question mark, or exclamation mark.

Example: _E_ Oh my gosh!

_S_ 1. My little brother insists on coming with us_._

_C_ 2. Tell him movies are bad for his health_._

_S_ 3. He says he is fond of movies_._

_Q_ 4. Does he know there are monsters in this movie_?_

_S_ 5. He says he needs facts for his science report_._

_S_ 6. He is writing about something that hatched from an old egg_._

_Q_ 7. Could he go to the library_?_

_Q_ 8. Could we dress him like us so he will blend in_?_

_E_ 9. You must be kidding_!_

_Q_ 10. Would he sit by himself at the movie_?_

_E_ 11. That would be too dangerous_!_

_S_ 12. Mom said she would give us money for candy if we took him with us_._

_E_ 13. That is awesome_!_

_C_ 14. Get your brother and go_._

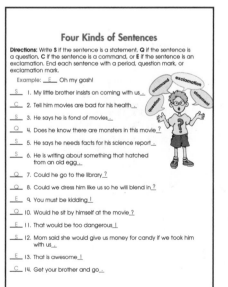

Page 226

Four Kinds of Sentences

Directions: For each pair of words, write two kinds of sentences (any combination of questions, commands, statements, or exclamations). Use one or both of the words in each sentence. Name each kind of sentence that you wrote.

Example:
pump crop
Question : _What kind of crops did you plant?_
Command : _Pump the water as fast as you can._

1. pinch health

2. fond fact

ANSWERS WILL VARY

3. insist hatch

exclamation command statement question

Page 227

Punctuation

A **sentence** is a group of words that tells a complete thought.

A sentence that tells something ends with a period (.).
A sentence that asks a question ends with a question mark (?).
A sentence that shows strong feeling ends with an exclamation point (!).
A sentence that gives a command ends with a period (.).

Directions: Read each sentence. Write the correct punctuation mark to end the sentence.

1. Do you want to go to the movies on Saturday ?
2. We are going to the theater at the mall .
3. I am going to buy a large popcorn and a bag of candy .
4. What do you like to eat at the movies ?
5. This movie is great !
6. Meet me outside .

Directions: Write four sentences about a move you have seen. Try to include at least two different kinds of sentences.

ANSWERS WILL VARY

Page 228

Capitalization

The first word in a sentence should begin with a capital letter.

Directions: Read each sentence. Underline with three short lines the first letter of each word that needs a capital letter. Rewrite the word correctly.

Example: _Today_ today is the first day of school.

1. Sam — sam takes the bus to school.
2. The — the children play soccer at recess.
3. Everyone — everyone has fun reading a story.
4. When — when will we do a science experiment?
5. Lunch — lunch is served in the cafeteria.
6. Our — our principal came to visit our class.
7. Students — students should be quiet in the library.
8. The — the teacher writes the homework on the board.
9. Clean — clean your desk before you go home.
10. Have — have a great day!

Page 229

Punctuation and Capitalization

Directions: In the paragraphs below, use periods, question marks, or exclamation points to show where one sentence ends and the next begins. Circle the first letter of each new sentence to show the capitalization.

Example: My sister accused me of not helping her rake the leaves . That is silly ! I helped at least a hundred times .

1. I toss out my fishing line . When it moves up and down, I know a fish is there . After waiting a minute or two, I pull up the fish . It is fun !

2. I tried putting lemon juice on my freckles to make them go away . Did you ever do that? It did not work . My skin just got sticky . Now, I am slowly getting used to my freckles .

3. Once, I had an accident on my bike . It was on my way home from school . What do you think happened? My wheel slipped in the loose dirt at the side of the road . My bike slid into the road !

4. One night, I dreamed I lived in a castle . In my dream, I was the king or maybe the queen . Everyone listened to my commands . Then, Mom woke me up for school . I tried commanding her to let me sleep . It did not work !

5. My dad does exercises every night to make his stomach flat . He says he does not want to grow old . I think it is too late . Do not tell him I said that !

Page 230

Punctuation and Capitalization

Directions: In the paragraphs below, use periods, question marks, and exclamation points to show where one sentence ends and the next begins. Circle the first letter of each new sentence to show the capitalization.

1. It was Christmas Eve . Santa and the elves were loading the toys onto his sleigh . The deer keepers were harnessing the reindeer and walking them toward the sleigh .

2. The reindeer were prancing with anxious anticipation of their midnight flight . Soon, the sleigh was overflowing with its load, and Santa was ready to travel . Crack went his whip . The reindeer pulled and tugged against their harnesses . The sleigh inched forward, slowly at first, then it climbed swiftly into the holiday night sky .

3. Everything was going smoothly . Santa and the reindeer made excellent time traveling from house to house and city to city . At each home, of course, the children had left snacks of cookies and milk for Santa .

4. Around 2 o'clock in the morning, Santa felt his red suit begin to get tight around his middle . "Hmm," he said to himself. "I have been eating too many snacks." He decided that he would have to cut back on his cookie calories .

5. The reindeer team guided Santa to his next stop . He hopped out of his sleigh, grabbed his bundle of toys, and jogged to the chimney . He climbed up to the chimney's opening and started down to the fireplace . Oops! Something awful happened! Santa got stuck! Oh, no! What do we do now? Wondered the reindeer.

Page 231

Capitalization

A **proper noun** names a special person, place, or thing. Capitalize the first letter in each word of a proper noun.

Examples: california cafe = California Cafe
malibu = Malibu

Directions: In the post card, underline with three short lines the first letter of each word that needs a capital letter.

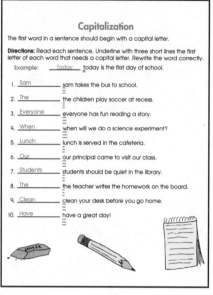

CALIFORNIA

Dear trudy,
My family and I are in los angeles, california. We have been to hollywood, santa monica beach, and rodeo drive in beverly hills. Tomorrow, we are going to visit disney land. I hope I will get to meet mickey mouse. Wish you were here!
Your friend, roberta

Trudy Little
3501 Courtland
Garden City, KS
67846

Directions: Rewrite Roberta's postcard with the correct capitalization.

Dear Trudy, My family and I are in Los Angeles, California. We have been to Hollywood, Santa Monica Beach, and Rodeo Drive in Beverly Hills. Tomorrow, we are going to visit Disney Land. I hope I will get to meet Mickey Mouse. Wish you were here! Your Friend, Roberta

Page 232

Capitalization

A person's name begins with a capital letter. The pronoun I is written as a capital letter.

Directions: Read each sentence. Underline with three short lines the first letter of each word that needs a capital letter. Write each sentence correctly.

Example:
The librarian helped tracy find a book about susan b. anthony.
The librarian helped Tracy find a book about Susan B. Anthony.

1. I learned that george washington was the first president.
   I learned that George Washington was the first president.

2. matthew and amelia are doing a project about thomas jefferson.
   Matthew and Amelia are doing a project about Thomas Jefferson.

3. elisa and I are studying about abraham lincoln.
   Elisa and I are studying about Abraham Lincoln.

4. harriet tubman helped rescue many people from slavery.
   Harriet Tubman helped rescue many people from slavery.

5. Many people admire helen keller's courage and intelligence.
   Many people admire Helen Keller's courage and intelligence.

6. Can I write a report about jackie robinson?
   Can I write a report about Jackie Robinson?

Page 233

Capitalization

Capitalize the first letter of each word in the names of holidays and special events.

Directions: Read each sentence. Underline with three short lines the first letter of each word that needs a capital letter. Rewrite each sentence correctly.

1. Did you watch the rose parade on new year's day?
   Did you watch the Rose Parade on
   New Year's Day?

2. The librarian helps us choose books during national book week.
   The librarian helps us choose books during National Book Week.

3. My family eats turkey and potatoes on thanksgiving day.
   My family eats turkey and potatoes on Thanksgiving Day.

4. The class planted a tree on arbor day.
   The class planted a tree on Arbor Day.

5. Our christmas tree is decorated with lights and ornaments.
   Our Christmas tree is decorated with lights and ornaments.

6. We watched fireworks at the park on independence day.
   We watched fireworks at the park on Independence Day.

Page 234

Capitalization

Capitalize the first letter of each word in geographical names and historical periods of time.

Examples: pacific ocean = Pacific Ocean
renaissance = Renaissance

Directions: Read each word. If the word should begin with a capital letter, rewrite it correctly on the line.

1. rocky mountains — Rocky Mountains
2. lake superior — Lake Superior
3. ocean —
4. kenya — Kenya
5. country —
6. middle ages — Middle Ages
7. dinosaur —
8. north pole — North Pole
9. stone age — Stone Age
10. river —
11. jurassic period — Jurassic Period
12. nile river — Nile River
13. europe — Europe
14. state —
15. atlantic ocean — Atlantic Ocean

Page 235

Abbreviations

An **abbreviation** is the shortened form of a word. Most abbreviations begin with a capital letter and end with a period.

Mr. = Mister	A.M. = Before Noon	St. = Street
Mrs. = Missus	P.M. = After Noon	Ave. = Avenue
Dr. = Doctor		Blvd. = Boulevard
		Rd. = Road

Weekdays: Sun. Mon. Tues. Wed. Thurs. Fri. Sat.
Months: Jan. Feb. Mar. Apr. Aug. Sept. Oct. Nov. Dec.

Directions: Write the abbreviation for each word.

Street	St.	Doctor	Dr.	Tuesday	Tues.
Road	Rd.	Mister	Mr.	Avenue	Ave.
Missus	Mrs.	October	Oct.	Friday	Fri.
Before Noon	A.M.	March	Mar.	August	Aug.

Directions: Rewrite each sentence using abbreviations.

1. On Monday at 9:00 before noon, Mister Jones had a meeting.
   On Mon. at 9:00 A.M., Mr. Jones had a meeting.

2. In December, Doctor Carlson saw Missus Zuckerman.
   In Dec., Dr. Carlson saw Mrs. Zuckerman.

3. One Tuesday in August, Mister Wood went to the park.
   One Tues. in Aug., Mr. Wood went to the park.

Page 236

Abbreviations

Use a **period** after an **abbreviation**.

Example: Monday = Mon.   December = Dec.

Do not use abbreviations in sentences.

Example: I like to skate on Mondays in December.

Directions: Fill in each blank with the correct abbreviation from the Word Bank.

1. Wednesday	Wed.	7. Rural Route	R.R.
2. January	Jan.	8. Thursday	Thurs.
3. Street	St.	9. Avenue	Ave.
4. Boulevard	Blvd.	10. Road	Rd.
5. February	Feb.	11. April	Apr.
6. Saturday	Sat.	12. Post Office	P.O.

Word Bank

Blvd.	St.
Jan.	Sat.
Wed.	Feb.
P.O.	R.R.
Rd.	Apr.
Ave.	Thurs.

Directions: Rewrite each sentence correctly on the lines below.

1. Every Mon. in Jan., they shovel driveways for the elderly.
   Every Monday in January, the shovel driveways for the elderly.

2. Their meetings are held each Tues. at Julie's house on Webster St.
   Their meetings are held each Tuesday at Julie's house on Webster Street.

3. During Feb., they visited nursing homes every Sun. evening.
   During February, they visited nursing homes every Sunday evening

Page 237

Capitalization

A **title** tells what a person is or does. It begins with a capital letter and ends with a period. An **initial** is the first letter of a person's first, middle, or last name.

Examples: **Mr. Rogers**
Dr. B.J. Honeycut

Directions: Write each name and title correctly.

1. dr seuss — Dr. Seuss
2. gen g patton — Gen. G. Patton
3. mr rogers — Mr. Rogers
4. mrs e roosevelt — Mrs. E. Roosevelt
5. miss gloria steinem — Miss Gloria Steinem
6. capt james t kirk — Capt. James T. Kirk
7. mr m twain — Mr. M. Twain
8. dr s freud — Dr. S. Freud
9. miss louisa m alcott — Miss Louisa M. Alcott
10. mr maurice sendak — Mr. Maurice Sendak
11. dr l pasteur — Dr. L. Pasteur
12. gen e braddock — Gen. E. Braddock

Page 238

Capitalization

Capitalize the first letter in each month of the year, in each day of the week, in a title of respect, and when abbreviating a title of respect.

Examples: january = January   tuesday = Tuesday
doctor jones = Doctor Jones   mrs. clark = Mrs. Clark

Directions: Read the story below. Underline with three short lines the first letter of each word that needs a capital letter. Rewrite the story correctly.

My baby brother, Nicholas, was born on sunday, september 8, 2002. On saturday, my mom went to see doctor nelson at the hospital. Our neighbors, mr. and mrs. Bigelow, let me sleep over at their house. My mom and Nicholas came home on monday.

My baby brother, Nicholas, was born on Sunday, September 8, 2002. On Saturday, my mom went to see Doctor Nelson at the hospital. Our neighbors, Mr. and Mrs. Bigelow, let me sleep over at their house. My mom and Nicholas came home on Monday.

Page 239

Capitalization

A specific name of a **person**, **place**, and **pet**, a **day of the week**, a **month of the year**, and a **holiday** each begins with a capital letter.

Directions: Read the words in the Word Bank. Write the words in the correct columns with the correct letters capitalized.

Word Bank

ron polsky	tuesday	march	april
presidents' day	saturday	woofy	october
blackie	portland, oregon	corning, new york	molly yoder
valentine's day	fluffy	harold edwards	arbor day
bozeman, montana	sunday		

People	Places	Pets
Ron Polsky	Bozeman, Montana	Blackie
Harold Edwards	Portland, Oregon	Fluffy
Molly Yoder	Corning, New York	Woofy

Days	Months	Holidays
Tuesday	March	President's Day
Saturday	April	Valentine's Day
Sunday	October	Arbor Day

Page 240

Book Titles

Capitalize the first and last words in a book's title. Capitalize all other words in a book's title except short prepositions, such as **of**, **at**, and **in**, conjunctions, such as **and**, **or**, and **but**, and articles, such as **a**, **an**, and **the**.

Examples:
Have you read <u>War and Peace</u>?
Pippi Longstocking in Moscow is her favorite book.

Directions: Underline the book titles. Circle the words that should be capitalized.

Example: murder in the blue room by Elliot Roosevelt

1. growing up in a divided society by Sandra Burnham
2. the corn king and the spring queen by Naomi Mitchison
3. new kids on the block by Grace Catalano
4. best friends don't tell lies by Linda Barr
5. turn your kid into a computer genius by Carole Gerber
6. amy the dancing bear by Carly Simon
7. garfield goes to waist by Jim Davis
8. the hunt for red october by Tom Clancy
9. fall into darkness by Christopher Pike
10. oh the places you'll go by Dr. Seuss

Page 241

Book Titles

All words in the title of a book are underlined or italicized.

Examples: <u>The Hunt for Red October</u> was a best-seller!
Have you read *Lost in Space*?

Directions: Underline the book titles in these sentences.

Example: <u>The Dinosaur Poster Book</u> is for eight-year-old children.

1. Have you read <u>Lion Dancer</u> by Kate Waters?
2. <u>Baby Dinosaurs</u> and <u>Giant Dinosaurs</u> were both written by Peter Dodson.
3. Have you heard of the book <u>That's What Friends Are For</u> by Carol Adorjan?
4. J.B. Stamper wrote a book called <u>The Totally Terrific Valentine Party Book</u>.
5. The teacher read <u>Almost Ten and a Half</u> aloud to our class.
6. <u>Marrying Off Mom</u> is about a girl who tries to get her widowed mother to start dating.
7. <u>The Snow</u> and <u>The Fire</u> are the second and third books by author Caroline Cooney.
8. The title sounds silly, but <u>Goofbang Value Daze</u> really is the name of a book!
9. A book about space exploration is <u>The Day We Walked on the Moon</u> by George Sullivan.
10. <u>Alice and the Birthday Giant</u> tells about a giant who came to a girl's birthday party.

Page 242

Titles

Titles of books are underlined when you write them by hand. When they are typed, titles of books are underlined or in italics.

Examples: <u>James and the Giant Peach</u>
James and the Giant Peach

Titles of stories, poems, and songs are always in quotation marks.

Examples: "Sleeping Beauty" (story)
"Paul Revere's Ride" (poem)
"Blue Suede Shoes" (song)

Directions: Read each sentence. Underline the title of a book. Put quotation marks around the title of a story, poem, or song.

1. Luis read <u>Number the Stars</u> for his book report.
2. "Stanley the Fierce" is a poem by Judith Viorst.
3. Laura Ingalls Wilder wrote <u>Little House in the Big Woods</u>.
4. Our class sang "America the Beautiful" for the veterans.
5. "The Gift of the Magi" is a good story.
6. Do you know how to play "Happy Birthday" on the piano?
7. "A Girl's Garden" is a poem by Robert Frost.
8. Last week, I checked out <u>Because of Winn-Dixie</u> from the library.
9. My dad read us the story "Tom Thumb" before we went to sleep.
10. Our class is reading <u>Sarah, Plain and Tall</u> this month.

Page 243

Commas

Commas are used to separate words in a series of three or more.

Example: My favorite fruits are apples, bananas, and oranges.

Directions: Put commas where they are needed in each sentence.

1. Please buy milk, eggs, bread, and cheese.
2. I need paper, pencils, and a folder for school.
3. Some good pets are cats, dogs, gerbils, fish, and rabbits.
4. Aaron, Mike, and Matt went to the baseball game.
5. Major forms of transportation are planes, trains, and automobiles.

Page 244

Commas

Use a comma to separate words in a series. A comma is used after each word in a series but is not needed before the last word. Both ways are correct. In your own writing, be consistent about which style you use.

Examples: We ate apples, oranges, and pears.
We ate apples, oranges and pears.

Always use a comma between the name of a city and a state.

Example: She lives in Fresno, California.
He lives in Wilmington, Delaware.

Directions: Write C if the sentence is punctuated correctly. Write X if the sentence is not punctuated correctly.

Example: __X__ She ordered shoes, dresses and shirts to be sent to her home in Oakland California.

1. __C__ No one knew her pets' names were Fido, Spot and Tiger.
2. __X__ He likes green beans lima beans, and corn on the cob.
3. __C__ Typing paper, pens and pencils are all needed for school.
4. __C__ Send your letters to her in College Park, Maryland.
5. __X__ Orlando Florida is the home of Disney World.
6. __C__ Mickey, Minnie, Goofy and Daisy are all favorites of mine.
7. __C__ Send your letter to her in Reno, Nevada.
8. __X__ Before he lived in New York, City he lived in San Diego, California.
9. __X__ She mailed postcards, and letters to him in Lexington, Kentucky.
10. __C__ Teacups, saucers, napkins, and silverware were piled high.
11. __C__ Can someone give me a ride to Indianapolis, Indiana?
12. __X__ He took a train a car, then a boat to visit his old friend.

Page 245

Page 246

Commas

Commas separate words in a list or series.

Examples: We will need to take a train, a helicopter, a bus, and a boat to get to the island.

Directions: Put commas where they belong in the story below.

We are on an expedition to visit these volcanoes: Mount Saint Helens, Mount Etna, Mount Pinatubo, Mount Pelee, and Mount Vesuvius. The members of our team are geologists, botanists, and volcanologists. They will help us study these volcanoes and learn more about the formation, the craters, the types of volcanoes, the types of eruptions, and the environmental impact. Violent explosions or blasts from the volcano can produce lava, rock, fragments, and gas. We will also look at the natural resources these volcanoes provide. The energy from volcanoes is used to heat homes in Iceland and greenhouses that grow vegetables and fruits. Geothermal steam produces electricity in Italy, New Zealand, the United States, and Mexico.

Page 247

Commas

Commas separate words or groups of words to help make the meaning of a sentence clear.

Use commas in a series of items.

Example: I love eating yogurt, toast, and cucumbers for breakfast!

Use commas when talking to people.

Example: Do you know where my shirt is, Andrew?

Directions: Write **C** if the sentence is punctuated correctly. Write **X** if the sentence is not punctuated correctly.

1. _X_ Bob is Sam going to the grocery store?
2. _C_ Sam is supposed to buy grapes, bananas, and apples.
3. _C_ Can you go with Sam, Bob?
4. _X_ Make sure to buckle your seatbelt drive safely and be careful in the parking lot.
5. _X_ Sam are you ready?

Page 248

Commas

Use a **comma** to set apart the name of someone who is being addressed. Use a comma to set apart introductory words, such as **yes**, **no**, and **well**.

Examples: **Kate**, do you think that butterflies are graceful?
Yes, they are very graceful and colorful.
I agree with you, **Jamal**, that we need more butterflies.

Directions: Add commas where they belong in each sentence below.

1. Monica, have you seen any butterflies fluttering around your yard?
2. Well, yesterday I saw one but just for a second.
3. When was the last time you saw butterflies in your garden, Betsy?
4. Meredith, can you name the four stages of the butterfly life cycle?
5. Yes, I can. They are the egg, larva, chrysalis, and adult butterfly.
6. Jeff, do you know the name of the butterfly's long feeding tube?
7. Yes, it is called the proboscis. The butterfly uses it to drink nectar.
8. Heather, did you know that Queen Alexandra's birdwing butterfly is the largest butterfly in the world?
9. No, I did not know that.
10. Well, did you know that butterflies are insects?
11. Yes, I knew that, Alyson.
12. Did you know, Dave, that butterflies like to warm up out in the sun?
13. No, but that must be because they are cold-blooded.
14. Yes, they cannot become more active until their bodies warm up.

Page 249

Commas

Use commas to separate the day from the year.

Example: May 13, 1950

Directions: Rewrite each date, putting the comma in the correct place. Capitalize the name of each month.

Example: Jack and Dave were born on february 22 1982.
February 22, 1982

1. My father's birthday is may 19 1948.
May 19, 1948
2. My sister was fourteen on december 13 1994.
December 13, 1994
3. Lauren's seventh birthday was on november 30 1998.
November 30, 1998
4. october 13 1996 was the last day I saw my lost cat.
October 13, 1996
5. On april 17 1997, we saw the Grand Canyon.
April 17, 1997
6. Our vacation lasted from april 2 1998 to april 26 1998.
April 2, 1998   April 26, 1998
7. Molly's baby sister was born on august 14 1991.
August 14, 1991
8. My mother was born on june 22 1959.
June 22, 1959

Page 250

Commas

Use a comma to separate the day of the month and the year. Do not use a comma to separate the month and the year if no day is given.

Examples: June 14, 1999
June 1999

Use a comma after **yes** or **no** when it is the first word in a sentence.

Examples: Yes, I will do it right now.
No, I do not want any.

Directions: Write **C** if the sentence is punctuated correctly. Write **X** if the sentence is not punctuated correctly.

Example: _C_ No, I do not plan to attend.

1. _C_ Yes, I told them I would go.
2. _C_ Her birthday is March 13, 1995.
3. _X_ He was born in May, 2003.
4. _C_ Yes, of course I like you!
5. _X_ No I will not be there.
6. _X_ They left for vacation on February, 14.
7. _C_ No, today is Monday.
8. _C_ The program began on August 12, 1991.
9. _X_ In September, 2007 how old will you be?
10. _X_ He turned 12 years old on November, 13.
11. _C_ No, I will not go to the party!
12. _C_ Yes, she is a friend of mine.
13. _C_ His birthday is June 12, 1992.
14. _X_ No I would not like more dessert.

Page 251

Commas

Capitalize the first letter in the name of a city and a state. Use a comma to separate the name of a city and a state.

Directions: Use capital letters and commas to write the names of the cities and states correctly.

Example: sioux falls south dakota — Sioux Falls, South Dakota

1. plymouth massachusetts — Plymouth, Massachusetts
2. boston massachusetts — Boston, Massachusetts
3. philadelphia pennsylvania — Philadelphia, Pennsylvania
4. white plains new york — White Plains, New York
5. newport rhode island — Newport, Rhode Island
6. yorktown virginia — Yorktown, Virginia
7. nashville tennessee — Nashville, Tennessee
8. portland oregon — Portland, Oregon
9. mansfield ohio — Mansfield, Ohio

Commas

Use a **comma** after the day in a date. Do not put a comma after the month if no day is given.

Examples: May 12, 2002   or   May 2002

Use a **comma** after each part of an address.

Example: 123 Main Street, Seattle, Washington

Use a **comma** between the city name and the state name when they are used together.

Example: Seattle, Washington

Directions: Rewrite the story putting the commas in the correct places.

My grandpa had a very interesting life! He was born on, August, 20 1943. He grew up in, Boston Massachusetts. In January, 1963, he moved to, Los Angeles California. My grandpa lived at 349, James Street Los Angeles California. On June, 8, 1964, he married my grandma at a church in, San Francisco California. My dad was born on, February 1 1966.

My grandpa had a very interesting life! He was born on August 20, 1943.

He grew up in Boston, Massachusetts. In January 1963, he moved to Los

Angeles, California. My grandpa lived at 349 James Street, Los Angeles,

California. On June 8, 1964, he married my grandma at a church in San

Francisco, California. My dad was born on February 1, 1966.

Page 252

Commas

Use a **comma** after the greeting and closing in a friendly letter.

Examples: **Greeting:**   **Closing:**
Dear Teresa,   Your friend,
                         Samantha

Directions: Put commas where they belong in the letter below.

Dear Donovan,

I can hardly wait to get to your house this weekend. My dad will be dropping me off on Saturday afternoon. We will have fun sleeping in your tree house. Can we build a campfire?

Your friend,
Simon

Directions: Write your own letter to a friend.

ANSWERS WILL VARY

Page 253

Commas

Use a **comma** in the greeting and closing of a letter. Also use a comma between the day and the year of a date. Use a comma to separate a city from its state.

Examples: **heading:**   Dear Grandma,
                  closing: Love, Megan
                  date: October 27, 2002
                  address: Tempe, Arizona

Directions: Put commas where they belong in each letter below.

Sunday, August, 22 1999

Aunt Betty,
The Little White House
Littleville, California

Dear Aunt Betty,

I am so excited to visit you. Did you get our Model T fixed yet? Remember how it scared everyone at the 4th of July parade? I will see you in two weeks.

Love,
Jennifer

Wednesday, August 25, 1999

Jennifer,
Big Brown Cottage
Bear Town, Washington

Dear Jenny,

I am also excited about your visit. Yes, my old car is fixed. We can drive to town to see my sisters. See you soon!

Love,
Aunt Betty

Page 254

Commas

Use a **comma** to set apart an introductory clause to make your meaning clear.

Example: Apart from his uncle, Abner is the strangest in the family.

Directions: Add commas where they belong in each sentence below.

1. At first, I thought I won the race.

2. In the gym, I saw a basketball game.

3. According to Billy, Molly and Jim were up late last night trying to find apples, cheese, and desserts.

4. Looking back at her younger brother, Molly stuck out her tongue!

5. After she left her aunt Susan, started to cry.

Page 255

Quotation Marks

Quotation marks show that someone is speaking. The opening quotation mark is used just before the first word, which begins with a capital letter. The closing quotation mark is used after the final punctuation mark. Make sure you use a comma to set apart quotations.

Example: "Follow me," he said.
                She replied, "I'll be right there."

Directions: Put quotation marks and the correct punctuation in each sentence below.

1. "Wow! This is beautiful!" Sean said.

2. Ling said, "I cannot see anything yet."

3. "Do you have any extra water?" Sean asked.

4. Ling said, "Yes, it is in my backpack."

5. "Good. It is going to be a hot day." Sean said.

6. "Stop!" Ling shouted.

7. "Why?" Sean asked.

8. "I think I saw a bear up ahead," Ling answered. "It is coming this way."

9. "Climb!" Sean yelled as he started up a tree.

Page 256

Quotation Marks

Quotation marks are punctuation marks that tell what a person says out loud. Quotation marks go before the first word and after the punctuation mark. The first word in a quotation begins with a capital letter if the quote is a complete sentence.

Example: Katie said, "Never go in the water without a friend."

Directions: Put quotation marks where they belong in each sentence below.

Example: "Wait for me, please," said Laura.

1. "John, would you like to visit a jungle?" asked his uncle.

2. The police officer said, "Do not worry. We will help you."

3. James shouted, "Hit a home run!"

4. My friend Carol said, "I really do not like cheeseburgers."

Directions: Answer each question below. Be sure to put quotation marks around your words.

1. What would you say if you saw a dinosaur?

ANSWERS WILL VARY

2. What would your best friend say if your hair turned purple?

Page 257

Punctuation: Quotation Marks

Use **quotation marks** before and after words that a person speaks out loud.

Examples: I asked Aunt Martha, "How do you feel?"
"I feel awful," Aunt Martha replied.

Do not put quotation marks around words that are a summary of what a person said out loud.

Examples: I asked Aunt Martha how she felt.
Aunt Martha said she felt awful.

Directions: Write **C** if the sentence is punctuated correctly. Write **X** if the sentence is not punctuated correctly.

Example: _C_ "I want it right now!" she demanded angrily.

1. _X_ "Do you want it now? I asked."
2. _X_ She said "she felt better" now.
3. _C_ Her exact words were, "I feel much better now!"
4. _C_ "I am so thrilled to be here!" he shouted.
5. _C_ "Yes, I will attend," she replied.
6. _X_ Elizabeth said "she was unhappy."
7. _C_ "I'm unhappy," Elizabeth reported.
8. _C_ "Did you know her mother?" I asked.
9. _X_ I asked "whether you knew her mother."
10. _C_ I asked, "What will dessert be?"
11. _C_ "Which will it be, salt or pepper?" the waiter asked.
12. _C_ "No, I don't know the answer!" he snapped.
13. _X_ He said "yes he'd take her on the trip."
14. _X_ Be patient, he said. "it will soon be over."

Page 258

Quotation Marks

Directions: Rewrite each sentence, putting quotation marks around the correct words.

1. Can we go for a bike ride? asked Katrina.

   "Can we go for a bike ride?" asked Katrina.

2. Yes, said Mom.

   "Yes," said Mom.

3. We should go to the park, said Mike.

   "We should go to the park," said Mike.

4. Great idea! said Mom.

   "Great idea!" said Mom.

5. How long until we get there? asked Katrina.

   "How long until we get ther?" asked Katrina.

6. Soon, said Mike.

   "Soon," said Mike.

7. Here we are! exclaimed Mom.

   "Here we are!" exclaimed Mom.

Page 259

Quotation Marks

Use quotation marks to set off a direct quotation. Also use quotation marks around the titles of poems, stories, T.V. shows, and reports.

Examples: The teacher said, "Kate, you got a 100 percent on your test."
Todd read the poem "The Owl and the Pussycat."

Directions: In each sentence below, put quotation marks where they belong.

1. Mr. Fry asked,"Sara, are you going to the park?"
2. Mom read me the poem"Who Has Seen the Wind?"
3. "The Magic School Bus is one of my favorite T.V. shows.
4. "Are you going to the game? Raquel asked.
5. Anna gave a report called"Tribes of the Northwest."
6. My brother can read the story"Little Red Riding Hood."
7. Maria remarked,"It is very cold today."
8. Terrence wrote a report titled"Inside the Super Computer."
9. "We Should get together tomorrow,"said Laura.
10. Have you read the poem called"Dancers' Delight?"
11. Monica said,"Raquel, we should play after school."
12. Jenny's report was titled"Great Modern Painters."

Page 260

Quotation Marks

Use quotation marks around the titles of songs and poems.

Examples: Have you heard the song "Still Cruising" by the Beach Boys?
"Ode to a Nightingale" is a famous poem.

Directions: Write **C** if the sentence is punctuated correctly. Write **X** if the sentence is not punctuated correctly.

Example: _C_ Do you know "My Bonnie Lies Over the Ocean"?

1. _X_ We sang The Stars and Stripes Forever" at school.
2. _C_ Her favorite song is "The Eensy Weensy Spider."
3. _X_ Turn up the music when "A Hard Day's "Night comes on!
4. _C_ "Yesterday" was one of Paul McCartney's most famous songs.
5. _C_ "Mary Had a Little Lamb" is a very silly poem!
6. _C_ A song everyone knows is "Happy Birthday."
7. _C_ "Swing Low, Sweet Chariot" was first sung by slaves.
8. _X_ Do you know the words to Home on "the Range"?
9. _C_ "Hiawatha" is a poem many people had to memorize.
10. _X_ "Happy Days Are Here Again! is an upbeat tune.
11. _C_ Frankie Valli and the Four Seasons sang "Sherry."
12. _X_ The words to "Rain, Rain" Go Away are easy to learn.
13. _C_ A slow song I know is called "Summertime."

Page 261

Apostrophes

An **apostrophe** shows where letters are missing in a contraction. A **contraction** is a shortened form of two words.

Example: Was not = wasn't

By adding an apostrophe and the letter **s** to the end of a person, place, or thing, you are showing that person, place, or thing to have ownership of something.

Example: Mary's cat

Directions: Write the apostrophe in each contraction below.

Example: We shouldn't be going to their house so late at night.

1. We didn't think that the ice cream would melt so fast.
2. They're never around when we're ready to go.
3. Didn't you need to make a phone call?
4. Who's going to help you paint the bicycle red?

Directions: Add an apostrophe and an **s** to each word below that shows ownership.

Example: Jill's bike is broken.

1. That is Holly's flower garden.
2. Mark's new skates are black and green.
3. Mom threw away Dad's old shoes.
4. Buster's food dish was lost in the snowstorm.

Page 262

Contractions

A **contraction** is a shortened form of two words. Apostrophes show where letters are missing.

Example: It is = it's

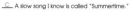

Directions: Write the words that make up each contraction.

we're _we_ + _are_   they'll _they_ + _will_

you'll _you_ + _will_   aren't _are_ + _not_

I'm _I_ + _am_   isn't _is_ + _not_

Directions: Write the contraction for each set of words.

you have _you've_   have not _haven't_

had not _had'nt_   we will _we'll_

they are _they're_   he is _he's_

she had _she'd_   it will _it'll_

I am _I'm_   is not _isn't_

Page 263

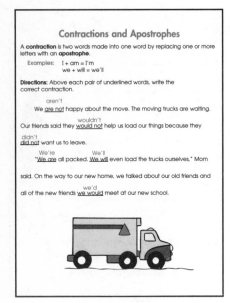

Contractions and Apostrophes

A **contraction** is two words made into one word by replacing one or more letters with an **apostrophe**.

Examples: I + am = I'm
we + will = we'll

Directions: Above each pair of underlined words, write the correct contraction.

aren't
We <u>are not</u> happy about the move. The moving trucks are waiting.

wouldn't
Our friends said they <u>would not</u> help us load our things because they

didn't
<u>did not</u> want us to leave.

We're   We'll
"<u>We are</u> all packed. <u>We will</u> even load the trucks ourselves," Mom

said. On the way to our new home, we talked about our old friends and

we'd
all of the new friends <u>we would</u> meet at our new school.

Page 264

Contractions and Apostrophes

Contractions are two words that are shortened and put together to make one word. An **apostrophe** replaces the missing letters.

Examples: does not = doesn't
cannot = can't

Directions: Draw a line from each pair of words to its matching contraction.

1. is not — weren't
2. are not — wasn't
3. was not — aren't
4. were not — isn't
5. have not — didn't
6. can not — haven't
7. do not — couldn't
8. did not — can't
9. could not — shouldn't
10. should not — don't

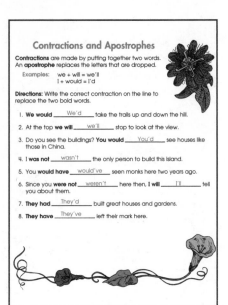

Do not use a contraction that ends in **n't** with another negative like **no**, **nothing, no one,** and **never.**

Examples: **Incorrect:** I didn't get no milk.
Correct: I didn't get any milk.

Directions: Rewrite each sentence correctly.

1. Molly doesn't have no tennis shoes.

Molly doesn't have any tennis shoes.

2. We aren't doing nothing on Saturday.

We aren't doing anything on Saturday.

Page 265

Contractions and Apostrophes

Contractions are made by putting together two words. An **apostrophe** replaces the letters that are dropped.

Examples: we + will = we'll
I + would = I'd

Directions: Write the correct contraction on the line to replace the two bold words.

1. **We would** ____We'd____ take the trails up and down the hill.

2. At the top **we will** ____we'll____ stop to look at the view.

3. Do you see the buildings? **You would** ____You'd____ see houses like those in China.

4. I **was not** ____wasn't____ the only person to build this island.

5. You **would have** ____would've____ seen monks here two years ago.

6. Since you **were not** ____weren't____ here then, **I will** ____I'll____ tell you about them.

7. **They had** ____They'd____ built great houses and gardens.

8. **They have** ____They've____ left their mark here.

Page 266

Contractions and Apostrophes

Directions: Circle the two words in each sentence that are not spelled correctly. Then, write the words correctly.

1. (Arn't) you going to (shere) your cookie with me?

Aren't   share

2. We (planed) a long time, but we still (wern't) ready.

planned   weren't

3. My (pensil) (hassn't) broken yet today.

pencil   hasn't

4. We (arn't) going because we don't have the correct (adress).

aren't   address

5. (Youve) (stired) the soup too much.

You've   stirred

6. (Weave) tried to be as (neet) as possible.

We've   neat

7. She (hasnt) seen us in this (darknes).

hasn't   darkness

Page 267

Capitalization and Punctuation Review

Directions: The following sentences have errors in punctuation, capitalization, or both. The number in parentheses ( ) tells you how many errors the sentence contains. Rewrite each sentence correctly.

1. I saw mr. Johnson reading <u>War And Peace</u> to his class. (2)

I saw Mr. Johnson reading War and Peace to his class.

2. Do you like to sing "Take me Out to The Ballgame"? (2)

Do you like to sing "Take Me out to the Ballgame?"

3. He recited Hiawatha to Miss. Simpson's class. (2)

He recited "Hiawatha" to Mrs. Simpson's class.

4. Bananas and oranges are among Dr smiths favorite fruits. (4)

Bananas and oranges are among Dr. Smith's favorite fruits.

5. "Daisy, daisy is a song about a bicycle built for two. (2)

"Daisy, Daisy" is a song about a bicycle built for two.

6. Good Morning, Granny Rose is a story about a woman and her dog. (1)

"Good Morning, Granny Rose" is a story about a woman and her dog.

7. Garfield goes to waist isnt a very funny book. (4)

Garfield Goes to Waist isn't a very funny book.

8. Peanut butter, jelly, and bread are Miss. Lees favorite treats. (2)

Peanut butter, jelly, and bread are Mrs. Lee's favorite treats.

Page 268

Homophones

Homophones are words that sound the same but are spelled differently and have different meanings.

Example:

sew   sow   so

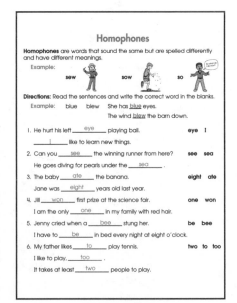

Directions: Read the sentences and write the correct word in the blanks.

Example: blue   blew   She has <u>blue</u> eyes.
The wind <u>blew</u> the barn down.

1. He hurt his left ____eye____ playing ball.   eye   I

____I____ like to learn new things.

2. Can you ____see____ the winning runner from here?   see   sea

He goes diving for pearls under the ____sea____.

3. The baby ____ate____ the banana.   eight   ate

Jane was ____eight____ years old last year.

4. Jill ____won____ first prize at the science fair.   one   won

I am the only ____one____ in my family with red hair.

5. Jenny cried when a ____bee____ stung her.   be   bee

I have to ____be____ in bed every night at eight o'clock.

6. My father likes ____to____ play tennis.   two   to   too

I like to play. ____too____ .

It takes at least ____two____ people to play.

Page 269

Homophones and Commonly Misused Words

Homophones are words that sound the same but are spelled differently and have different meanings.

Directions: Answer each riddle below with a homophone from the Word Bank.

Word Bank				
main	meat	peace	dear	to
mane	meet	piece	deer	too

1. Which word has the word **pie** in it? _____piece_____

2. Which word rhymes with **ear** and is an animal? _____deer_____

3. Which word rhymes with **shoe** and means **also**? _____too_____

4. Which word has the word **eat** in it and is something you might eat? _____meat_____

5. Which word has the same letters as the word **read** but in a different order? _____dear_____

6. Which word rhymes with **train** and is something on a pony? _____mane_____

7. Which word, if it began with a capital letter, might be the name of an important street? _____main_____

8. Which word sounds like a number but has only two letters? _____to_____

9. Which word rhymes with **greet** and is a synonym for **greet**? _____meet_____

10. Which word rhymes with **cease** and can mean quiet? _____peace_____

Page 270

Common Corrections

Some words look and sound very much alike but have very different meanings.

Directions: Finish each sentence below with the correct word from the Word Bank.

Word Bank		
series	lose	bear
serious	loose	bare

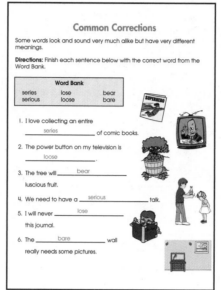

1. I love collecting an entire _____series_____ of comic books.

2. The power button on my television is _____loose_____

3. The tree will _____bear_____ luscious fruit.

4. We need to have a _____serious_____ talk.

5. I will never _____lose_____ this journal.

6. The _____bare_____ wall really needs some pictures.

Page 271

Common Corrections

Some words look and sound very much alike but have very different meanings.

Directions: Look at the words and their meanings below. Then, write the correct word to complete each sentence.

their: pronoun that shows possession or ownership
there: at or in that place
angel: a figure with halo and wings
angle: two lines that connect at a single point
accept: to say yes
except: not including or otherwise
intend: to plan
attend: to be present at

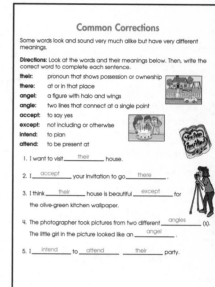

1. I want to visit _____their_____ house.

2. I _____accept_____ your invitation to go _____there_____.

3. I think _____their_____ house is beautiful _____except_____ for the olive-green kitchen wallpaper.

4. The photographer took pictures from two different _____angles_____ (s). The little girl in the picture looked like an _____angel_____.

5. I _____intend_____ to _____attend_____ _____their_____ party.

Page 272

Common Corrections

Some words look and sound very much alike but have very different meanings.

Directions: Finish each sentence below using the correct word from the Word Bank.

Word Bank		
united	whether	now
untied	weather	know

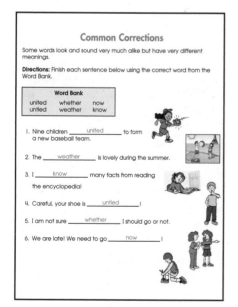

1. Nine children _____united_____ to form a new baseball team.

2. The _____weather_____ is lovely during the summer.

3. I _____know_____ many facts from reading the encyclopedia!

4. Careful, your shoe is _____untied_____!

5. I am not sure _____whether_____ I should go or not.

6. We are late! We need to go _____now_____!

Page 273

Common Corrections

Some words look and sound very much alike but have very different meanings.

Directions: Look at the words and meanings below. Write the correct word to finish each sentence.

thorough: complete
through: in one side and out the other
then: at that time
than: a comparison
mere: a tiny bit
mirror: a reflective surface

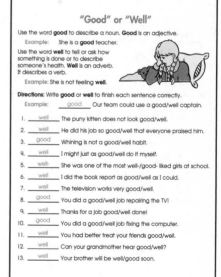

1. I am taller _____than_____ you by five inches!

2. Please do a _____thorough_____ job when you sweep the floor.

3. There was a _____mere_____ drop of ketchup left in the bottle!

4. The ball went _____through_____ the glass window!

6. Do your homework and _____then_____ we will go play.

7. Do you have a _____mirror_____ I could use so that I can fix my hair?

Page 274

"Good" or "Well"

Use the word **good** to describe a noun. **Good** is an adjective.

 Example: She is a **good** teacher.

Use the word **well** to tell or ask how something is done or to describe someone's health. **Well** is an adverb. It describes a verb.

 Example: She is not feeling **well**.

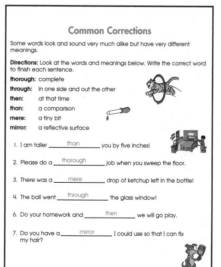

Directions: Write **good** or **well** to finish each sentence correctly.

 Example: _____good_____ Our team could use a good/well captain.

1. _____well_____ The puny kitten does not look good/well.

2. _____well_____ He did his job so good/well that everyone praised him.

3. _____good_____ Whining is not a good/well habit.

4. _____well_____ I might just as good/well do it myself.

5. _____well-_____ She was one of the most well-/good- liked girls at school.

6. _____well_____ I did the book report as good/well as I could.

7. _____well_____ The television works very good/well.

8. _____good_____ You did a good/well job repairing the TV!

9. _____well_____ Thanks for a job good/well done!

10. _____good_____ You did a good/well job fixing the computer.

11. _____well_____ You had better treat your friends good/well.

12. _____well_____ Can your grandmother hear good/well?

13. _____well_____ Your brother will be well/good soon.

Page 275

"Your" or "You're"

The word **your** shows possession.

Examples: Is that **your** book?
I visited **your** class.

The word **you're** is a contraction for **you are**.
A **contraction** is two words joined together as one.
An **apostrophe** shows where letters have been left out.

Examples: **You're** doing well on that painting.
If **you're** going to pass the test, you should study.

Directions: Write **your** or **you're** to finish each sentence correctly.

Example: __You're__ Your/You're the best friend I have!

1. __You're__ Your/You're going to drop that!
2. __Your__ Your/You're brother came to see me.
3. __your__ Is that your/you're cat?
4. __you're__ If your/you're going, you'd better hurry!
5. __your__ Why are your/you're fingers so red?
6. __your__ It's none of your/you're business!
7. __Your__ Your/You're bike's front tire is low.
8. __You're__ Your/You're kidding!
9. __your__ Have it your/you're way.
10. __your__ I thought your/you're report was great!
11. __you're__ He thinks your/you're wonderful!
12. __your__ What is your/you're first choice?
13. __your__ What's your/you're opinion?
14. __you're__ If your/you're going, so am I!
15. __you're__ Your/You're welcome.

Page 276

"Good" or "Well" and "Your" or "You're"

Directions: Finish each sentence with the correct word: **good, well, your** or **you're**.

1. Are you sure you can see ___well___ enough to read with the lighting you have?

2. ___You're___ going to need a paint smock when you go to art class tomorrow afternoon.

3. I can see ___you're___ having some trouble. Can I help with that?

4. The music department needs to buy a speaker system that has ___good___ quality sound.

5. The principal asked, "Where is ___your___ hall pass?"

6. You must do your job ___well___ if you expect to keep it.

7. The traffic policeman said, "May I please see ___your___ driver's license?"

8. The story you wrote for English class was done quite ___well___.

9. That radio station you listen to is a ___good___ one.

10. Let us know if ___you're___ unable to attend the meeting on Saturday.

Page 277

"Its" or "It's"

The word **its** shows ownership.

Examples: **Its** leaves have all turned green.
Its paw was injured.

The word **it's** is a contraction for **it is**.

Examples: **It's** better to be early than late.
It's not fair!

Directions: Write **its** or **it's** to finish each sentence correctly.

Example: ___It's___ Its/It's never too late for ice cream!

1. ___Its___ Its/It's eyes are already open.
2. ___It's___ Its/It's your turn to wash the dishes!
3. ___Its___ Its/It's cage was left open.
4. ___Its___ Its/It's engine was beyond repair.
5. ___Its___ Its/It's teeth were long and pointed.
6. ___Its___ Did you see its/it's hind legs?
7. ___It's___ Why do you think its/it's mine?
8. ___It's___ Do you think its/it's the right color?
9. ___Its___ Don't pet its/it's fur too hard!
10. ___It's___ Its/It's from Uncle Harry.
11. ___It's___ Can you tell its/it's a surprise?
12. ___Its___ Is its/it's stall always this clean?
13. ___It's___ Its/It's not time to eat yet.
14. ___It's___ She says its/it's working now.

Page 278

"Can" or "May"

The word **can** means **am able** to or to be able to.

Examples: I can do that for you.
Can you do that for me?

The word **may** means **be allowed** to or **permitted to**. May is used to ask or give permission. **May** can also mean **might** or **perhaps**.

Examples: May I be excused?
You may sit here.

Directions: Write **can** or **may** to finish each sentence correctly.

Example: ___May___ Can/May I help you?

1. ___can___ He is smart. He can/may do it himself.
2. ___may___ When can/may I have my dessert?
3. ___can___ He can/may speak French fluently.
4. ___may___ You can/may use my pencil.
5. ___may___ I can/may be allowed to attend the concert.
6. ___can___ It is bright. I can/may see you!
7. ___May___ Can/May my friend stay for dinner?
8. ___may___ You can/may leave when your report is finished.
9. ___can___ I can/may see your point!
10. ___can___ She can/may dance well.
11. ___Can___ Can/May you hear the dog barking?
12. ___Can___ Can/May you help me button this sweater?
13. ___may___ Mother, can/may I go to the movies?

Page 279

"Its" or "It's" and "Can" or "May"

Directions: Finish each sentence with the correct word: **its, it's, can,** or **may**.

1. "It looks as though your arms are full, Diane. ___May___ I help you with some of those things?" asked Michele.

2. The squirrel ___can___ climb up the tree quickly with his mouth full of acorns.

3. She has had her school jacket so long that it is beginning to lose ___its___ color.

4. How many laps around the track ___can___ you do?

5. Sometimes you can tell what a story is going to be about by looking at ___its___ title.

6. Our house ___may___ need to be painted again in two or three years.

7. Mother asked, "Jon, ___can___ you open the door for your father?"

8. ___It's___ going to be a while until your birthday, but do you know what you want?

9. I can feel in the air that ___it's___ going to snow soon.

10. If I am careful with it, ___may___ I borrow your CD player?

Page 280

"Sit" or "Set"

The word **sit** means to rest.

Examples: Please **sit** here!
Will you **sit** by me?

The word **set** means to put or place something.

Examples: **Set** your purse there.
Set the dishes on the table.

Directions: Write **sit** or **set** to finish each sentence correctly.

Example: ___sit___ Would you please sit/set down here?

1. ___set___ You can sit/set the groceries there.
2. ___set___ She sit/set her suitcase in the closet.
3. ___set___ He sit/set his watch for half past three.
4. ___sit___ She is a person who cannot sit/set still.
5. ___Set___ Sit/Set the baby on the couch beside me.
6. ___set___ Where did you sit/set your new shoes?
7. ___sit___ They decided to sit/set together during the movie.
8. ___set___ Let me sit/set you straight on that!
9. ___sit___ Instead of swimming, he decided to sit/set in the water.
10. ___set___ He sit/set the greasy pan in the sink.
11. ___set___ She sit/set the file folder on her desk.
12. ___sit___ Do not ever sit/set on the refrigerator!
13. ___set___ She sit/set the candles on the cake.
14. ___set___ Get ready! Get sit/set! Go!

Page 281

"They're," "Their," "There"

The word **they're** is a contraction for **they are**.

Examples: **They're** our very best friends!
Ask them if **they're** coming.

The word **their** shows ownership.

Examples: **Their** dog is friendly.
It's **their** bicycle.

The word **there** shows place or direction.

Examples: Look over **there**.
There it is.

Directions: Write **they're, their,** or **there** to finish each sentence correctly.

Example: ___There___ They're/Their/There is the sweater I want!

1. ___their___ Do you believe they're/their/there stories?
2. ___there___ Be they're/their/there by one o'clock.
3. ___there___ Were you they're/their/there last night?
4. ___they're___ I know they're/their/there going to attend.
5. ___their___ Have you met they're/their/there mother?
6. ___there___ I can go they're/their/there with you.
7. ___their___ Do you like they're/their/there new car?
8. ___They're___ They're/Their/There friendly to everyone.
9. ___they're___ Did she say they're/their/there ready to go?
10. ___their___ She said she would walk by they're/their/there house.
11. ___there___ Is anyone they're/their/there?
12. ___there___ I put it right over they're/their/there!

Page 282

"Sit" or "Set" and "They're," "There," or "Their"

Directions: Finish each sentence with the correct word: **sit, set, they're, there,** or **their.**

1. Her muscles became tense as she heard the gym teacher say, "Get ready, get ___set___, go!"
2. When we choose our seats on the bus, will you ___sit___ with me?
3. ___There___ is my library book! I wondered where I had left it!
4. My little brother and his friend said ___they're___ not going to the ball game with us.
5. Before the test, the teacher wants the students to sharpen ___their___ pencils.
6. She blew the whistle and shouted, "Everyone ___sit___ down on the floor!"
7. All the books for the fourth graders belong over ___there___ on the top shelf.
8. The little kittens are beginning to open ___their___ eyes.
9. I'm going to ___set___ the dishes on the table.
10. ___They're___ going to be fine by themselves for a few minutes.

Page 283

"This" or "These"

The word **this** is an adjective that refers to a specific thing. **This** always describes a singular noun. Singular means **one**.

Example: I'll buy **this** coat.
(Coat is singular.)

The word **these** is also an adjective that refers to specific things. **These** always describes a plural noun. Plural means **more than one**.

Example: I will buy **these** flowers.
(Flowers is a plural noun.)

Directions: Write **this** or **these** to finish each sentence correctly.

Example: ___these___ I will take this/these cookies with me.

1. ___these___ Do you want this/these seeds?
2. ___these___ Did you try this/these nuts?
3. ___this___ Do it this/these way!
4. ___this___ What do you know about this/these situation?
5. ___these___ Did you open this/these doors?
6. ___this___ Did you open this/these window?
7. ___these___ What is the meaning of this/these letters?
8. ___these___ Will you carry this/these books for me?
9. ___These___ This/These pans are hot!
10. ___this___ Do you think this/these light is too bright?
11. ___these___ Are this/these boots yours?
12. ___this___ Do you like this/these rainy weather?

Page 284

Double Negatives

Only use one **negative word** in a sentence. **Not, no, never,** and **none** are some negative words.

Examples:
Incorrect: No one nowhere was sad when it started to snow.
Correct: No one anywhere was sad when it started to snow.

Directions: Circle the word in parentheses that makes each sentence correct.

1. There wasn't (no, (any)) snow on our grass this morning.
2. I couldn't find (no one, (anyone)) who wanted to build a snowman.
3. We couldn't believe that (no one, (anyone)) wanted to stay inside.
4. We shouldn't ask ((anyone), no one) to go ice skating with us.
5. None of the students could think of (nothing, (anything)) to do at recess except to play in the new-fallen snow.
6. No one (never, (ever)) thinks it is a waste of time to go ice skating on the pond.

Directions: Write the correct word on each line to replace the negative word in parentheses.

1. You shouldn't (never) ___ever___ play catch with a snowball unless you want to be covered in snow.
2. Isn't (no one) ___anyone___ else going to eat icicles?
3. There wasn't (nothing) ___anything___ wrong with using fresh snow to make our fruit drinks.
4. The snowman outside isn't (nowhere) ___anywhere___ as large as the statue in front of our school.
5. Falling snow isn't (no) ___any___ fun if you cannot go out and play in it.

Page 285

Word Usage Review

Directions: Finish each sentence by writing the correct word in the blank.

1. ___good___ You have a good/well attitude.
2. ___well___ The teacher was not feeling good/well.
3. ___well___ She sang extremely good/well.
4. ___good___ Everyone said Josh was a good/well boy.
5. ___You're___ Your/You're going to be sorry for that!
6. ___you're___ Tell her your/you're serious.
7. ___Your___ Your/You're report was wonderful!
8. ___You're___ Your/You're the best person for the job.
9. ___It's___ Do you think its/it's going to have babies?
10. ___Its___ Its/It's back paw had a thorn in it.
11. ___It's___ Its/It's fun to make new friends.
12. ___its___ Is its/it's mother always nearby?
13. ___may___ How can/may I help you?
14. ___may___ You can/may come in now.
15. ___Can___ Can/May you lift this for me?
16. ___can___ She can/may sing soprano.
17. ___sit___ I will wait for you to sit/set down first.
18. ___set___ We sit/set our dirty boots outside.
19. ___their___ It is they're/their/there turn to choose.
20. ___There___ They're/Their/There is your answer!
21. ___they're___ They say they're/their/there coming.
22. ___this___ I must have this/these one!
23. ___these___ I saw this/these gloves at the store.
24. ___these___ He said this/these were his.

Page 286

Proofreading

Directions: Proofread the sentences. Write **C** if the sentence has no errors. Write **X** if the sentence contains errors.

Example: ___C___ The new Ship Wreck Museum in Key West is exciting!

1. ___X___ Another thing I liked was the litehouse.
2. ___X___ Do you remember Hemingways address in Key West?
3. ___C___ The Key West Cemetery is on 21 acres of ground.
4. ___X___ Ponce de leon discovered Key West Florida.
5. ___X___ The cemetery in key west is on francis street.
6. ___X___ My favorete tombstone was the sailor's.
7. ___C___ His wife wrote the words.
8. ___X___ The words said, at least I know where to find him now!
9. ___C___ The sailor must have been away at sea.
10. ___X___ The trolley ride around Key West isnt boring.
11. ___X___ Do you why it is called Key West?
12. ___C___ Can you imagine a lighthouse in the middle of your town?
13. ___X___ It is interesting that Key West is the more southern city.
14. ___X___ Besides Harry Truman and Hemingway did other famous people live there?

Page 287

Proofreading: Capitalization

When you are reviewing your own or another student's writing, it helps to use proofreading marks to show where corrections are needed.

To show where a capital letter should be, write three short lines below the letter that needs to be capitalized.

Example: the mosleys took a trip to maryland.

Directions: Read the paragraph below. Write three short lines under letters that should be capitalized.

the white house was the first official building in washington, d.c. construction began on october 13, 1792. it is located at 1600 pennsylvania avenue in washington, d.c. it is the home of the president of the united states. the president and his family live in one section of the house. every american president except george washington has lived in the white house. the other section is used for the president's office. the white house is a beautiful building.

Page 288

Proofreading: Inserting Words and Punctuation

When you are reviewing your own or another student's writing, it helps to use proofreading marks to show where corrections are needed. Show where a punctuation mark or word is needed by using a carat (∧).

Example: Mary Jo Patty and Serena splashed in the lake ∧

Directions: Use the proofreading mark to insert punctuation marks where they are needed in the paragraph and letter below.

"A picnic at the lake is a wonderful idea," exclaimed Mary Jo. "I will bring cherry pie, ham sandwiches, and potato chips."

Patty replied, "Great, I will bring a blanket, an umbrella and lemonade."

"Can I come," Serena asked. "I could bring toys and games."
"Sure, you can come," Patty said. "We will have lots of fun."

> 1543 Treetop Lane
> Forrester, Illinois 56284
> July 23, 2002
>
> Dear Mary Jo,
> Thank you for inviting me to the picnic at the lake. It was really fun. I enjoyed splashing in the lake and riding in the boat. Your ham sandwiches tasted terrific. I hope we can go to the lake again.
> Your friend,
> Serena

Page 289

Proofreading

Proofreading means searching for and correcting errors by carefully reading and rereading what has been written. Use the proofreading marks below when correcting someone's writing, including your own.

To insert a word or a punctuation mark that has been left out, use a carat (∧).
went
Example: We ∧ to the dance together.

To show that a letter should be capitalized, put three lines under it.
Example: Mrs. jones drove us to school.

To show that a capital letter should be lower case, draw a diagonal line through it.
Example: Mrs. Jones Drove us to school.

To show that a word is spelled incorrectly, draw a horizontal line through it and write the correct spelling above it.
walrus
Example: The welres is an amazing animal.

Directions: Proofread the two paragraphs below using proofreading marks.

The Modern ark
My book report is on the modern ark by Cecilia Fitzsimmons. The book tells about 80 of worlds endangered animals. The book also has an ark and animals inside for kids put together.

Their House
Their house is a great book! The author's name is Mary Towne. they're house tells about a girl name Molly. Molly's family buys an old house from some person named warren. Then their big problems begin!

Page 290

Proofreading

Proofreading marks help us to revise our writing. These marks show where changes should be made.

¶ Indent a paragraph
∧ Insert something
ꝰ Take something out
≡ Capitalize
/ Make lowercase

Directions: Edit the paragraph below. Use proofreading marks.

Margaret Thatcher was the first female prime minister in Great Britain. A prime minister is like a president. Mrs. Thatcher was born in a town called grantham in 1925. She went to school at the University of oxford. She became a chemist Later, she married a man named denis. After passing the bar examination, she became a tax lawyer. Mrs. Thatcher got involved in politics in 1959. She became the prime minister of Great Britain in 1979.

a   c
Proofreding prakticee

Page 291

Proofreading

Directions: Proofread the paragraphs using proofreading marks. There are seven capitalization errors, three missing words, and eleven errors in spelling or word usage.

Key West
key West has been tropical paradise ever since Ponce de Leon first saw the set of islands called the keys in 1513. Two famous streets in Key West are named duval and whitehead. You will find the cemetery city cemetery on Francis Street. The tombstones are funny!

The message on one is, "I told you I was sick!"
On sailor's tombston is this message his widow:
"At lease I no where to find him now."

The cemetery is on 21 acres in the midle of town. The most famous home in key west is that of the author Ernest Hemingway. Hemingway's home was at 907 whitehead Street.
He lived their for 30 years.

Page 292

Proofreading

Directions: Proofread and correct the errors in the description below. There are eight errors in capitalization, seven misspelled words, a missing comma, and three missing words.

More About Key West
learn
a good way to lern more about key West is to ride the trolley. Key West has a great troley system. The trolley you will take on a tour of the salt ponds. You can also see three red brick forts. The troley tour goes by a 110-foot-high lighthouse. It is rite in the middle of the city. Key west is the only city with a lighthouse in the midle of iit. It is also the southernmost city in the United States.

visit
If you have time, the new Ship Wreck Museum. Key west was also the hom of former president Truman Harry truman. During his presidency, truman spent many vacations on key west.

Page 293

Page 294

Paragraphs

A **paragraph** is a group of sentences that tell about one main idea. It begins with a **topic sentence**. **Supporting sentences** tell more about the topic. The paragraph ends with a **concluding sentence**.

Example: **Topic Sentence:** States the main idea.

Supporting Sentences: Give more detail about the main idea.

Concluding Sentence: Rephrases the topic sentence and summarizes the main idea.

Directions: Underline the topic sentence in this paragraph. Number each of the supporting sentences. Circle the concluding sentence.

My dog is the smartest dog in the world. [1] Her name is Lulu. [2] She can fetch the newspaper when Dad asks her to. [3] When Mom is sad, Lulu cheers her up by licking her face. [4] I really like it when Lulu helps me find my lost tennis shoe. (Lulu is the best dog!)

Page 295

Paragraphs

A **paragraph** is a group of sentences that tell about one main idea. The **topic sentence** tells the main idea of the paragraph. The **supporting sentences** tell more about the main idea. The **concluding sentence** rephrases the main idea or connects it to the next paragraph.

Directions: Write a concluding sentence for each paragraph.

1. It looks like rain. Heavy gray clouds are collecting in the sky. The icy wind is blowing through my sweater. Drops splatter the sidewalk and my glasses.

   ANSWERS WILL VARY

2. The flowers bloom in brilliant colors. Daffodils smile with their yellow faces. Purple irises complement the pink tulips. Many people cut the white daisies to put in vases.

3. Birds build nests to prepare a home for their eggs. First, they find a safe place for a nest. Then, they collect twigs, branches, and leaves. Finally, the birds arrange the nest.

Page 296

Paragraphs

A **paragraph** is a group of sentences that tell about one main idea. It begins with a topic sentence. The **topic sentence** tells the main idea of the paragraph. The rest of the paragraph relates to the main idea.

Directions: Write a topic sentence for each paragraph.

ANSWERS WILL VARY

_____ First, I put on my helmet. Next, I practiced balancing on the bike. My mom gave me a little push, and I was on my way. I pedaled as fast as I could. I steered carefully. I was riding by myself!

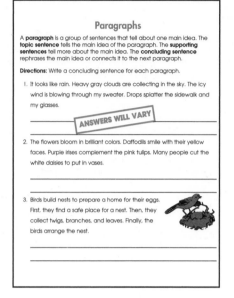 _____ We go outside and eat our snacks. When the teacher excuses us, we race out to the field. Some kids play on the jungle gym and others swing on the swing set. A game of soccer is organized. Everyone has fun at recess.

_____ We use computers to help us write reports. We use them to surf the web and learn new things. Computers ring up our purchases at the store. They can even make phone calls for us. The computer is a wonderful invention.

_____ He spills milk on the table at snack time. He talks when the teacher is talking and gets sent to the principal's office. He fools around in line for the bus. Bradley Johnson is always in trouble.

Page 297

Paragraphs

A **paragraph** is a group of sentences that tell about one main idea. The **topic sentence** tells the main idea of the paragraph. The **supporting sentences** tell more about the main idea.

Directions: Write three supporting sentences for each topic sentence.

Police officers are very helpful.

ANSWERS WILL VARY

I was really scared during the thunderstorm.

My favorite amusement park ride is the bumper cars.

Saturday is the best day of the week.

Page 298

Write Your Own Paragraph

My Topic:

Topic sentence

Supporting Sentence 1

ANSWERS WILL VARY

Supporting Sentence 2

Supporting Sentence 3

Concluding Sentence

Page 299

Proofreading: Paragraphs

When you are reviewing your own or another student's writing, it helps to use proofreading marks to show where corrections are needed. Use this symbol (¶) to show where a new paragraph should begin.

A **paragraph** is a group of sentences that tell about one main idea. It begins with a topic sentence. Supporting sentences tell more about the topic. The paragraph ends with a concluding sentence.

Directions: Insert a proofreading mark (¶) where each new paragraph should begin in the report below.

¶Birds are unique animals. Birds hatch out of eggs, and many are born without feathers. Birds have bills instead of mouths, but they do not have teeth. They can cool their bodies while flying through the air or panting at rest. These features make birds special animals.¶There are different kinds of birds. Ostrich are the largest birds. They can be almost 8 feet tall. Bee hummingbirds are the smallest birds and are no more than 2½ inches tall. Hummingbirds are the only birds that are capable of flying backward. Penguins use their wings as oars when swimming through water. Woodpeckers drum on trees to create nesting holes and to communicate with other woodpeckers.¶Bird feathers have many different uses. The bright colors can attract mates or scare away other birds. Feathers can act as camouflage to protect birds. They help protect birds from cold weather. They are water-repellent on swimming birds. Feathers are important to birds' survival.